Magical American Jew

Magical American Jew

The Enigma of Difference in Contemporary Jewish American Short Fiction and Film

Aaron Tillman

LEXINGTON BOOKS
Lanham • Boulder • New York • London

Published by Lexington Books
An imprint of The Rowman & Littlefield Publishing Group, Inc.
4501 Forbes Boulevard, Suite 200, Lanham, Maryland 20706
www.rowman.com

Unit A, Whitacre Mews, 26-34 Stannary Street, London SE11 4AB

British Library Cataloguing in Publication Information Available

Library of Congress Cataloging-in-Publication Data

Names: Tillman, Aaron, author.
Title: Magical American Jew: the enigma of difference in contemporary Jewish American short
    fiction and film / Aaron Tillman
Description: Lanham ; Boulder ; New York ; London : Lexington Books, [2017] | Includes biblio-
    graphical references and index.
Identifiers: LCCN 2017043596 (print) | LCCN 2017044476 (ebook) | ISBN 9781498565035 (elec-
    tronic) | ISBN 9781498565028 (cloth : alk. paper)
Subjects: LCSH: American literature--Jewish authors--History and criticism. | Judaism and literature-
    -United States--History--20th century. | Jews in literature. | Jews in motion pictures. | Jews--
    identity.
Classification: LCC PS153.J4 (ebook) | LCC PS153.J4 T55 2017 (print) | DDC 813/.6098924--dc23
LC record available at https://lccn.loc.gov/2017043596

∞™ The paper used in this publication meets the minimum requirements of American National Standard for Information Sciences Permanence of Paper for Printed Library Materials, ANSI/NISO Z39.48-1992.

Printed in the United States of America

Contents

Acknowledgments   vii

Introduction: Magical American Jew: The Enigma of Difference
in Contemporary Jewish American Short Fiction and Film   1

1   Postmodern Neurotic: Jewish American Excess and the
Narrative Body in Woody Allen's *Annie Hall*   13

2   Presuming the Dominant Gaze: Spirits of Shame in Cynthia
Ozick's "Levitation"   33

3   Collecting Pain: Masochism, Identity, and Archiving
Trauma Testimony in Melvin Jules Bukiet's "The Library of
Moloch"   51

4   "Jewish, Here in the Back": Magical and Comical Discord
between Religiosity and Ethnicity in Nathan Englander's
"The Gilgul of Park Avenue" and Steve Stern's "The Tale of
a Kite"   71

5   "Through the Rube Goldberg Crazy Straw": Ethnic
Mobility and Narcissistic Fantasy in *Sarah Silverman: Jesus Is
Magic*   93

Conclusion: Portraying the Impossible: Franz Kafka and the
Magical Influence of an Enigmatic Artist   115

Bibliography   133

Index   141

About the Author   149

Acknowledgments

For Shira, Jonah, Livya, and Mia.

Thank you to my parents, Rhoda and Stephen Tillman, for their love and support, and to my in-laws, Susan and Joel Lewin, for providing the summer space necessary to complete this project.

This book would not have been possible without the guidance and wisdom of Naomi Mandel—a true mentor and friend.

I am also grateful for the feedback I received from Ryan Trimm, Peter Covino, Evelyn Sterne, David Gitlitz, and Brendan O'Malley.

Thank you to Lindsey Porambo for believing in this project and providing the resources necessary to make it real.

Earlier versions of some of these chapters have appeared in various publications.

An earlier version of "'Jewish, Here in the Back': Magical and Comical Discord between Religiosity and Ethnicity in Nathan Englander's 'The Gilgul of Park Avenue' and Steve Stern's 'The Tale of a Kite'"[1] appeared in *Symbolism: An International Annual of Critical Aesthetics*, Rüdiger Ahrens, Klaus Stierstorfer (eds.) Vol. 12/13, (Special Focus: Jewish Magic Realism); Berlin/Boston: De Gruyter, 2013, 170–91.

An earlier version of "'Through the Rube Goldberg Crazy Straw': Ethnic Mobility and Narcissistic Fantasy in *Sarah Silverman: Jesus Is Magic*" appeared in *Studies in American Humor* 3.20 (2009): 58–84.

An earlier version of "Presuming the Dominant Gaze: Spirits of Shame in Cynthia Ozick's 'Levitation'" appeared in *The CEA Critic* 71.2 (Winter 2009): 57–72. Reprinted with permission by Johns Hopkins University Press.

NOTE

1. The version that appeared in *Symbolism* was titled "'Jewish, Here in the Back': The Magical and Comical Call of an Enigmatic Difference in Nathan Englander's 'The Gilgul of Park Avenue' and Steve Stern's 'The Tale of a Kite.'"

Introduction

*Magical American Jew: The Enigma of Difference in
Contemporary Jewish American Short Fiction and Film*

Efforts to describe contemporary Jewish American identities often reveal more questions than concrete articulations, more statements about what Jewish Americans are *not* than what they are. A review of contemporary writings about Jewish American literature and culture bares a residue of paradoxical phrases—"comfortably uncomfortable," "insider-outsider," "ambiguously located," "near invisible territory of literary limbo."[1] Laura Levitt discusses several "contradictions" unique to American Jews. In her assessment—which comes out of an examination of the differing views of Jewish identification and secularism that emerged after European and Eastern European waves of Jewish immigration—"Jews do not fit into the now long accepted litany of differences—race, class, gender, sexuality."[2] For Levitt, "*religion* . . . and even *ethnicity* have never been able to fully or accurately describe what it means to be a Jew in the United States."[3] Peter Novick raises similar questions: "What *does* differentiate American Jews from other Americans? On what grounds can a distinctive Jewish identity in the United States be based?"[4] In an effort to answer, Novick displays a difficulty similar to Levitt's:

> These days American Jews can't define their Jewishness on the basis of distinctively Jewish religious beliefs, since most don't have much in the way of distinctively Jewish religious beliefs. They can't define it by distinctively Jewish cultural traits, since most don't have any of these either. American Jews are sometimes said to be united by their Zionism, but if so, it is of a thin and abstract variety: most have never visited Israel; most contribute little to, and know even less about, that country.[5]

While one could argue that attention to and knowledge of Israel has increased since Novick's study was published in 1999—since September 11, 2001, especially, coverage of the Middle East and Israel's ongoing conflicts would be harder to ignore—the difficulty Novick raises regarding Jewish identity has not gone away.

In her introduction to a 2008 collection of essays on *American Jewish Identity Politics*, Deborah Dash Moore suggests that starting in the late twentieth century, "Jewish identity acquired a self-conscious valence

1

lacking for an earlier generation."[6] She cites a familiar series of questions and complications: "What did it mean to be an American Jew? Was this a religious question? A question of ethnicity? Perhaps a political question? How did Jews understand themselves as individuals and as members of a group in the United States?"[7] For Dash Moore, "Jewish identity [was] ambiguously located among changing American interpretations of ethnicity, religion, people, and race."[8]

Such ambiguity is common in contemporary writings about Jewish American cultural identity. Henry Bial states most pointedly: "It is not easy to speak of a 'Jewish American identity' or even of 'American Jews,'[9] suggesting, however, that "Jewish studies as a discipline often proceeds as if it were possible to define an 'authentic' Jewish culture."[10] Andrew Furman writes of the "double bind" for Jewish American writers and academics, citing his own difficulty when applying for jobs at universities which were largely not "interested in an Americanist specializing in Jewish American fiction."[11] He suggests that the successes of "Saul Bellow, Philip Roth, and Bernard Malamud" pushed Jewish American writers out of the multicultural curriculum and toward, but not quite into, the dominant canon. For Furman, this "golden age of Jewish American fiction . . . has hemmed in contemporary Jewish American writers to a near invisible territory of literary limbo between the mainstream and the multicultural realm of literary discourse."[12] He further contends that the "socioeconomic factor—the disproportionate flow of Jewish Americans into the professions as the concomitant material success of Jewish Americans since World War II (although several poor Jews do exist)—plays a significant role in the exclusion of contemporary Jewish American writers from the multicultural canon."[13] The "near invisible territory" that Furman describes in academia can be seen as emblematic of Jewish culture itself.

Substantial or not, the exclusions, double binds, and persistent questions that pervade contemporary discussions of Jewish American literature and culture speak to the elusive difference felt by many Jewish Americans. Yet for many, the (in)abilty to assert this difference, this cultural uniqueness, is a crucial concern. David Biale, Michael Galchinsky, and Susannah Heschel speak of the discomfort of this concern, describing "the consciousness Jews have of themselves as occupying an anomalous status: insiders who are outsiders and outsiders who are insiders. They represent that boundary case whose very *lack* of belonging to a recognizable category creates a sense of unease."[14] But how do you understand and articulate a *sense* that has made its way through Jewish history and persists even in times and places of relative comfort? It is this enigma—bubbling out of "contradictions" and some implicit "lack"—that I explore in *Magical American Jew*.

What I am characterizing as enigmatic is the indefinite yet undeniable difference that informs "the consciousness [American] Jews have of themselves." According to Levitt, "[t]o remain marked as other even in the process of becoming citizens, of becoming incorporated into the nation, still haunts contemporary Jewish experience as well as efforts to explain Jewish difference."[15] These efforts to "explain Jewish difference," to communicate what "still haunts contemporary Jewish experience," present a singular challenge to American Jews and Jewish American artists who have attempted to shade the subtle markings of difference so they are more visible, attempted to provide the apparitions of history with a material presence, so they are apparent enough to acknowledge and discuss. *Magical American Jew* explores how certain Jewish American writers and filmmakers have employed magical realist techniques in their efforts to portray the enigmatic difference that Jewish Americans have felt and continue to feel. Within this study, I limit the still-wide pool of contemporary American Jews by focusing on largely assimilated and secular Jewish Americans whose habits, values, and identities are not determined by religious law.[16] The goal of *Magical American Jew* is not to identity and discuss an exhaustive list of Jewish American magical realist sources, but to provide substantive analyses of select works that reveal aspects of the enigmatic difference that shapes contemporary Jewish American identity.

Similar to the indefinite position of Jewish Americans, the magical realist mode does not fit easily into any singular category. As indicated above, it is often characterized as a *mode* of literary expression, rather than a genre within literature, which suggests that it "can characterize works belonging to several genres, periods or national literatures."[17] Although it is often described as a mode, magical realism has been used to *label* fictional and filmic works (as well as other works of art) and fiction writers and filmmakers (as well as other artists). However, scholars such as Jeanne Delbaere-Garant warn readers, theorists, and critics to "refrain, at least when referring to contemporary works in English, from speaking of 'magic realist writers,' for magic realism is often used only sporadically in an author's oeuvre, and sporadically even in those of his or her texts commonly regarded as 'magic realist.'"[18]

Works associated with magical realism tend to be those that possess a "co-presence" of the natural and supernatural that is treated as normal by the narrator. These works are often grounded in realistic settings, focus on characters who struggle with realistic concerns, yet allow various extensions of reality—the materialization of memories, the hyberbolic extensions of time or space—to coexist (without narrative question or pause) with those bound by realistic conventions. Although *Magical American Jew* focuses on Jewish American short fiction and film, the ways in which magical realism highlights complex identity negotiations works well in the study of U.S. ethnic literature as a whole.[19]

When the natural and the supernatural coexist, there is unique space in which to represent the dichotomies of ethnic identities. While the term ethnic comes from "the Greek *ethnikos*, a word that pejoratively denotes 'otherness' akin to the Hebrew term *goy* . . . [i]n the latter half of the twentieth century . . . *ethnic* and *ethnicity* have come to mean cultural . . . difference, located squarely in cultural customs rather than any essential racial makeup."[20] These "cultural customs" relate to established pasts, out of which came various traditions, languages, superstitions, religions, delicacies, and other cultural ingredients that have nourished the actions and interactions of communities for generations. Magical realism allows the convergence of past places, times, and traditions to coexist in a natural way in the "present." The untroubled narrative treatment provides readers and viewers with a more vivid view of the often hybrid identities that make up the ethnic imagination. While demonstrating the value of the magical realist mode through analyses of contemporary works of Jewish American short fiction and film, a further aim is to encourage its use in the study of U.S. ethnic literature more broadly.[21]

Employing a co-presence of the natural and supernatural as a means to represent marginalized identities can be traced back to the short fiction of Franz Kafka whom I see as a pivotal practitioner of what is now referred to as magical realism.[22] Significantly, Kafka used magical realist techniques to convey his own unique position as a German-speaking Jew in Prague who was keenly aware of—was able to *sense*—the vile waves of discrimination that would lead, over a decade after his own death in 1924, to the extermination of his entire family in the events of the Holocaust. If not the first, Kafka was certainly one of the most influential writers to marry the magical and the marginalized. Through stories such as "The Metamorphosis," "A Report to an Academy," and many others, Kafka portrayed the pressures, performances, and political anxieties that come with assimilation and marginalization, and he radically changed the literary landscape.

It is in the co-presence of worlds—exhibited by Kafka and others—where one can make the distinction between magical realism and the genres of fantasy or science fiction. The latter genres exist in a *singular* supernatural world, rather than a world in which realistic settings and circumstances are *simultaneously* cohabited by supernatural figures or occurrences that are treated as no less ordinary than the mundane details of real life. Robert Stam contends "With 'magic realism,' the word 'realism' remains the substantive, 'magic' only the qualifier."[23] As *magic* is the qualifier in "magic realism," *Jewish* is the qualifier in Jewish American. In each case, there are questions about the connection between the construction of words: What is the relationship between the magical and the real, the Jewish and the American? It is through examining the "qualifier[s]" and their relationships to their "substantive[s]"—addressing the questions of meaning and the significance that arises—where the enigma of Jewish American difference can be productively explored.

While there has been important work on the magical realist literary mode—Amaryll Beatrice Chanady, Frederic Jameson, Wendy Faris, Lois Parkinson Zamora, Robert Stam, Rawdon Wilson, and Shannin Schroeder have made notable, contemporary contributions to the ongoing debate about the features of this mode—and cultural and literary critics such as Hana Wirth-Nesher, Jonathan Freedman, Emily Miller Budick, Andrew Furman, Victoria Aarons, Dean Franco, and many others have written sustained works on aspects of the Jewish American literary tradition, there are markedly few studies that deal directly with Jewish American magical realism,[24] despite its presence in the work of writers and filmmakers as prominent as Bernard Malamud, Philip Roth, Cynthia Ozick, Steve Stern, Nathan Englander, Nicole Krauss, Woody Allen, and Joel and Ethan Coen. By concentrating on a diverse selection of Jewish American short fiction and film, addressing a range of subjects from archiving Holocaust testimony to satirical Jewish American humor, I am able to shed light on other facets of contemporary American society—including aspects of media, ethnicity, marginalization, and other pertinent topics. My intention with the chapters of *Magical American Jew* is to highlight the complexities and contradictions that emerge in the examination of Jewish American identity, while analyzing how magical realist techniques can enable a uniquely cogent portrayal of enigmatic elements of difference.

Although little scholarly attention has been paid to *Jewish American* magical realism, as referenced in the notes, there are two fairly recent books that focus on U.S. ethnic magical realism: *Uncertain Mirrors: Magical Realisms in U.S. Ethnic Literatures* (2009), by Jesús Benito, Ana Mª Manzanas, and Begoña Simal, and the anthology *Moments of Magical Realism in U.S. Ethnic Literatures* (2012), edited by Lyn Di Iorio Sandín and Richard Perez, both of which are addressed in greater depth in the conclusion. Additionally, in Shannin Schroeder's 2004 book *Rediscovering Magical Realism in the Americas*, Schroeder makes a compelling connection between U.S. ethnic writers and the magical realist mode. However, Schroeder's discussion is primarily about the presence of consumer and popular culture within North American magical realism, characterizing the mode "as an effective means for discussing North America's socioeconomic condition,"[25] rather than an effective means to illustrate anomalous cultural positions. While I value and directly engage with Schroeder's discussions of postmodernism and popular culture,[26] *Magical American Jew* is primarily concerned with the ways in which the magical realist mode has been used to highlight aspects of the enigmatic difference that, I argue, permeates contemporary Jewish American identities.

As referenced in the notes, there is limited scholarship devoted to Jewish American magical realism, but there are two evocative articles, offering important points of view, that are addressed in *Magical American Jew*. The more recent is Caroline Rody's "Jewish Post-Holocaust Fiction and the Magical Realist Turn," which is integrated and discussed most directly in the conclusion. An earlier essay, Tamara Kaye Sellman's "Jewish Magical Realism," provides a broader, but valuable overview and discussion of Jewish works that stretch the boundaries of realism. Sellman suggests "[p]opulations that are restricted often rely upon diffusions of reality to keep up hope and to explain what is often otherwise inexplicable." She goes on to posit that "[m]agical realism captures that merging between concrete reality and subjective realism, not to rationalize it, but to show how people enduring oppressive conditions must live among and between these worlds in order to survive psychically."[27] Sellman's articulation is compelling, particularly her suggestion that "diffusions of reality" can help "explain what is often otherwise inexplicable"; however, I would not characterize *contemporary* Jewish American conditions as "oppressive." As Andrew Furman suggests, a greater barrier to understanding and articulating Jewish American identity exists in "the assumption that Jews in America . . . have simply not suffered enough of late to be considered a minority or multicultural group."[28]

It is in the effort to address the questions and complications about Jewish American identity that *Magical American Jew* analyzes selections of contemporary Jewish American short fiction and film that feature contemporary American characters grappling with aspects of Jewish American difference. These fictions and films are all set in the contemporary United States and none of the protagonists are faced with any great oppression or alienation.[29] However, in each case, the figures at the center of these works are influenced by a self-consciousness that affects them and their surroundings, and their circumstances either include magical elements or lead to magical outcomes. With Levitt's endeavors to examine the "diversity of Jewish expression"[30] in mind, *Magical American Jew* focuses expressly on stories and films that use magical realist techniques to express the enigmatic positions of secular Jews in the contemporary United States—the losses and gains, restrictions, compromises, compulsions to remember, identity quests, power positions, and excesses.

The fictions and films discussed in this study can be or have been classified as works of magical realism. More directly in some cases, I address this classification (or lack of it), pulling from an assortment of scholarship on the literary mode. In an effort to consider the complexities that arise when discussing Jewish American identity, I investigate aspects of difference that are pertinent to contemporary American Jews: the consequences of experiencing and imagining difference, the presumptions about difference and conformity, the pressures that demand and sustain difference, the methods used to express difference, and the shifting manifestations and "types" of personified and performed difference.

It is with one of the *types* mentioned above in mind that I devote the first chapter of *Magical American Jew* to a discussion of Woody Allen's film *Annie Hall*. I argue for the film as an example of Jewish American magical realism that relies on postmodern techniques: meta-narratives, over-lapping layers of media, an awareness of itself as art and artifact. The self-consciousness and reflexivity characteristic of postmodernism helps to portray a persona who is grappling with feelings of isolation and insecurity. The effort to compensate for these feelings creates behavioral excess that accentuates difference and exposes a heightened level of discomfiture. *Annie Hall* uses magical realist techniques to illustrate this excess, which, in the context of the film, is a residual of negotiating with the enigma of Jewish American difference. Working with scholarship on magical realism, postmodernism, and contemporary media—most notably from Wendy Faris, Lois Parkinson Zamora, Shannin Schroeder, Amaryll Beatrice Chanady, Vivian Sobchack, Judith Halberstam, Ira Livingston, and Christian Moraru—I demonstrate that the augmented narrative body not only represents the excess that is associated with Jewish American difference, but amounts to a postmodern presence, which bears affective import that is crucial to the experience of the film.

To delve into the affective forces that influence Jewish American identities, chapter 2 analyzes Cynthia Ozick's short story "Levitation," concentrating on the presence of shame. Although guilt is an affect often linked with the Jewish American persona, it is shame, I argue, that plays a greater affective role within American Jewish communities, and it is shame that is at work in "Levitation." Shame takes several forms in the story, and this chapter argues for the value of analyzing these forms to gain greater insight on Jewish American difference. Within this chapter, I discuss the manifestations and exchanges of shame that drive this unique work of fiction. I elucidate the distinction between shame and guilt— primarily relating to guilt's association with behavior and shame's with self-esteem. It is in the perception that "some quality of the self has been brought into question,"[31] where magical realism finds fertile ground—in this case, leading to the levitation of all the Jews at an urban party away from common ground. The shame that results from the presumption of difference gets internalized and incorporated into Jewish identity, and it is this identity that consumes, infects, drives, and ultimately divides the protagonists of Cynthia Ozick's magical realist tale.

While chapter 2 challenges the common association between Jews and guilt and posits shame as a more discerning lens through which to view Jewish American difference—a difference that is influenced by a history in which the Holocaust is a principal concern—chapter 3 focuses more directly on memory and the masochistic extreme that can be imagined if one were to position the Holocaust at the center of contemporary Jewish American identity. Although chapter 2 and chapter 3 each analyze a short story that features a Holocaust survivor and each concludes with a magical ending, the chapters speak to different aspects of the enigmatic. Shame gives us access to understanding and thinking about the enigma of difference, while memory—and the consistent call "to remember"—

shows us how the enigmatic is enhanced and identity is troubled for many contemporary American Jews.

Melvin Jules Bukiet's short story "The Library of Moloch," the story at the center of chapter 3, concludes in a blazing video archive as a Holocaust witness speaks through a video screen to the archivist whose obsessive pursuit for traumatic testimonies turns into a masochistic search for ethnic identification. This premise reveals some of the complexities and potential consequences of positioning the Holocaust at the center of Jewish identity. Another important aspect of this chapter speaks to Walter Benn Michaels's critique of "the dependence of identity on memory"[32] and the complications and contradictions that arise for Jewish Americans who are compelled to remember an atrocity that most have never experienced and many have characterized as inexpressible and unknowable. In recent decades, Jews have made an active commitment to archive the Holocaust. This important effort has allowed representations of this horror to be inserted (on many levels, through many channels) into the Jewish consciousness; it has become a significant part of how Jews and Jewish Americans define themselves and has been a significant force in the formation of Jewish American identities. This chapter explores the masochistic potential of founding one's identity too centrally on this connection.

Chapter 4 addresses the tensions that arise from the perceived separation between religiosity and ethnicity, between Judaism and Jewishness. Significantly, I argue that the perceptions and practices of Judaism and Jewish ethnicity complicate the "fundamental dichotomy" of religious and ethnic identities, reinforcing the enigmatic difference that marks contemporary Jewish American communities. Anchoring my discussion in analyses of Nathan Englander's short story "The Gilgul of Park Avenue" and Steve Stern's short story "The Tale of a Kite," this chapter aligns humor with magic, demonstrating how magical realist and comical modes work in conjunction to illustrate the enigma of difference that permeates contemporary Jewish American literature and culture.

Just as the magical realist narratives found in "Gilgul" and in "Kite" subvert conventional notions of reality, the humor featured in each story subverts stable structures, classifications, and categories. Through my discussion of the magical and comical modes in Englander's story and in Stern's story, I am able to highlight the fallacy of a stable Jewish American identity—or the equivalently aberrant idea of a purely religious or a purely ethnic Jewish American identity—and illustrate the heterogeneous and continuously changing character of contemporary American Jewry.

Chapter 5 extends the discussion of humor into an analysis of Sarah Silverman's performance film *Jesus Is Magic*, in which she mobilizes her Jewish American ethnicity in an effort to magnify a narcissistic persona and satirize twenty-first century American media culture. As with chapter 1, the final body chapter of *Magical American Jew* returns to the influence and utilization of media, moving from the twentieth century neurotic figure found in *Annie Hall* to the twenty-first century narcissistic figure found in *Jesus Is Magic*. Throughout her film, Silverman employs fantastic diversions from her stage performance—extensions comparable to those found in Allen's film. As with *Annie Hall*, the extensions in *Jesus Is Magic* point to a certain excess, offering Silverman's *film* audience more explicit insight into the mind of her character—an assimilated and narcissistic Jewish American woman who maintains a unique and curious connection to her Jewish American identity. To help analyze the ideas of Jewish American identity raised in Silverman's piece—noting the influence of contemporary American media culture on her character's intermittent moves to identify herself as Jewish, as American, as "white"—I draw from scholarship on ethnic studies and ethnic humor, addressing the ideas of Werner Sollers, Joseph Boskin, John Lowe, Lois Leveen, Alan Dundes, and others.

The conclusion of *Magical American Jew* places greater emphasis on Franz Kafka and his essential influence on the Jewish American artists featured in this study. The concluding chapter addresses Kafka's own ambiguous cultural identity, as a German speaking Jew living in Prague at the turn of the twentieth-century, and highlights the rich tradition of mystical and fabulist Jewish storytelling—biblical and secular—that influenced and inspired Kafka, as well as the artists whose works are analyzed most closely in *Magical American Jew*. I also address some of the Jewish American magical realist fictions and films that are not discussed at length in the preceding chapters—fiction from Isaac Bashevis Singer, Bernard Malamud, and Philip Roth, along with original films and filmic adaptations from Joel and Ethan Coen, Scott McGehee and David Siegel, Liev Schreiber, and an additional work from Woody Allen. I close out the conclusion by examining some of the ways that the magical realist mode has been and can be used to consider U.S. ethnic literatures and cultures more broadly.

By examining the magical elements within these varied works of short fiction and film, *Magical American Jew* is shedding light on the productive and destructive tensions that have contributed to the creation and (mis)understanding of contemporary Jewish American identities. The magical realist mode animates the aspects of difference that impact the way American Jews imagine themselves and offers a mode of expression and articulation that is uniquely apt for expressing the enigma of Jewish American difference.

NOTES

1. The phrases noted come from: Dean Franco, "Re-Placing the Border in Ethnic Literature," *Cultural Critique* 50 (Winter, 2002): 104–34, 114; Victoria Aarons, "The Outsider Within: Women in Contemporary Jewish-American Fiction," *Contemporary Literature* 28.3 (Autumn, 1987): 378–93, 382; Deborah Dash Moore, "Introduction," in *American Jewish Identity Politics*, ed. Deborah Dash Moore (Ann Arbor: U Michigan P, 2008), 9; Andrew Furman, *Contemporary Jewish American Writers and the Multicultural Dilemma: Return of the Exiled* (Syracuse: Syracuse UP, 2000), 4.

2. Laura Levitt, "Impossible Assimilations, American Liberalism, and Jewish Difference: Revisiting Jewish Secularism," *American Quarterly* 59.3 (2007): 807–32, 807.

3. Ibid., 809.

4. Peter Novick, *The Holocaust in American Life* (New York: Mariner, 2000), 7.

5. Ibid., 7.

6. Deborah Dash Moore, "Introduction," in *American Jewish Identity Politics*, ed. Deborah Dash Moore (Ann Arbor: U Michigan P, 2008), 1.

7. Ibid., 1–2.

8. Ibid., 9.

9. Henry Bial, *Acting Jewish: Negotiating Ethnicity on the American Stage and Scree* (Ann Arbor: U Michigan P, 2005), 12.

10. Ibid.

11. Andrew Furman, *Contemporary Jewish American Writers and the Multicultural Dilemma: Return of the Exiled* (Syracuse: Syracuse UP, 2000), 2.

12. Ibid., 4.

13. Ibid., 4.

14. David Biale, Michael Galchinsky, and Susannah Heschel, "Introduction: The Dialectic of Jewish Enlightenment," in *Insider/Outsider: American Jews and Multiculturalism*, eds. David Biale, Michael Galchinsky, and Susannah Heschel (Berkeley: UCP, 1998), 1–13, 5 (emphasis added).

15. Levitt, "Impossible Assimilations," 807.

16. The protagonist Charles, from Nathan Englander's story "The Gilgul of Park Avenue," might be a minor exception here. As discussed in chapter 4, Charles was not raised Jewish, but was magically endowed with a "Jewish Soul." Once this magical transformation takes place, he makes an effort to adhere to Jewish law more closely than most of the other characters discussed in this study. However, Charles is not always sure why he is following the laws as he does. He has difficulty explaining what being Jewish really means (consistent with many contemporary American Jews); he steals his mezuzah from a neighbor's doorframe, and he views God as a secondary element to being Jewish.

17. Amaryll Beatrice Chanady, *Magical Realism and the Fantastic: Resolved Versus Unresolved Antinomy* (New York: Garland, 1985), 2.

18. Jeanne Delbaere-Garant, "Psychic Realism, Mythic Realism, Grotesque Realism Variations on Magic Realism in Contemporary Literature in English," *Magical Realism: Theory, History, Community*, ed. Lois Parkinson Zamora and Wendy B. Faris (Durham, NC: Duke UP, 1995), 249–66, 249. We see the sporadic use referenced by Delbaere-Garant in the works discussed in this study, specifically in Cynthia Ozick's "Levitation," Melvin Jules Bukiet's "The Library of Moloch," and Nathan Englander's "The Gilgul of Park Avenue." In the first two pieces, the magical realist moments are largely reserved for the endings, eliciting questions about the significance of these supernatural turns and the circumstances that lead up to them. In "Gilgul," the magical premise is embedded in the opening details and the story proceeds from there.

19. As addressed in more depth in the conclusion, there are two fairly recent books that focus on U.S. ethnic magical realism: *Uncertain Mirrors: Magical Realisms in U.S. Ethnic Literatures*, by Jesús Benito, Ana Mª Manzanas, and Begoña Simal, and the anthology *Moments of Magical Realism in U.S. Ethnic Literatures*, edited by Lyn Di Iorio Sandín and Richard Perez.

20. Dean Franco, *Ethnic American Literature: Comparing Chicano, Jewish, and African American Writing* (Charlottesville: UVP, 2006), 18.

21. Along with a discussion of the books cited above, this aim is fleshed out more in the conclusion.

22. Angel Flores, Alejo Carpentier, and others have made efforts to claim magical realism as a "genuinely Latin American" (Flores 116) mode of literature. However, many scholars of magical realism, including Flores, draw "the current to Kafka" (Chanady 19) who lived in Prague and wrote in German and persists as an implicit challenge to these regional claims. Rawdon Wilson discusses "the geographical fallacy" of such claims, arguing that this move "collapses many levels of textual evidence and seems, flatly, to deny the parallels between Latin American (or Anglo-Indian or Canadian) magical realism and the tradition of European fantasy exemplified by, say, Kafka or Bulgakov" (222–23).

23. Robert Stam, *Literature through Film: Realism, Magic, and the Art of Adaptation* (Malden, MA: Blackwell, 2005), 316.

24. Tamara Kaye Sellman's article "Jewish Magical Realism: Writing to Tell the Tale" references a number of literary works that could be categorized as "Jewish Magical Realism," but suggests a paucity of scholarship devoted expressly to the subject. In a more recent and substantial article, Caroline Rody's "Jewish Post-Holocaust Fiction and the Magical Realist Turn" argues that there has been an "eruption" of Jewish American magical realist fiction that contain postmodern, post-Holocaust plots of quests for origins" (39). I engage most directly with Rody's article in the conclusion. There was also a special issue of the Berlin-based journal *Symbolism: An International Annual of Critical Aesthetics* that dedicated a portion of the issue to "Jewish Magic Realism." My essay "Jewish, Here in the Back," an earlier version of chapter 4, was published in this special issue and is one of two essays in the journal that focus exclusively on Jewish American magical realist texts. The other essay, by the Israeli scholar and professor Meyrav Koren-Kuik, examines the use of magical realism in Dara Horn's novels.

25. Shannin Schroeder, *Rediscovering Magical Realism in the Americas* (Westport, CT: Praeger, 2004), 74.

26. Most notably in chapter 1, dealing with Woody Allen's film *Annie Hall*.

27. Tamara Kaye Sellman, "Jewish Magical Realism: Writing to Tell the Tale," *Margin*, April 20, 2006.

28. Furman, *Contemporary Jewish American Writers and the Multicultural Dilemma*, 5.

29. The one exception can be found in Steve Stern's "The Tale of a Kite." Although the exact year is never mentioned, there are details that suggest the story is set just prior to World War II and a greater degree of cultural tension seems to exist.

30. Levitt, "Impossible Assimilations," 826.

31. Donald L. Nathanson, "A Timetable for Shame," *The Many Faces of Shame*, ed. Donald L. Nathanson (New York: Guilford, 1987), 1–63, 4.

32. Walter Benn Michaels, "'You Who Was Never There': Slavery and the New Historicism—Deconstruction and the Holocaust," in *The Americanization of the Holocaust*, ed. Hilene Flanzbaum (Baltimore: Johns Hopkins UP, 1999), 181–97, 189.

ONE

Postmodern Neurotic

*Jewish American Excess and the Narrative Body in
Woody Allen's* Annie Hall

When writing about Jewish American acculturation, many have referenced the well worn quip "Jews are just like everyone else, only more
so."[1] Laura Levitt suggests this joke speaks to the "excess that always
marks . . . [Jews] as other. . . . The harder U.S. Jews try to fit in, the more
they end up demonstrating their Jewish difference."[2] Implicit in the oft-
stated joke is the discomfort and self-consciousness, even paranoia, about
how one does *not* fit in—the insecurities that inspire the effort to try
"harder." These insecurities, which come from a real and imagined sense
of difference, can prevent the unconscious ease of natural action; it is
relatable to the "double-consciousness" put forward by W. E. B. Du Bois
who describes the "peculiar sensation . . . of always looking at one's self
through the eyes of others, of measuring one's soul by the tape of a world
that looks on in amused contempt and pity."[3] While I am not trying to
claim the double-consciousness described by Du Bois for all Jewish
Americans, I do make the connection to the real and imagined perception
of difference that has influenced some Jewish American values, actions,
and identities, and influenced the portrayals of contemporary American
Jews in works of fiction and film.

Woody Allen's acclaimed film *Annie Hall* employs postmodern techniques and the magical realist mode to illustrate the type of late-twenti-
eth-century Jewish American excess[4] discussed in the opening paragraph—a behavioral excess that I argue is a product of grappling with
enigmatic aspects of Jewish American difference. Similar to magical realism, postmodernism is a slippery concept that has garnered debate about

13

its origin, meaning, and application. Linda Hutcheon, a prominent scholar of postmodernism, suggests that most theorists see postmodernist art as "marked primarily by an internalized investigation of the nature, the limits, and the possibilities of the language or discourse of art. On the surface, postmodernism's main interest might seem to be in the processes of its own production and reception, as well as in its own parodic relation to the art of the past."[5] Hutcheon argues "that postmodernism is a fundamentally contradictory enterprise: its art forms (and its theory) use and abuse, install and then subvert convention in parodic ways, self-consciously pointing both to their own inherent paradoxes and provisionality and, of course, to their critical or ironic re-reading of the art of the past."[6] In the context of *Annie Hall*, the parodies, paradoxes, installations, and subversions all contribute to the experience of excess. Part of what makes Allen's film so effective is its ability to exhibit this excess through an augmentation of the narrative body.

In *Annie Hall*, the protagonist is more than the diminutive human figure Alvy Singer (played by Woody Allen) whose body and voice appear to direct and demand our attention, but rather, what I argue is, a postmodern presence comprised of all that fractures and multiplies this representative persona. It is the compilation of embodied memories and fantasies, disembodied voices, cartoons, subconscious-subtitles, dreams, conversing split-screens, and voiceover narratives that are interacting with and affecting the on-screen characters as well as the audience. These narrative splits and extensions are representative of the behavioral excess of Alvy Singer who has become emblematic of an ethnic "type" that still exists in the twenty-first century.[7] This type is often associated with certain neurotic behaviors, stemming from "problems of anxiety, fearfulness, and social inhibition."[8] Freud notes a tendency for neurotics to "contrive . . . to feel themselves scorned"[9] and a "compulsion to repeat" adverse behaviors.[10] These behavioral tendencies are exhibited by and through Allen's film. In this chapter, I elaborate on the augmented narrative body of *Annie Hall* and illustrate how magical realist and postmodern techniques are used to evoke a multi-faceted Jewish American persona.

In *Annie Hall*, characters, actions, and circumstances are often depicted with comic exaggeration and a unique conflation of the fantastic and the real. Discussing the "hyperbole of magical realism," Lois Parkinson Zamora and Wendy B. Faris note how "excess is a hallmark of the [magical realist] mode."[11] In their description, they suggest that

> magical realism is a mode suited to exploring—and transgressing—
> boundaries, whether the boundaries are ontological, political, geographical, or generic. Magical realism often facilitates the fusion, or coexistence, of possible worlds, spaces, systems that would be irreconcilable in other modes of fiction. The propensity of magical realist texts

to admit a plurality of worlds means that they often situate themselves on liminal territory between or among those worlds. [12]

We can imagine how the "coexistence" of the natural and supernatural relies on an augmentation of space and time. In *Annie Hall*, this augmentation is displayed through various narrative extensions, including overlapping aspects of media, as well as dreams, fantasies, and memories, each portrayed with a distinct material presence. However, as Amaryll Chanady and others have discussed, the presence of dreams, fantasies, and memories "does not make a story into an example of magical realism, unless the imagined events are presented as objectively real. If the situation is described as a dream, the supernatural is invalidated, and the phenomenon explained." [13] Part of what makes *Annie Hall* an example of magical realism has to do with the ordinary narrative treatment of extraordinary circumstances and events. The film consistently pushes and transgresses narrative boundaries, and offers a "plurality" of otherwise "irreconcilable" worlds, but never pauses to explain the continuous course of fantastic occurrences. In one example, Alvy, Annie, and Alvy's friend Rob travel back to Alvy's childhood home, located beneath a rollercoaster in the Coney Island section of Brooklyn—a journey that covers both space and time. In this case, Alvy, Annie, and Rob physically enter into the past, watching Alvy's parents argue in the den before Aly leads his guests into the living room to witness a party that took place in 1945. At one point, Rob even poses a few questions to Alvy's aunt Tessie, who responds without looking directly at him. The narrative never stops to question how or why this takes places, but incorporates the interactions into the narrative in a magically real way.

Consistent with other scholars of magical realism, Jon Thiem suggests "one of the main advantages of magical realism as a literary mode lies in its extraordinary flexibility, in its capacity to delineate, explore, and transgress boundaries." [14] *Annie Hall* transgresses boundaries in a myriad of ways, and these transgressions contribute to an understanding of Jewish American excess. Along with the magical layers, this behavioral and self-conscious excess is exhibited through intertextual extensions that stem from and communicate a keen awareness of difference. Although examples are discussed throughout this chapter, one instance can be found in the clip of *The Sorrow and the Pity*—Marcel Ophüls's 251-minute documentary on the collaboration between France's Vichy government and Nazi Germany—that is shown in the film, signifying the Holocaust, the media's role in disseminating images and representations of the Holocaust, the influence that such representations and historical realities has on contemporary identity construction, and much more. From the very beginning, we see how the expanding boundaries of Allen's film become emblematic of the excess that exposes and divulges aspects of Jewish American difference.

The process of extension and construction that is so prominent throughout *Annie Hall* is in stark contrast to the film's spare opening: simple text, *Annie Hall*, in white letters over a black background; the credits follow in silence. The first image is of Woody Allen, playing the protagonist Alvy Singer—the presumed subject. The first sound is Allen/ Alvy breathing in, giving life to the narrative body. The camera is still; Alvy Singer stands before a flat beige background and speaks directly into the camera—at the audience, at himself, at an imagined analyst— opening with "an old joke: ahm, two elderly women are at a Catskill mountain resort, and one of them says: 'Boy, the food at this place is really terrible'; the other one says: 'Yeah, I know, and such small portions.'" [15] The image of Alvy Singer and the joke that he opens with are suggestive of a particular Jewish American identity; while reference to "a Catskill mountain resort" conjures certain associations, [16] we are presented with a persona who privileges humor and holds a comically bleak view of life. The second "important joke" he tells in this opening scene is attributed to Sigmund Freud and Groucho Marx—two prominent Jewish figures who are associated with neurosis and excess: "I would never want to belong to any club that would have someone like me for a member." He describes this as the "key joke of [his] adult life in terms of [his] relationships with women," [17] furthering the characterization to reveal a persona who is self-reflective enough to *acknowledge* an inherent discontent with whomever he involves himself with romantically. The opening scene concludes with an admission that he may be going through a "life crisis" since he turned forty, discussing his aging image and projecting this image into the future, hopeful that he will get better as he gets older, becoming the "balding virile type, instead of the distinguished gray." Then he sighs and reveals the most present crisis: he and Annie—the title character—are no longer together, something he is still trying to "get his mind around." [18] His attempt to discuss this breakup leads, in a psychoanalytic move, back to his childhood; he describes himself as a "reasonably happy kid . . . [who was] brought up in Brooklyn during World War II." [19]

Following the opening scene, the narrative takes us into the past, revealing a representation of Alvy Singer as a child, sitting in an analyst's office with his mother who laments to the doctor that Alvy has been depressed and has stopped doing his homework. When asked for an explanation, Alvy discloses the source of his depression and the underlining crisis in his life: "'The universe is expanding. . . . [T]he universe is everything, and if it's expanding, someday it will break apart and that would be the end of everything!'" Dr. Flicker's advice—"We've gotta try to enjoy ourselves while we're here!" [20]—is significant. It reinforces the anxiety of the expanding universe—and impending death—and applies pressure to "enjoy ourselves while we're here." The doctor's advice is also indicative of the Jewish diaspora, where moments of comfort were never lasting, but expansion and movement were never ending.

This diasporic perspective would be particularly keen in Brooklyn during World War II, when Alvy receives this advice from Dr. Flicker. But even in the twenty-first century, the diaspora still influences Jewish identity. Dean Franco suggests that "America is home [for Jews] precisely because it is diasporic; neither the homeland nor the Jewish nation, America is a place where Jews can be comfortably uncomfortable, physically and socially safe, not pejoratively marked as interlopers exactly, but different all the same."[21] Franco's description relates to the second "important joke" referenced above—"I would never want to belong to any club that would have someone like me for a member." In this case, it is the "club" of America. The United States must remain "comfortably uncomfortable" if Jews are to remain Jews, which is to say different. Returning to the words of Dr. Flicker, the advice to "enjoy ourselves while we're here" has a place in Jewish/Yiddish culture. Not only is a reminder of mortality implicit in the statement—related to the opening joke about the elderly women at the Catskill resort, by which Alvy attributes his view of life: "full of loneliness, and misery, and suffering, and unhappiness, and it's all over much too quickly"[22]—but Jewish culture, particularly as portrayed in literature, on stage, and on screen,[23] has a history of humor during hard times, as well as a tendency to "kvetch" about one's unfortunate plight.[24] The heavy laughter that follows the doctor's statement plays up the theatricality and anxiety of his advice.

Out of the doctor's laughter, we see the image of a house tucked beneath a Coney Island roller coaster—one might imagine a "comfortably uncomfortable" residence—and we hear the first notes of music. Over the soft, rumbling ascension of the rollercoaster and the sounds of a muted horn, we hear the disembodied voice of the adult Alvy Singer, providing voiceover narration about memory and childhood. Although his analyst has suggested that he exaggerates his childhood memories, in the context of the film, hyperbole becomes reality, evident at this particular moment in the location of his childhood home beneath a Coney Island rollercoaster, to which he attributes his "nervous" personality. Alvy claims to have a "hyperactive imagination" which has caused him to have "some trouble between fantasy and reality."[25] This assertion is represented by a scene showing the young Alvy Singer running in front of three men in military uniforms and one woman in a red dress who pauses before the still lens and puckers her red lips to offer a kiss to the camera. Fantasies of virility and sexuality are represented in this brief clip, as Alvy equates himself with the masculine[26]—mainstream, gentile—strength of the military, while simultaneously suggesting that he is the recipient (in bodily absentia) of this woman's flirtatious affection. Already we can see how fantasy is an early extension of the narrative. But Alvy's mention of fantasy, and the position of Alvy's childhood home beneath a Coney Island rollercoaster that he links to his personality, should not be confused with an attempt at explanation that "would eliminate its position of equivalence with respect to our conventional view of reality."[27] In Allen's film, Alvy is a child prone to fantasies—particularly sexualized fantasies—whose childhood house *is* beneath a Coney Island rollercoaster. Not only is a scene played out in which the young Alvy sips a shaking spoon of soup as a rollercoaster roars overhead, but as referenced earlier, the adult Alvy returns to his old house—still beneath the rollercoaster—with Annie and his friend Rob, and as they talk to and about the figures from Alvy's past, the house periodically shakes as the ride roars overhead. These scenes, along with others discussed later in the chapter, illustrate the "hyperbole of magical realism" and serve to "integrate . . . the supernatural into the code of the natural, which must redefine its borders."[28]

In *Annie Hall*, the magical and postmodern work in conjunction with one another. Shannin Schroeder notes how "innovative postmodern features, including metafiction, eclecticism, multiplicity, discontinuity, and the erasure of boundaries, are the frequent tools of magical realists."[29] Such "postmodern features" are constitutional characteristics in *Annie Hall*, which exhibits a profusion of metafictional moments, resists a chronological sequence, collapses the barriers between past and present, actor and audience, and incorporates layers of visual media, including television, film, and photography. Discussing the presence of and relationship between such visual media, Vivian Sobchack suggests "Cinematic technology *animates* the photographic and reconstitutes its materiality, visibility, and perceptual verisimilitude in a difference not of degree but of kind. The *moving picture* is a visible representation not of activity finished or past but of activity coming into being and being."[30] Sobchack elaborates on this cinematic being (and coming into being), marking it as a formal distinction between photography—which she relates "with loss, with pastness, and with death"[31]—and the animated presence of film, made up of parts that constitute a body:

> That is, articulated as separate shots and scenes, discontiguous spaces and discontinuous times are synthetically gathered together in a coherence that is the cinematic lived body: the camera its perceptive organ, the projector its expressive organ, the screen its discrete and material center of meaningful experience. In sum, the cinematic exists as an objective and visible *performance* of the perceptive and expressive structure of subjective lived-body experience.[32]

The postmodern and magical realist components that animate *Annie Hall* allow the film to function as an ethnically charged and materially excessive "lived-body experience."

While there is an important performative component to the excess found in *Annie Hall*, it is different from the "objective and visible *performance*" which Sobchack attributes to the materiality of film. In *Annie Hall*, aspects of Jewish American identity are performed in the way that "gender proves to be performative—that is, constituting the identity it is perported to be"[33]—in Judith Butler's important theorization. For Butler, "identity is performatively constituted by the very 'expressions' that are said to be its results."[34] Butler forces us to think about how and why people behave as they do and how and why these behaviors are interpreted as they are. According to Henry Bial, who works with concepts posited by Butler, "analysis of significant performances created by Jews in American theater, film, and television over the last half century is essential to understanding the shifting formulation of Jewish identity over the same period."[35] Bial devotes portions of his study to "Jews in the diaspora . . . especially in the postwar United States, where barriers to assimilation and intermarriage are lower than ever before, [and] the traditional approach to performing Judaism has been destabilized."[36] Working with related claims made by Stephen Whitfield and Arnold Band, Bial posits that within "less affiliated homes, popular drama has become increasingly more important as a source of information on how to *act* Jewish."[37] He quotes Egon Mayer who suggests that one can identify the "longing for Jewishness reflected time and time again in Jews who flock to Woody Allen movies."[38] In *Annie Hall*, the magical realist and postmodern techniques enhance the "expressions" of Jewish American behavioral excess and aid in "understanding the shifting formulation of Jewish identity."

As suggested earlier, the opening frames of *Annie Hall*, particularly the "trouble between fantasy and reality" depicted on screen, are consistent with the excess and hyperbole that are featured throughout the film. As the initial voiceover in *Annie Hall* takes us through Alvy's past, we settle in an elementary school classroom where we witness the young Alvy Singer kissing one of his schoolmates. The teacher scolds him, but the Alvy who responds is not the boy whom we watched kissing his classmate, but the forty-year old Alvy Singer, now sitting in the back of the room, defending himself for "expressing a healthy sexual curiosity." The interaction continues as the girl whom Alvy kisses exclaims: "For God sakes Alvy, even Freud speaks of a latency period!"[39] But Alvy cannot wait for the emergence of latent urges; he has revealed the source of his anxieties to a medical professional who made it clear that "We've gotta try to enjoy ourselves while we're here!"

Beyond the movement into Alvy's past that this classroom scene provides—initially accompanied by the disembodied voice of his present—the emergence of his present figure, arguing with a manifestation from his past, is an example of the magical realist co-presence that is at work in the film, transgressing conventional realist boundaries, notably regarding time. In this case, we have a "present time" narrator providing the context for a scene in the past in which the forty-year-old Alvy Singer appears and interacts. Even with the dispersal of subject positions (young

Alvy, older Alvy, narrator), the flow of the narrative never falters; events just play themselves out—no questions asked, no explanations required—and the film's narrative body continues to grow.

The classroom scene progresses as the narrative voice asserts itself again, admitting that he sometimes wonders what his classmates are doing today, leading a few of the children from this room to stand up and respond, revealing a range of occupations and interests that includes a boy who "runs a profitable trust company" to a girl who admits that she is "into leather." When these pronouncements have finished, the scene cuts to a television screen, where Alvy Singer, who "wound up a comedian," is being interviewed on a talk show by Dick Cavett.[40] The voice-over transitions into the speaking voice of the Alvy figure on television, providing yet another play on time and space, media within media. The intertextual nature of *Annie Hall* makes it easy to see the film as extending beyond the singular, where even the author does not stand alone.

Soon after Alvy's appearance on the screen within the screen, we are offered a different modulation of time and space, where a still camera shows people walking along a New York City sidewalk; Alvy Singer's voice can be heard talking to his friend Rob about the anti-Semitic comments that he believes have been directed at him. This begins as a "voice-off," in which the voices of Alvy and Rob are off screen. Alvy's paranoia, which speaks to real and imagined difference, is packaged in fairly simple dialogue, yet gestures toward complex layers of fiction and media. As Rob questions his friend's mild hysteria—suggesting that Alvy's a paranoid conspiracy-theorist—Alvy insists that an acquaintance at NBC replied to his query about lunch by saying "*Jew* eat?" instead of "Did you eat?"[41] He relates another experience at a record store where the clerk told him about a sale on Wagner, a recommendation which Alvy interprets as anti-Semitic. The voice-off itself "may also serve to make the viewer/listener think about different levels of the film's fiction,"[42] since it's not immediately evident whether the voice is sharing the same time and space as the figures on screen.

When Alvy and Rob finally do emerge into the focus of the frame, the camera glides back at the same pace, tracking their walk until the end of the scene when they move past the camera. We see here how "the very mobility of its vision structures the cinematic subject (both film and spectator) as always in the act of displacing itself in time, space, and the world; thus, despite its existence as materially embodied and synoptically centered (on the screen or as the spectator's lived body), it is always eluding its own (as well as our) containment."[43] The elusion in this scene is heightened by the initial move to lock the viewer's eye on a singular location where it must wait for the bodies to arrive, grounded only by the voices of Alvy and Rob—which remain constant and audible to the audience—yet unstable still, as Rob refers to Alvy as "Max," an uncertain and ethnically ambiguous name. Soon after entering the visual frame, Rob looks at his watch and asks whether Alvy will be late for his date with Annie, whom Alvy has arranged to meet for a movie; as Alvy responds, the figures move past the camera, and the audience is held back before a short jump in time takes us to where Alvy is already waiting.

The play with time and space continues at the Beekman theater where Annie arrives late (after the audience), emerging out of a taxi two minutes after the movie they had planned to watch has begun. As a result, Alvy insists on seeing a different film, one they can watch from start to finish. He suggests *The Sorrow and the Pity*, and though Annie is not interested in a "four hour documentary about Nazis" — another reference to time, as well as a gesture toward Alvy's Jewish identity — Alvy seems to get his way, as the next frame finds them in line at The New Yorker theater (where they and the audience have relocated), suffering through the pedantic ramblings of a man in line behind them.[44] Annie is upset because she slept through a therapy session, a comment that contributes to the layers of time, space, and characterization. As the viewer eventually learns, these sessions are a product of her relationship with Alvy; he pays for the analysis that ultimately helps her find the strength and rationale to leave him, her psychoanalytic benefactor. (Of course, psychoanalysis has its own history of unearthing remnants from the past and making them a consideration in the present.)

While in line at The New Yorker theater, we are not only steeped in postmodern meta-narratives — films within films, conversations over conversations — but we get a closer look at the diversions and extensions of Alvy Singer who is consumed by the pontificating professor in line behind him, while selectively returning to the conversation he is holding with Annie about her depression and their "sexual problem," for which he insists she claim exclusive responsibility. Even at the heart of the present crisis that has inspired the film — the break-up with Annie that he cannot get his "mind around" — Alvy's attention is dividing and expanding, branching away from confrontation and emotion, compensating for a heightened awareness and an inability to deal with crisis directly. The overlapping subject matter gains postmodern import when considering the disquisition of the Columbia professor who speaks to his date about various media-related topics; he begins by lamenting the lack of "cohesive structure" in the latest Fellini film. After some brief pauses during which Alvy and Annie's conversation emerges, the professor moves from "indulgent filmmakers" to Samuel Beckett to the theorist and critic Marshall McLuhan and the "influence of television." Unable to bear it any longer, Alvy steps out of line and addresses the camera directly, "breaking the fourth wall" to ask what one is to do when "stuck on a movie line with a guy like this behind you?" The professor then steps out of line to defend himself before the judgment of the camera. In the famous conclusion to this scene, Alvy pulls Marshall McLuhan himself out from behind a billboard and allows him to put the pedantic professor in his place —

telling him that he has no idea what he's talking about. The scene ends with Alvy facing the camera once again, suggesting how great it would be if life were really like this.[45]

While this scene is notable for its humor and originality, it does elicit questions relevant to the enigma of difference. In this case, the questions are about what is and what is not real. In the film, as discussed before, Alvy's childhood home *is* beneath a Coney Island rollercoaster. This is reinforced by the narrative voice and Alvy, Rob, and Annie's return visit to Alvy's home. But at The New Yorker theater, the viewers are told that what was just on screen was *not* real, or at least not real in some extra-textual sense of the word. So the questions emerge: How are we meant to understand the events we have already viewed? How are we meant to understand the events we will go on to view? These questions are related to the cultural and national ambivalence that many American Jews have experienced. In terms of difference, what is real and what is not? How are Jewish Americans the same as every American, yet also different? For Alvy Singer in particular, how real is the anti-Semitism that he cites? How pervasive is his paranoia? These uncertainties lead to the behavioral excess that is communicated through Allen's film.

The themes and cinematic moves that dominate the scene at The New Yorker also serve to "complicate . . . the divisions between *high* and *low* culture, elite and mass consciousness"[46] that are linked directly to post-modernism. Such divisions are dramatized throughout *Annie Hall*. Another such example centers on Alvy's relationship with his second wife, Robin. In this scene, Alvy and Robin are at a party of New York intellectuals; as they enter the living room of the host who is going to publish Robin's book, Robin rattles off a few of the more prominent guests, among whom are department chairs from Princeton and Cornell. When Alvy makes a joke about finding "two more chairs . . . [to make] a dining room set," Robin asks why he is being so "hostile." He answers that he wants to "watch the Knicks on television." In the next shot, we find Alvy alone in a bedroom watching the Knicks game, alienating himself from the "high" culture of New York intellectuals to watch basketball on television. When Robin finds him, she demands to know what he "finds so fascinating about a group of pituitary cases trying to stuff the ball through a hoop." His response is "that it's physical." He proceeds to pull his wife onto the bed, hoping to instigate another form of physical activity. Reacting to his wife's objections, Alvy says: "It'll be great . . . because all those Ph.D.s are in there . . . discussing models of alienation, and we'll be in here quietly humping."[47] Alvy's desire to isolate himself from the social gathering and engage in physical activity (after watching a different sort on television) not only becomes emblematic of his own alienation, but can be seen as an attempt to find a respite from the self-consciousness and paranoia that add to his excess. Ironically, his comments meant to disparage members of the party for their ruminations and conversations—being too cerebral and not physical enough—are no different from the tendencies and inclinations that he has shown, only his ruminations and conversations are more about life and death, anti-Semitism, identity, and difference.

A correlative scene that demonstrates a slightly different tension between the physical and mental takes place with Annie and Alvy on a weekend alone in the Hamptons. After Alvy thwarts Annie's attempt to smoke marijuana before they have sex, Annie exercises her power by splitting away from her body, represented on screen as a phantom spirit stepping out of bed: a ghost removing itself from its shell. When Annie's spirit asks Alvy if he knows where she left her sketch pad, Alvy responds to the phantom figure by making it clear that her body is not enough. We see how magical realist inversion—the extraordinary made ordinary—is at work; instead of lingering on the supernatural occurrence of a fractured individual (mind body split), our attention is diverted to Annie's drawing pad and her mundane attempt to pass time, as well as Alvy's frustrated desire. What is staged here is a disjunction of desire, relevant to one of the opening jokes of the film: "I would never want to belong to any club that would have someone like me for a member." In many ways, Alvy belongs to the appropriate club, one in which he is *not* entirely desired as a member. And as I discuss later in the chapter, Annie comes to stand as a symbol of America herself.

In terms of postmodernism and magical realism, the scene in the Hamptons is revealing. We can read this scene as one of bodily extension and dispersed subjectivity. Annie takes independent action to remove herself from her body and create something in her sketch pad. It is important to note that the mind/body separation is *not* caused by marijuana or any other drug that might explain away the supernatural. In fact, it is the *lack* of such influences that instigates the move, the magical reality reinforced by the ordinary narrative treatment. Annie's move to enhance her own individual pleasure through marijuana is also a move away from the person with whom she would experience that pleasure, someone with whom she is not entirely comfortable. Meanwhile, Alvy's desire is attached to a longing for understanding and control. After stopping Annie from smoking marijuana—an urge he does not understand—he substitutes his own fantasy in its place, putting a red light bulb in the lamp: their hotel room connoting a red light district, where relations of power and pleasure exist on a server-client basis.

Alvy's initial introduction to Annie takes place at another convergence of physicality and power dynamics. Alvy is playing doubles tennis with his friend Rob—who continues to call him Max—and two women, one of whom is Annie Hall. As they approach the court, Rob tries to gear the conversation toward the impending game, but Alvy is fixated on the idea that the "failure of the country to get behind New York City is . . . anti-Semitism." He goes on to clarify that he is "not discussing politics or economics . . . [but] foreskin."[48] Here, he calls attention to the absence (or presence) of physical extension and its ethnic implications. We also see another example of Alvy's paranoia: the feeling that his club (the U.S.) would never fully want him as a member.

Following the game, Alvy accepts Annie's offer for a ride in her "VW," the specific reference to her German car an implicit reminder of Alvy's ethnicity. Although he makes no outward mention of the car, the fact that Annie is driving a Volkswagen is significant, perhaps more so for a Jewish audience. The VW reference can be seen an example of "double-coded" speech, comparable to a later scene at a delicatessen where Annie orders a "pastrami on white bread with mayonnaise," something which triggers a small, eye-rolling reaction from Alvy.[49] There's a similar scene in Allen's 1986 film *Hannah and Her Sisters* in which Allen's character decides he wants to convert to Catholicism, so he goes out and buys white bread and mayonnaise.[50] Henry Bial maintains that "When considering the performance of Jewishness in mass culture . . . it is necessary to address the way the work speaks to at least two audiences: a Jewish audience and a general or gentile audience."[51] He notes that "theoretically there are as many variant readings of the performance as there are spectators, [but] in practice readings tend to coalesce around certain culturally informed subject positions: a 'Jewish' reading and a non-Jewish or 'gentile' reading."[52] For Bial, "double-coded performance of Jewishness . . . does not typically carry meanings that are opposed to one another, nor does it usually imply hostility of the performer toward the audience or (vice versa). Rather . . . the Jewish reading of a performance is most commonly *supplemental* to the dominant or gentile reading."[53] It is this supplemental argument that contributes most directly to the portrayal of excess that I am arguing is on display in *Annie Hall*. It is an augmentation of the subject matter—extensions of meaning—through intertextual and magical realist means.

After their tennis match, Annie and Alvy wind up in Annie's apartment where she pours some white wine in a water glass for Alvy and invites him outside on her deck. After a few brief exchanges, Annie reveals that Alvy is "what Grammy Hall would call a real Jew." She proceeds to admit that her grandmother "hates Jews; she thinks they just make money."[54] The awkwardness that follows, and Alvy's decision to change the subject and prolong the conversation, suggests an inclination to deemphasize difference—to be just like everyone else—while exposing the struggle between ethnic identity/sensitivity and mainstream acceptance that exists throughout the film. It gives us a new perspective on an earlier scene, when Alvy takes Annie to see *The Sorrow and the Pity*—a moment that takes place earlier in the film, but chronologically later in the relationship. As their relationship develops, Alvy asserts aspects of his cultural identity through the mode of media; *The Sorrow and the Pity* serves as a reminder of the harsh realities of the Holocaust and the history that has contributed to Alvy's ethnic identity.

The excess that exists as an integral part of his personality has formed, in part, from grappling with a difference that demands both acknowledgement and denial, an inclination to have it both ways: accepted as the same, yet acknowledged as different. As many diversions into art and media as this film offers, we never stray too far from a reminder of Alvy's cultural identity, enhanced through his courtship of Annie Hall, one that can be viewed as a courtship of the Midwestern American WASP who initially sees him as a glaring ethnic type, a "real Jew." While the Jewish *religion* never really plays a role, Alvy's identity as an ethnic Jew — a contributing source of his personality — is central.

Alvy's cultural self-consciousness is shown most visibly during an Easter dinner with Annie's family. It is here where he imagines that he is being viewed as an Hasidic Jew, the image of this fantasy depicted on screen: the frowning face of Grammy Hall followed by Alvy Singer dressed in Hasidic attire, with a black hat and suit, a long brown beard and long curly sideburns — the materialization of Du Boisian "Double Consciousness." To reinforce his self-awareness, Alvy addresses the camera directly, taking the opportunity to describe Annie's family to the audience. He characterizes Annie's grandmother as a "classic Jew hater," but also suggests that the members of her family "really look American . . . very healthy, you know they never get sick or anything." This is a drastic difference from his own family who emerge from the right of the screen, quickly taking up most of the space with their crowded, dimly lit dining room — a contrast to the spacious, well-lit dining room of the Halls — and their loud discussion of ailments and death. Across the split screen, Annie's mother asks Alvy's mother how they plan to spend the holidays; she replies: "We fast." Mr. Singer clarifies that they do not eat "to atone for [their] sins." When Mrs. Hall claims not to understand what sins they're referring to, Mr. Singer admits that he's not sure himself.[55]

This scene represents another example of a magical realist transgression, in this case across space and time. In the universe of the film, the conversation takes place; it is an actual (and comical) exchange, which is treated as natural within the context of the narrative. This scene also represents the most direct reference to Jewish religion, and yet it features an ambivalence about the customs and traditions that contribute to Jewish identity. In terms of the cinematic medium, it uses "juxtaposition to highlight discordant perspectives . . . [and it] suggests the permeability of the boundary that divides them as it calls attention to the split-screen device."[56] Ruth D. Johnston notes how the "doubling of perspectives is in turn triangulated by that of the spectator, who, thanks to the split-screen, is in a position to laugh in appreciation at the subtle play between identity and difference."[57] The ethnic divide is displayed directly; the Singers

magically appear as an imposing, foreign entity, their "traditions hav-
[ing] little authority within the dominant culture."[58] Lois Leveen suggests that within "a predominantly Christian society, Jews will always be
in a problematic deterritorialized state—not quite at home, not quite con-
forming to the assumed behavior and beliefs."[59] This generalized perception informs and extends the narrative of *Annie Hall*, illustrating the excess of a persona that is divided and deterritorialized, doubled as "an
ethnic minority and a member of the dominant culture,"[60] compensating
for a continuing crisis of identity.

The desire to assimilate often forces the ethnic subject to divert attention away from cultural difference to something more neutral, as Alvy
does during his first conversation in Annie's apartment. It is on Annie's
deck, after Annie labels him (via Grammy Hall) a "real Jew," where he
shifts the conversation to Annie's photographs. This conversational shift
sets up another of the narrative extensions, where "thinking" subtitles,
meant to reveal what is really going on in the heads of Annie and Alvy,
emerge over a conversation on the aesthetics of photography, which Alvy
characterizes as an art form in which "the medium enters in as a condition of the art form itself"—the subtitle reading: "I don't know what I'm
saying. She senses I'm shallow." Here, we get a clear depiction of how
"postmodernism merges language and metalanguage, reflection and self-
reflection."[61] The subtitles emphasize the extended consciousness, and
heightened self-consciousness, that are significant aspects of the medium
and the message of the film, and the subtitles juxtapose image and text,
allowing each to communicate and represent (or re-present) divergent
thoughts and ideas.

Throughout *Annie Hall*, the audience is addressed directly, as are figures from Alvy's memories and fantasies, along with extras who appear
at first to be parts of the cinematic landscape. One of the more notable
extensions of the narrative exists after Alvy unloads his anxieties about
women to a policeman's horse, suggesting to this equestrian creature that
his tendency to fall for the wrong woman is exemplified by his childhood
attraction for the wicked queen over Snow White. This sets up a movement into cartoon, where an animated replica of Alvy Singer appears
beside a giant version of the wicked queen; the disembodied voices of
Alvy and Annie speak for these cartoon figures, reinforcing the "postmodernism . . . [that] entails a reflexive recognition of our lived relation
within the world of the simulacra. This is a world lived at the level of
consumption, images, media, and the popular."[62] The scene concludes as
a cartoon version of Rob, the same size as Alvy, suggests that he has other
women with whom he wants to set Alvy up.

The cartoon segment transitions into a date with a woman who describes her sexual experience with Alvy as "Kafkaesque." This reference
highlights ethnicity and intertextuality, as well as excess, bodily extension, and the process of grappling with inexplicable circumstances (not

quite as extreme as waking from uneasy dreams as a dung beetle or delivering a report to an academy about a life formerly led as an ape, but aspects of self-consciousness and heightened feelings of difference are still quite present). While in bed with this woman, Alvy receives a desperate call from Annie who pleads with him to come to her apartment for what turns out to be a spider in her bathtub.[63]

The scene at Annie's apartment is not as outwardly remarkable as some of the others, but what adds to the ordinary dimensions are the series of photographs of Alvy holding a live lobster that are on Annie's wall. These are worth considering for a few reasons. The photographs were taken by Annie during an earlier scene in the movie, now standing as a marker of time. These photographs are a tangible re-presentation, aligned with memory. Thinking back to Sobchack's claims about the association of photographs "with loss, with pastness, and with death," we have a gesture toward the past relationship—the relationship that has passed on and died. Artifacts and bodily extensions are also called back to the audience's attention, as the frozen and framed images show Alvy holding a formerly live body (the lobster), while he is in Annie's apartment to kill another animal body (the big black spider), for which he grabs Annie's tennis racket, a nod to Annie and Alvy's initial meeting. As Vivian Sobchack argues, "the intentional temporal and spatial fluidity of the cinema expresses and makes visible . . . the nonlinear and multidirectional movements of *subjectivity* as it imagines, remembers, projects forward. In this way the cinematic makes time visibly *heterogeneous*."[64] Sobchack further maintains that "subjective" and "objective" time "exist *simultaneously* in a demonstrable state of *discontinuity* as they are, nonetheless, actively and constantly *synthesized as coherent* in a specific lived-body experience (that is, a particular, concrete, and spatialized history and a particularly temporalized narrative)."[65] This lived-body experience is projecting and performing a condition of crisis, reaching out of and returning to common themes, spaces and times.

Another recurring scene that enhances our postmodern condition of crisis involves another performance-within-a-performance, as Annie takes the stage once again, this time to sing—conveniently—"Seems Like Old Times." Following this performance, Alvy stands in the way of Annie's opportunity to discuss her singing career—and a potential recording contract—with the producer, Tony Lacey (Paul Simon); instead, the audience is once again shown a clip from *The Sorrow and the Pity*, suggesting that this is the alternative that Alvy has forced upon her. The conflict between Annie and Alvy is highlighted further with the split screen display of their psychoanalytic sessions—once again, Alvy's side is darker, set on the right, and takes up a larger portion of the screen (just like Annie's only more so). They both acknowledge to their analysts that Annie seems to be making "progress" in the sessions that Alvy is paying for, a reality that causes them both to have a doubled and split reaction:

Annie feels guilty and proud, while Alvy feels victimized and magnani-
mous.[66]

The next movement in the film takes us to California, where the audience gets to experience a world of anxious creation, a fantasy land where
Rob has relocated, describing it as having "no crime, no mugging." Rob
takes Alvy and Annie to the control room of his television show—perhaps an implicit reference to *Oz*—demonstrating how the laugh track
works, projecting yet another performance-within-performance, one with
a different kind of technological presence (an expressive one), which
Alvy characterizes as "immoral." Annie and Alvy's relationship ends
upon their return from California, a place that comes to signify an antipo-
dal space for Alvy, one which he can only represent as subversive and
absurd.[67]

The film winds down with a final, postmodern meta-extension, as we
see the play that Alvy has written on his relationship with Annie. Alvy's
play ends differently, altering the ineffectual conclusion to their "real"
relationship: Sunny, the character based on Annie, cannot let Artie, the
Alvy-inspired-character, walk away without her. At the end of the re-
hearsal for this play, the camera cuts to Alvy who speaks directly into the
camera, acknowledging the flaws in his script: "Whadya want? It was my
first play." He claims to have tried to "get things to come out perfect in
art because . . . it's real difficult in life," acknowledging the compensatory
role that a narrative can play, while simultaneously performing in a narrative with compensatory extensions of its own: one which he tries to
align with "life."[68]

With Annie's version of "Seems Like Old Times" playing in the background, Alvy tells the audience that he ran into her again, and that she
was taking friends to see *The Sorrow and the Pity,* a move he characterizes
as a "personal triumph." The frame cuts to Alvy shaking hands with
Annie and her friends outside of a movie theater where the marquee
reads: "OPHULS PRIZE FILM THE SORROW AND THE PITY." The
movie draws closer to its conclusion by projecting a montage of clips
from the film we are still watching, followed by a scene where Annie and
Alvy leave each other on the street, having just gotten together to talk
about old times.[69] As Vivian Sobchack relates:

This temporal simultaneity not only 'thickens' the cinematic present
but also extends cinematic presence spatially—both expanding the space
in every image between the here, where the enabling and embodied cinematic eye is situated, and the there, where its gaze locates itself in its
objects, and embracing a multiplicity of situations in such visual/visible
cinematic articulations as double exposure, superimposition, montage,
and parallel editing.[70]

In many ways, the ending reinforces the excess of the postmodern
narrative body. As the film comes to a close, the audience sees Annie and
Alvy parting on the street through the window of a restaurant, as if the

viewer were inside the restaurant watching a scene outside. However, we hear the narrative voice of Alvy Singer telling the joke that closes the film, meant to sum up Alvy's feelings about relationships: "This guy goes to a psychiatrist and says 'Doc . . . my brother's crazy; he thinks he's a chicken.' And . . . the doctor says, 'Well why don't you turn him in?' And the guys says, 'I would, but I need the eggs.'" After Alvy and Annie have walked out of the frame, the audience is left to watch the flow of traffic through the restaurant window, while listening to the disembodied voice of Alvy Singer who suggests that this joke captures the "totally irrational and crazy and absurd" nature of relationships that humans both desire and need.[71] It also gestures toward the magical realist mode, which "integrate[s] . . . the supernatural into the code of the natural": in the world of the joke, the eggs are real and necessary. These conflicts and apparent contradictions are presented as rooted facets of the ethnic type portrayed in Allen's film, part of the condition that we struggle to articulate and understand. In *Annie Hall*, the condition is one of excess, growing out of and exposing aspects of an enigmatic difference.

The continuous experimentations and extensions found in *Annie Hall* call attention to the cinematic medium itself and allow us to see the film as a heterogeneous presence, an expressive *being* immersed in representations of identities. It is a postmodern and magical realist creation, aware of itself, able to critique and perform at the same time, mimetic, yet entirely original. To illustrate the excess of this Jewish American neurotic identity, the film is augmented to take more space, represent more life, employ more technology, and encompass a multifaceted persona that is trying to get its "mind around" an expanding universe, an enigmatic ethnic difference, and a fissure in a personal relationship with the dominant culture, presented in the form of a WASP woman from the Midwest, who goes by the name of Annie Hall.

NOTES

1. This phrase can be found in a number of writings about Jewish American assimilation and acculturation. Paula Fredriksen takes it as the title of her critical review of David Biale's 2005 (thousand plus page) study *Culture of the Jews: A New History*. Other contemporary writers who have also referenced the phrase (and are included in *Magical American Jew*) include Charles E. Silberman, Laura Levitt, Andrew Furman, and Peter Novick.

2. Laura Levitt, "Impossible Assimilations, American Liberalism, and Jewish Difference: Revisiting Jewish Secularism," *American Quarterly* 59.3 (2007): 807–32, 809.

3. W. E. B. Du Bois, *The Souls of Black Folk* (New York: Simon & Schuster, 2005), 7.

4. It is important to note that by "Jewish American excess" I am referring to a *behavioral* excess—as I mention in the opening paragraph, "the insecurities that inspire the effort to try 'harder'"—not a material excess. Although the insecurities might *lead* some to a materialistic lifestyle, money and material goods are different from the self-conscious behavior that is implicit in the joke cited in the opening sentence of this chapter.

5. Linda Hutcheon, "The Politics of Postmodernism: Parody and History," *Cultural Critique* 5 (Winter, 1986–1987): 179–207, 179.

6. Ibid., 180.

7. Henry Bial writes about how *Annie Hall*, more than any other Allen film, "is so explicitly framed as an intercultural encounter, Alvy's mode of acting Jewish—as the humorous sexual schlemiel—stakes a claim as an archetype of Jewish masculinity" (98). He also cites Kathryn Bernheimer who suggests that Allen should "be credited with providing audiences with a detailed profile of a specific Jewish personality" (qtd. in Bial, 98). While this neurotic "type" still exists, chapter 5 of *Magical American Jew* addresses a shift from the late-twentieth century neurotic excess portrayed by Woody Allen to the twenty-first century narcissistic excess performed by Sarah Silverman in her film *Jesus Is Magic*.

8. C. Keith Conners, "Symptom Patterns in Hyperkinetic, Neurotic, and Normal Children," *Child Development* 41.3 (1970): 667–82, 669.

9. Sigmund Freud, *Beyond the Pleasure Principle*, trans. James Strachey (New York: Norton, 1961), 22.

10. Ibid., 41.

11. Lois Parkinson Zamora and Wendy B. Faris, "Introduction: Daiquiri Birds and Flaubertian Parrot(ie)s," in *Magical Realism: Theory, History, Community*, ed. Lois Parkinson Zamora and Wendy B. Faris (Durham: Duke UP, 1995), 1–11, 1.

12. Ibid., 5–6.

13. Amaryll Beatrice Chanady, *Magical Realism and the Fantastic: Resolved Versus Unresolved Antinomy* (New York: Garland, 1985), 29.

14. Jon Thiem, "The Textualization of the Reader in Magical Realist Fiction," in *Magical Realism: Theory, History, Community*, ed. Lois Parkinson Zamora and Wendy B. Faris (Durham: Duke UP, 1995), 235–48, 244.

15. Woody Allen, *Annie Hall*, DVD, dir. Woody Allen, Metro-Goldwyn-Mayer Studios Inc., 1977.

16. One could say that reference to "a Catskill mountain resort" is already coded, suggesting something particular to a Jewish audience. This "double-coded" idea is discussed in greater detail later in the chapter.

17. Allen, *Annie Hall*.

18. Ibid.

19. Ibid.

20. Ibid.

21. Dean Franco, "Re-Placing the Border in Ethnic Literature," *Cultural Critique* 50 (2002): 104–34, 114.

22. Allen, *Annie Hall*.

23. Examples range from the stories of Sholom Aleichem to the fiction of Grace Paley, to the stage and screen productions of *Fiddler on the Roof* and *Brighton Beach Memoirs* (along with many other stories, novels, plays, and films by Neil Simon and others).

24. There are many sources on this subject. One example can be found in Michael Wex's book *Born To Kvetch: Yiddish Language and Culture in All Its Moods* (2005). And as mentioned in the body of the chapter, one can also see this in the opening joke of the film (about elderly women at a Catskill resort), and Alvy's explanation of its significance to him.

25. Allen, *Annie Hall*.

26. As noted earlier, Henry Bial and others have written about how Allen's performance—particularly in *Annie Hall*—of "the humorous sexual schlemiel . . . stakes a claim as an archetype of Jewish masculinity" (98). His body type and persona enhances the fantasy of this particular scene.

27. Chanady, *Magical Realism and the Fantastic*, 30.

28. Ibid.

29. Shannin Schroeder, *Rediscovering Magical Realism in the Americas* (Westport, CT: Praeger, 2004), 61.

30. Vivian Sobchack, *Carnal Thoughts: Embodiment and Moving Image Culture* (Berkeley: UCP, 2004), 146.

31. Ibid.

32. Ibid., 152.

33. Judith Butler, *Gender Trouble: Feminism and the Subversion of Identity* (New York: Routledge, 1990), 25.

34. Ibid.

35. Henry Bial, *Acting Jewish: Negotiating Ethnicity on the American Stage and Screen* (Ann Arbor: U Michigan P, 2005), 13–14.

36. Ibid., 13.

37. Ibid. (emphasis added).

38. Egon Mayer, "From an External to an Internal Agenda," in *The Americanization of the Jews*, eds. Robert M. Seltzer and Norman J. Cohen (New York: NYUP, 1995), 432.

39. Allen, *Annie Hall*.

40. Ibid.

41. Ibid. For a study that examines paranoia about anti-Semitism (among other perceptions), see Gary A. Tobin and Sharon L. Sassler's *Jewish Perceptions of Antisemitism*.

42. Timothy Corrigan and Patricia White, *The Film Experience: An Introduction*, 3rd ed. (Boston: Bedford/St. Martin's Press, 2012), 192.

43. Sobchack, *Carnal Thoughts*, 150.

44. Allen, *Annie Hall*.

45. Ibid.

46. Marita Sturken and Lisa Cartwright, *Practices of Looking: An Introduction to Visual Culture* (Oxford: OUP, 2001), 239.

47. Allen, *Annie Hall*.

48. Ibid.

49. Ibid.

50. Woody Allen, *Hannah and Her Sisters*, DVD, dir. Woody Allen, Orion Pictures Corporation, 1986.

51. Bial, *Acting Jewish*, 16.

52. Ibid.

53. Ibid., 17.

54. Allen, *Annie Hall*.

55. Ibid.

56. Ruth D. Johnston, "Joke-Work: The Construction of Jewish Postmodern Identity in Contemporary Theory and American Film," in *You Should See Yourself: Jewish Identity in Postmodern American Culture*, ed. Vincent Brook (New Brunswick: Rutgers UP, 2006) 207–29, 213–14.

57. Ibid., 214.

58. Lois Leveen, "Only When I Laugh: Textual Dynamics of Ethnic Humor," *MELUS* 21.4 (1996): 29–55, 40.

59. Ibid., 48.

60. Ibid., 49.

61. Christian Moraru, *Memorious Discourse: Reprise and Representation in Postmodernism* (Madison: Fairleigh Dickinson UP, 2005), 128.

62. Sturken and Cartwright, *Practices of Looking*, 239.

63. Allen, *Annie Hall*.

64. Sobchack, *Carnal Thoughts*, 150.

65. Ibid., 150–51.

66. Allen, *Annie Hall*.

67. Ibid.

68. Ibid.

69. Ibid.

70. Sobchack, *Carnal Thoughts*, 151.

71. Allen, *Annie Hall*.

TWO

Presuming the Dominant Gaze

Spirits of Shame in Cynthia Ozick's "Levitation"

As suggested earlier in this study, Jewish cultural identity in the United States is uniquely indeterminate. As involved in social, political, economic, artistic, educational, even athletic arenas of the "mainstream" as some might be, as assimilated, acculturated, and secular as plenty have become, many Jewish Americans are compelled to maintain an ethnic identity that gestures to the margins. For secular American Jews, the effort to define and portray this identity can be an onerous, often paradoxical process. The external pressures that exact this process—educational, social, political, religious—are as varied as the affects of those who are compelled to engage in it: shame, pride, guilt, spite, wonder, disgust. Although guilt might be the affect most commonly linked to the Jewish American persona, its kissing cousin, shame, offers greater potential for examining the enigma of Jewish American difference.

Before getting into the analytical and representational potential of shame, it is worth looking into the relationship between American Jews and guilt, and highlighting some of the distinctions between guilt and shame. Starting with the former: the association between Jewish Americans and guilt—from survivor's guilt to the guilt of success and failure—is far reaching and fairly broad, but the most common and pervasive association sprouts out of the stereotype of the Jewish American mother. This stereotype of the overbearing, meddling, and overprotective matriarch has infiltrated the cultural consciousness of the United States; it rears its head in jokes, on T-shirts, in movies—the list goes on. Alan Dundes discusses how the "[t]he J.A.M. [Jewish American Mother] is depicted as enjoying the role of the martyr. One might even say that the Jewish American Mother suffers from a martyr complex. She is mater as martyr! She is never happier than when she has something to complain about, with the complaint intended to produce feelings of guilt in her children."[1] Through a significant portion of his discussion, Dundes provides his readers with an assortment of jokes, citing "the J.A.M.'s uncanny ability to use solicitude as a devastating weapon to create feelings of guilt."[2] Joyce Antler discusses how this overbearing figure of Americana is most often portrayed as employing "stratagems for ensuring that her children remain . . . dependent . . . [t]he main technique [of which is] . . . the cultivation of guilt."[3] In Antler's book *You Never Call! You Never Write!: A History of the Jewish Mother*—guilt implicit in her title—she points to the 1960s and suggests that the breadth of the Jewish mother stereotype can be linked to the widespread commercial success of three books: Dan Greenberg's guidebook *How to Be a Jewish Mother*, Bruce Jay Friedman's novel *A Mother's Kisses*, and Philip Roth's novel *Portnoy's Complaint*.[4] Of the latter novel, Antler cites a review by Mordecai H. Levine, published in 1970 in the *CLA Journal*, in which Levine asserts that *Portnoy's Complaint* contains "the caricature to end all caricatures of the Jewish mother."[5] Dundes too cites Roth's novel,[6] as does Martha A. Ravits who argues "[t]he comic stereotype of the Jewish mother . . . is a cultural construct developed by male writers in the United States in the 1960s."[7] According to Ravits, *Portnoy's Complaint* provides "[t]he most memorable and fully elaborated caricature of the Jewish mother."[8] Indeed, Alexander Portnoy, the narrator of Roth's novel, describes his mother as being "imbedded in [his] consciousness," and he devotes a significant portion of his narrative addressing—in one form or another—his mother and the guilt she has inspired in him, pleading with his therapist to help him escape his fate as "the smothered son in the Jewish joke."[9] One example of the guilt with which Alex feels burdened is related to his therapist (and the reader) in the form of a joke: A Jewish G.I. named Milty meets and marries a Japanese girl while stationed overseas. Before his return, Milty calls his mother to tell her the news. He's surprised when she suggests that they stay in her small apartment. When Milty asks whether there's enough room for all of them, she replies: "'Milty darling . . . don't you worry, there'll be all the room you want: as soon as I hang up, I'm killing myself.'"[10] Within this joke, the themes of which may be familiar to some, guilt is tied to specific actions or inactions—behavior—and meant to serve as an affective obstacle for a member of an in-group.

Although the portrayal of the Jewish American mother is indeed a "construct" that may very well have been perpetuated by Roth and others, the guilt represented in the joke cited above relates, in part, to the consequences of intermarriage that can carry a special degree of guilt. For Jews, guilt derived from intermarriage can be the most keenly felt and the most paradoxical at the same time. Since arriving to the United States, many Jewish immigrants and early Jewish Americans prioritized the effort to assimilate, to downplay differences, and to meld into American society. However, for some Jews—even secular Jews—intermarriage takes the melding too far, as it can result in the erasure of Jewish lineage and Jewish identity. Some go so far as to portray intermarriage as a victory for Hitler who tried to eliminate the Jews from the earth.[11] Although most would take a far softer stance—Calvin Goldscheider, in particular, makes the argument that "intermarriage cannot have the same meaning in modern context of generations as it did in the former context of rejection and escape"[12]—fear over the loss of Jewish identity can still lead to the dissemination of guilt. So if guilt targets behavior and is instigated, in some cases, by fear, where does shame come into play? What is the difference between guilt and shame?

According to Donald L. Nathanson, "guilt refers to punishment for wrongdoing, for violation of some sort of rule or internal law. . . . Guilt implies action, while shame implies that some quality of the self has been brought into question. Experience teaches us that . . . unwarranted opinions about the self, when exposed, will be punished by shame."[13] June Price Tangney and Ronda L. Dearing survey much of the work that has been done on shame and guilt—from the psychoanalytic studies to the anthropological—and discuss the distinctions between the two, pitting their own findings against those that came before. In describing the differences between these "moral" and "self-conscious" emotions, Tangney and Dearing demonstrate a view consistent with Nathanson "that shame is associated with a focus on the self whereas guilt is associated with a focus on a specific behavior."[14] Silvan Tomkins suggests that "guilt is about moral transgression; shame is about inferiority."[15] Andrew P. Morrison contends that shame "emphasizes . . . the eye of the self gazing inward."[16] Almost without exception, those who study and write about shame and guilt make a distinction between the two affects, most often citing guilt as an affective response to behavior and shame an affect that "is bound up with how the self feels about itself."[17] It is the contention of this chapter that when investigating the enigmatic difference of Jewish Americans, it is more productive to focus on the presence of shame, and the self-conscious sense of self that is associated with it, than to dwell on the presence of guilt, and the feelings associated with specific behaviors, regardless of how widespread the stereotypes of those feelings and behaviors may be.

The multitude of jokes about guilt—some referenced above—have helped to perpetuate the association with Jews. Shame, however, is more difficult to discuss and more difficult to make jokes about, since it is not necessarily tied to specific behavior. But an analysis of shame reveals more about the complexities, contradictions, spirits, and splits of Jewish American identity. Many of these characteristics are found in Cynthia Ozick's magical realist short story "Levitation." Ozick's "Levitation" is a pertinent story through which to consider the active life of Jewish history, an important part of Jewish self-perception, and a useful story through which to consider the magical realist representation of Jewish American identity. Additionally, shame's elusive, nebular quality aligns well with an enigmatic difference and makes it an apt emotion to illustrate through magical realist means. Throughout the course of this chapter, various components of shame—especially its reliance on a real or imagined witness—are discussed along with the details, circumstances, and magical portrayals contained within Ozick's "Levitation."

As a means of moving toward Ozick's story, it is worth noting another distinction between shame and guilt, raised by Tangney and Dearing. According to their clinical studies, "when shamed, participants felt more isolated—less as though they belonged—than when experiencing guilt."[18] They suggest that those who feel shame have "less control" over the origins and methods of alleviation. As with many ethnic groups, Jewish Americans have, to various degrees, grappled with issues of isolation, belonging, and control. Thinking in terms of national and ethnic culture, one cannot look past centuries of Jewish history, and the emotions that feed the "diasporic imagination," to use Matthew Frye Jacobson's term, which "has more to do with how one sees and thinks about the world than with where one ultimately chooses to live."[19] For many Jews, the world has been a place where one has had to work for admittance and grapple with a history of exclusion and exile. The *choice* contained in Jacobson's articulation can be striking—especially when relating diaspora with exile—yet it is germane when thinking of the enigmatic nature of Jewish American identity.

For contemporary American Jews, diaspora seems to embody choice in two significant ways: the choice to stay in the United States rather than "return" to the Jewish homeland of Israel, and the choice to hold onto the Jewish diaspora as a means—in part, at least—to hold onto and understand one's ethnic identity. But is the latter really a choice? For secular American Jews who are compelled to maintain a cultural connection—for a variety of factors, not all of their choosing[20]—what options exist? Revisiting the statements made by Dean Franco—cited in chapter 1—"America is home precisely because it is diasporic; neither the homeland nor the Jewish nation, America is a place where Jews can be comfortably uncomfortable, physically and socially safe, not pejoratively marked as interlopers exactly, but different all the same."[21] Part of what gets internalized by American Jews—and contributes to, but does not entirely define Jewish American identity—comes from the inability to ignore the subtle and not-so-subtle markers of difference that have been impressed upon the garment (and branded on the skin) of Jewish history. These markers can lead to the behavioral excess discussed in chapter 1 and contribute to feelings of self-consciousness and isolation—the sense that one does not belong—discussed by Tangney and Dearing.

As involved in the formation and expression of U.S. culture as some have and continue to be, many Jewish Americans remain—on some level at least—uneasy about issues of national and ethnic identity. Victoria Aarons suggests "the very tension in the fiction of Jewish-American writers is the insider-outsider *paradox*, the ability of the Jew to be at once insider and outsider, in terms of both America and Judaism."[22] She cites the "self-consciousness" that results from this paradox, referencing Cynthia Ozick's description of herself as "a third-generation American Jew (though the first to have been native-born) perfectly at home and yet perfectly insecure, perfectly acculturated and yet perfectly marginal."[23] Aarons continues her discussion by arguing the "self-consciousness on the part of the Jewish writer . . . extends to the characters' visions of themselves and to their perceived place in America."[24] In "Levitation," Ozick uses magical realist techniques to animate (and elevate) Jewish American difference and highlight the self-conscious aspects of her central characters. This self-consciousness—a characteristic of shame—emerges in the eyes and actions of these characters, ultimately leading them in markedly different directions.

Cynthia Ozick's short story "Levitation" tells the story of a married couple, Lucy and Feingold, who are planning a party in their New York City apartment. Feingold is a cautious editor and a marginal novelist who, although Jewish, has "always known he did not want a Jewish wife." He is characterized as "pale" and "powerless" and obsessed with historical Jewish atrocities. Although Lucy is the daughter of a minister, she always wanted to "marry out of her tradition." At a young age, she imagined herself as "an Ancient Hebrew" and before marriage, she converted to Judaism. Like her husband, Lucy is a novelist, but her books are about "domestic life," rather than the fictionalized accounts of atrocity and trauma that consume her husband.[25]

The present time action of the story takes place at their party where none of the New York "luminaries" whom they invited show up. Despite a full apartment, Lucy and Feingold are both affected by the absence of these figures, each handling the disappointment in different ways. Lucy is committed to movement, and is described as "swimming" around her apartment. Feingold is more outwardly melancholic, confining himself to the living room where a group of Jewish guests has gathered. Feingold instigates conversation about Jewish history, but defers to a Holocaust survivor who captures the small crowd with his testimony of trauma. The story ends with Lucy standing outside the living room, witnessing the ascension of this group of Jews who levitate out of sight, absorbed by the atrocities of the past.[26]

Before examining the details of Ozick's story, it is important to consider the initial characterizations of Feingold and Lucy. In Jewish tradition, the religion of a child is determined on the maternal line; Feingold's wish to marry a non-Jew can be seen as a wish to end his Jewish lineage.

Considering his obsession with the atrocities of Jewish history—the most recent of which proposed a "final solution" for Jews—his sweeping desire to marry a gentile can also be seen as an act of self-negation. Sara Ahmed speaks of this self-negation, characterizing shame as "an intense feeling of the subject 'being against itself.'"[27] What is important to note here, in terms of differentiating between shame and guilt, is that for Feingold, it is not a matter of falling in love with a gentile woman and experiencing guilt as a result, but rejecting the prospect of marrying a Jewish woman, and as a result, rejecting a part of himself. As a man obsessed with historical efforts to drive out or eliminate Jewish peoples, his *desire* to drive the Jewish connection out of himself (or dilute it at least) can be linked more closely to feelings of shame than feelings of guilt. Ironically and conveniently, we find a related desire—with significant differences, as we will later explore—in Lucy who rejects the religion in which she was raised (and her father devoted his life), as well as the contemporary time and place where she developed her identity, in favor of the romanticized (and comic) idea of becoming an "Ancient Hebrew."

Moving on with the initial characterizations of our heroes, their occupations—writing and editing—are also significant in terms of the "double play of concealment and exposure [that] is crucial to the work of shame."[28] Ahmed argues that "in shame, the subject's movement back into itself is simultaneously a turning away from itself." She suggests "shame . . . conceals and reveals what is present in the present."[29] For Lucy and Feingold, the act of writing can be seen as a manifestation of "concealment and exposure." As novelists, they hide behind imagined characters, inside imagined settings, all while revealing personal truths, exploring uncomfortable histories, and exposing fundamental vulnerabilities. As writers, they both believed that they should "never writ[e] about writers. Your protagonist always has to be someone *real*."[30] Already, Lucy and Feingold have made themselves less-than-real, representations rather than individuals. By exploring their lives and identities—Feingold through Jewish history and Lucy through an autobiographically-grounded story of domesticity—they are moving into and turning away from themselves.

It is also telling to consider Feingold's work at a barely profitable publishing house. He is an editor who rarely accepts a manuscript that he likes, for fear that it might not sell. On the few occasions when he does risk exposure—in this case, through the assertion of his own judgment and taste—he is "brutal to the writer . . . knock[ing] the paragraphs about until they [a]re as sparse as his own."[31] As a result, Lucy refuses to share any of her work with him, yet she indulges in frequent conversations about writing with her husband, and Lucy and Feingold each feels grateful to be married to another writer.

A similar such "double play" can be found in the decision to throw a party. Parties are forums where a performative concealment is often at play. Hosts and guests can hide behind affective party masks, yet they are subjected to wider exposure as the number of witnesses is significantly greater. For Lucy and Feingold, the party is emblematic of their social positions. They are keenly aware of those who are "above" them—demonstrated by their effort to compile "a list of luminaries"—and they aspire to be accepted within this loftier culture, yet they remain isolated.[32] Although their apartment fills up, Feingold is convinced that the important people are elsewhere, stopping his wife to exclaim: "'No one's here!'"[33] Through this claim, which Lucy does not refute, Feingold reduces himself, his wife, and his guests to nothing—a group of *no-ones*—yet another act of self-negation.

The party fosters other manifestations of shame as well. According to Ahmed, "[t]he very physicality of shame—how it works on and through bodies—means that shame also involves the de-forming and re-forming of bodily and social spaces, as bodies 'turn away' from the others who witness the shame."[34] Although Ahmed's claims about the "physicality of shame" is rather sweeping, one does see—in the portrayal of Lucy and Feingold, at least—some physical manifestations of their emotions, portrayed through the descriptions of their bodies as well as the party space itself. Even before the physical and social space of their apartment undergoes a magical transformation, Lucy tries to stay clear of her husband's gaze, as well as the gaze of everyone at the party. In an effort to avoid being stopped, "Lucy sw[i]m[s] by blank-eyed." The party itself is described as having "washed and turned like a sluggish tub." The consistent references to water highlight a certain de-forming and re-forming: Lucy becomes a fish, the apartment a tub, and Feingold an anchor, weighted down—for the time being, at least—by his shame in the present and obsession with the past.[35]

Although Lucy and Feingold avoid each other's eyes and the eyes of most of the party guests, the eyes that are eliciting shame are the imagined eyes of the people who are not at the party, the imagined eyes of the dominant witness—the gentile mainstream—who make Lucy and Feingold self-conscious of themselves and their efforts to fit in and rise in some imaginary social sphere. As Tangney and Dearing contend (as well as Tomkins and Ahmed in slightly different language), "Shamed people . . . feel exposed. Although shame doesn't necessarily involve an actual observing audience that is present to witness one's shortcomings, there is often the imagery of how one's defective self would appear to others."[36] In their discussion of the subject-object confusion that can occur with shame, Tangney and Dearing describe "a split in self-functioning in which the self is both agent and object of observation and disapproval. An observing self witnesses and denigrates the focal self as unworthy and reprehensible."[37] Returning to *Portnoy's Complaint*, we find an explicit articulation of such self-consciousness, expressed by the narrator whose obsession with "the goyim" and "the *shikes*" leads to his melodramatic proclamation (to an imagined father and semi-present doctor): "don't tell me we're just as good as anybody else, don't tell me we're Americans just like they are. No, no, these blond-haired Christians are the legitimate residents and owners of this place."[38] A similar description is found in *Annie Hall*—noted in chapter 1—when Alvy Singer is eating Easter dinner with Annie's family and suggests to the viewing audience that the members of her family "really look American," a contrast to his own family who soon emerge on the other side of a split screen.[39] Although much has changed since the publication of Roth's novel and the release of Allen's film, these same splits—regarding national and cultural identity—can be found in subtle ways even today. They emerge through reminders of otherness and difference (see note 20), and become a part of Jewish American identity, in all its enigmatic glory. At the end of "Levitation," as we will see, there is a unique play on such self-conscious "imagery" where Lucy imagines herself *as* the dominant witness.

Before the shift that takes place at the end—when Lucy is grounded, statue-like, while Feingold and the living room Jews are carried away by the spirits of history—there are many distinctions made between the afflictions felt by Lucy and those felt by Feingold. At the party, in the most social of spaces, the descriptions of their actions are telling: as mentioned before, Lucy swims, weightless, while Feingold mopes, suggesting a heavy step and a body burdened by the persistent pull of gravity. Regarding their novels, Lucy writes about the trials of a "housebound woman" while Feingold writes about the weight of Jewish history. Their apartment is filled with Feingold's books (many on Jewish history), while Lucy is said to read *Emma* continuously and exclusively. Lucy herself acknowledges the strain of her husband's historical obsession in her novel, an excerpt of which is included in "Levitation." She has used her own apartment as the setting for her book, and in the brief passage provided—after describing the heavy volumes that line the shelves—there are the lines: "Oh God, the weight, the weight."[40]

In many ways, the germs of characterization and identification can be found in the names of the heroes: Feingold and Lucy. Last names offer links to history, while first names emerge from a wider variety of sources, and are more prone to the movements of trend and current culture. Last names are anchored to geographical and familial pasts, which for Jews— almost without exception—connects them to tales of survival and atrocity. In the collection *Who We Are: On Being (and Not Being) a Jewish American Writer*, Isaac Bashevis Singer's famous statement, "Every writer must have an address," is referenced several times, by several writers. In regard to Singer's dictum, Cynthia Ozick discusses how "address means more than geography; it means being addressed by a literary tradition inherent in one's language, meaning the particular history secreted in the very syllables of language. . . . In this sense . . . I am a Jewish writer."[41] She goes on to suggest that "for everyone alive in the century we have left behind, the cataclysm of murder and atrocity that we call the Holocaust is inescapable and indelible, and inevitably marks—stains—our moral nature; it is an event that excludes no one."[42] Lucy is affected by this same history, but what draws her to Feingold is a desire to realize a romantic vision that is at odds with the contemporary reality of her husband. She wants to be a biblical Hebrew, not a newfangled American Jew grappling with issues of identity. She had imagined Feingold's identity as more stable and concrete than it actually is. What she discovers is that she and her husband are both grappling, but from different vantage points, from different addresses. She is the child of a Presbyterian minister who practices in the mainstream United States; her gaze is projected from national soil, and her name is indicative of her birth religion and the eyes of her nation. Although in Jewish tradition, first names are often used to commemorate deceased relatives, in the case of Lucy—the daughter of a minister—her name is more naturally associated with Saint Lucy, an autonym which signifies light and (in the context of the story) her eventual role—real or imagined—as dominant witness. According to *The Oxford Dictionary of Saints*, Lucy's "usual emblem . . . [is] her eyes, which were reputed to have been torn out and miraculously restored."[43] From Lucy's perspective, her restoration takes place at the end, when she imagines herself as detached from Feingold's diaspora, judging him from her new vantage point, with her newly restored vision.

Eyes are significant when considering affective responses—particularly to shame—and they play an important role in Ozick's story. Beyond the suggestion that shame requires a witness[44]—real or imagined—and the obvious implication of eyesight that goes along with the act of witnessing, a response to the experience of shame is often located in the eyes and in the face.[45] There is significant attention to Lucy's eyes throughout the story. As noted earlier, she avoids the eyes of her husband and her party guests while moving "blank-eyed" around the apartment. She is described as having "huge, intent, sliding eyes, disconcertingly luminous." When she sees her husband's agnostic friend from the Seminary who officiated her conversion, she becomes self-conscious, "her great eyes wheel[ing]."[46] It is this shift of the eyes—after Lucy sees her husband's friend, and the guest whom this friend has brought—where we find a shift in the fiction itself, a turning point that puts the story on its magical path: one that divides Lucy from Feingold, and leads Lucy to presume the dominant gaze, projecting her imagined beam directly upon Feingold and the living room of *others*. However, before a full examination of this magically real split, we should consider how Lucy and Feingold are characterized as a couple.

There are several references to the secondary status of Lucy and Feingold. They are described as "absorbed by power . . . [yet] powerless. They lived on pity." One might imagine them on both sides of this pity: pitying and being pitied. The narrative tells of their excessive sympathy "toward everyone in the least way victimized," and their "attract[ion] to bitter lives." They see themselves in these lives, and as evidenced at the party— their disappointment in the absence of "luminaries" and the presence of the "falsehood[s]" and "figment[s]" — they are ashamed of what they see. Once again, we can imagine them split between sides: ashamed before the imagined eye of the dominant witness, while witnessing at the same time.[47] Returning again to Ahmed's assertion—cited earlier in the chapter: "shame is bound up with how the self feels about itself." For Lucy and Feingold, the most explicit description comes from their collective point of view:

About their own lives they had a joke: they were "secondary-level" people. Feingold had a secondary-level job with a secondary-level house. Lucy's own publisher was secondary-level; even the address was Second Avenue. The reviews of their books had been written by secondary-level reviewers. All their friends were secondary-level . . . the wearisome hacks of small Jewish journals.[48]

Lucy's theory is that "they were . . . sunk in a ghetto," and while her husband continues with his "morbid investigations into Inquisitional autos-da-fé," she seeks out the humor in women who stay home, suggesting: "Jews and women! They were both beside the point."[49] Again, we see the "focus on the self"[50] that is so much a part of the work of shame. But this is different from the self-obsession of narcissism (discussed most directly in chapter 5), since it depends on the *notion* of an external witness. For Lucy, she uses comedy to divert her eyes from the ghetto where she has located herself (and imagined that others have located her) as a woman and as a Jew. Feingold on the other hand remains absorbed in "Inquisitional autos-da-fé," in a sense, sentencing himself to a life fettered by marginalization and shame.

Following Feingold's declaration that "'No one is here!'" he enters the living room with the intention of instigating a discussion about God or death. He considers a few of the horrific events of Jewish history before reflecting on the curious fact "that Magna Carta and the Jewish badge of shame were issued in the same year, and that less than a century afterward all the Jews were driven out of England."[51] This moment speaks to the existence of shame (and the anxieties of American Jews) in several ways. Beyond the mention of the humiliating badge that marked Jewish people throughout Europe in the early thirteenth century—and served as a legal doctrine that barred Jews from exercising the rights of other citizens—it addresses the conflicting realities that undermined their ability to understand the "rules of the game," to feel grounded and secure in law and in land. Magna Carta was meant to establish the groundwork for constitutional human rights, yet Jewish families were marked as less than human, and those who had lived in the same place for centuries were uprooted. Throughout history, some of the recurring realities for Jews have been the conflicts, contradictions, indignities, and atrocities that have forced them to construct their identities, to some extent at least, with a "diasporic imagination." Such continuous identity construction, as subtle as it may seem today, contributes to the enigmatic culture whose affects, inherent connections to exile, and anomalous national and ethnic status can harbor spirits of shame. It is the contention of this chapter, and *Magical American Jew* as a whole, that facets of this difference can be imagined, depicted, and animated through magical realist means.

A characteristic magical realist move is to animate—provide material presence for—a deceased figure from the past.[52] Although ghosts do not play an explicit role in "Levitation," there are specters of history that influence the actions of characters and propel the magical conclusion of the story. Cynthia Ozick has spoken about the active presence of Jewish history on several occasions through several different mediums: essays, fictions, interviews. For a 1989 *New York Times* article, when asked why she writes about the Holocaust when she has "no history of personal suffering in the Holocaust," her response speaks directly to this presence: "If you're talking about why do I write about people affected by the Holocaust, it's because I believe that after the Holocaust, and through knowledge of it, everybody is a witness, not just those who went through it and came out alive. . . . For the Jews of Poland before the Holocaust, the Spanish Inquisition was a full presence in their lives." She goes on to say that she "grew up always as a witness—of the Inquisition, of the pogroms, of the Crusades, of the Holocaust, all at once."[53] Although Ozick's liberal use of the term "witness" —different from the "witness" discussed in terms of shame—can be troubling for some,[54] her point relates to how the spirits of Jewish history continue to influence Jewish identity and perception. Even for American Jews who have been able to enjoy a certain comfort and stability, the presence of the past serves as an essential reminder of the Jewish diaspora: the persistent "questions and accusations of character" that have, to some extent at least, driven and partially defined Jews throughout history. These spirits of history, along with the national, social, and ethnic negotiations that take place for many Jewish Americans, make magical realism a particularly productive and useful mode of expression, one that allows for realistic circumstances to coexist with the present spirits of history.

In "Levitation," the persistent "presence" of Jewish history is a significant part of what drives Feingold and Lucy apart. What obsesses Feingold, and what he cannot escape—the past that influences his identity—Lucy finds tedious and dull. Lucy begins to feel like an anxious tourist in the haunted and enigmatic culture of her husband. In the latter half of the story, she separates herself from her husband and the gathering of Jews, and imagines herself as a mainstream witness to the *others* who have congregated in the living room; isolated from this ethnic assemblage, she is self-conscious and defensive. Dean Franco suggests "ethnicity—cultural difference—not only indicates a minority group, but interpellates a dominant other, a dialectic where neither position is stable, but always shifting in response to the gaze of the other."[55] This mutually shifting gaze that Franco describes—emblematic of the shifting ground on which a cross-section of Americans have found themselves—emerges as a prominent tension in the story, and the force that distinguishes and divides Lucy and Feingold.

As mentioned earlier, the arrival of Feingold's friend from the Seminary—the agnostic friend "who had administered her [Lucy's] conversion"—instigates the separation-by-levitation that concludes the story. For Lucy, his presence makes her self-conscious about her gentile roots—her "address." She wonders whether she is looked upon as a sinner: "she felt tested. Sometimes she spoke of Jesus to the children. She looked around—her great eyes wheeled—and saw that everyone in the living room was a Jew." But the separation—and Lucy's observation of it—takes on a magical life with the emergence of another guest, a Holocaust survivor who arrives with Feingold's friend from the Seminary. In her examination of this person, she determines that he's "a refugee" who may be blind. "It was hard to tell where the eyes were under that ledge of skull." She identifies this refugee as having "the face of Jesus"—the ultimate witness for Lucy—and suggests that his whisper is "the voice Feingold was waiting to hear." Through Lucy's point of view, the exchange of gazes—between the daughter of a Presbyterian minister and this haunted ethnic group—becomes evident. She is self-conscious of how she being perceived by the congregation of Jews—how she *imagines* she is being perceived, at least—yet presumes the ability to scrutinize *them* through gentile eyes.[56]

The appearance of the "refugee" reminds Lucy of her father. She watches as this man closes his eyes to demonstrate how God's eyes had been closed during the Holocaust. "Again Lucy looked around. It pained her how intense Jews could be. . . . *They* were intense all the time . . . was it because they had been Chosen, was it because they pitied themselves every breathing moment? Pity and shock stood in all their faces."[57] Where pity had once been something they shared—"They lived on pity"—now Feingold is the exclusive heir; in this case, Lucy sees Feingold pitying himself while she imagines herself removed from this same sort of sympathetic or self-pity. When Lucy ceases to sympathize with her husband's intensity regarding his history and enigmatic position in society—discovering that "she is bored by the shootings and the gas and the camps, [and] she is not ashamed to admit this"[58]—she becomes detached from the ethnic community of her husband; she imagines a return to a place in the mainstream majority where she is interpellated as a dominant figure, uncertain why her husband and the other *intense* Jews can't simply forget about the past and move on.

While the Jews in the living room become *othered* by Lucy's gaze—from her point of view, she witnesses their "pity and shock"—Ozick allows the reader to consider the gaze of the *witness* from another vantage point. The "refugee," labeled as such by Lucy and referenced this way in the narrative—*labeling* an act indicative of a dominant subject, refugee a name indicative of diaspora—refers to himself as "the witness." In this case, he is witness to the horrors of the Holocaust when God had His eyes closed. As he speaks of the atrocities and indignities that continue to affect Jews in the present, Lucy feels disconnected, unable to sympathize and relate. Only by imagining Jesus standing in as every Jew can she feel something; "otherwise it was only a movie."[59] It is at this point when the separation becomes even greater. Lucy remains outside of the living room, standing like a statue of Saint Lucy. She watches and listens as the past—so much a part of the Jewish present—takes life (becomes animated in the magical realist mode) through the voice of the refugee, the voice of this ethnic emblem: "For a long time the refugee's voice pinched them and held them, so that you had to look. His voice made Lucy look and look . . . Then Lucy saw the fingers of the listeners—all their fingers were stretched out." The voice of the refugee—drawing in Feingold and the contemporary American Jews—melds the group into a singular spectacle. This ethnic collective is generalized by Lucy's point of view (she imagines herself as the dominant witness), and it is portrayed—magically—as not fully rooted to American soil. The room begins to rise from the ground, "levitating on the little grains of the refugee's whisper." Stretching her neck to witness the ascent,[60] Lucy determines that only Christ could carry her away, suggesting that the Jews are being abducted "by a messenger from the land of the dead." Feingold's identity is informed by this "land of the dead"; Ozick's use of the magical can be seen as a way of enhancing this connection and this separation.[61]

With the room of Jews rising, Lucy drifts off into an "illumination"—a term significant of vision, light, and enlightenment. She imagines herself in the park with her children, watching peasant performers—spectacles with "heavy dark skins . . . ears and noses that look like dried twisted clay . . . gold teeth [or] . . . no teeth." Their "eyes are in a trance" as they sing in ancient tongues and wear "the drugged smiles of dervishes." Lucy is fascinated by these exotic *others*: those outside of the mainstream with their far off gazes and histories filled with whirling movements and atrocities. Lucy imagines the dancers as snakes, and laments "how she has lost true religion on account of the Jews." This illumination acts as a bridge—a transition—to Lucy's move to reestablish herself as part of the mainstream, and imagine herself as a dominant delegate, positioned to witness a congregation of *others*.[62]

From Lucy's point of view, Feingold is lifted by the spirits of the past, out of his home and away from his American life, "away from the others who witness the shame."[63] Lucy is weighted by the position she presumes: her dominant (statue-like) position as a representation of the mainstream, separated from her husband and his diasporic community.

As the living room rises out of sight, Lucy strains to hear the faint sounds of this community, convinced that she knows what they are discussing: "Death and death and death. The word is less a human word than an animal's cry; a crow's. Caw caw. It belongs to storms, floods, avalanches. Acts of God. 'Holocaust,' someone caws dimly from above; she knows it must be Feingold. He always says this word over and over and over. [64] History is bad for him: how little it makes him seem!" [65]

Despite the transition cited above, Lucy's transformation is still quite drastic. She not only relates the Jews of the living room with the dead, but she marginalizes them further by comparing them to animals, referencing the Holocaust—the not-so-distant past—when Jews were herded like cattle onto trains and carted away to be slaughtered. But Lucy's transformation is not without its origin and impetus. The shame, indignity, and inhumanity of Jewish historical atrocities—which obsess her husband and (as discussed in detail in chapter 3) *must not be forgotten*—are alive in her household and have contributed to Feingold's understanding of his ethnic identity. As David Biale, Michael Galchinsky, and Susannah Heschel (among others) contend, "At a time when Jews are enjoying their greatest acceptance as part of the majority, never before has Jewish identity been founded so centrally on a history of victimization, consisting primarily in the memory of the Holocaust." [66] Indeed, this history is a significant part of what many secular American Jews cling to for ethnic identification, but it is not everything, and it is not digested and understood in any universal way. However, the "spectacle" of the ethnic group is often generalized in sweeping and singular ways, as demonstrated by Lucy—the dominant point of view at the end of Ozick's story.

Lucy and Feingold are both imagining the dominant witness—presuming the dominant gaze—only from polar addresses: same road, same affective center. Both are self-conscious before (and behind) the eyes of this witness, but Ozick features Lucy's point of view at the end to highlight the affective spectacle, the generalized conglomerate of *others*. Lucy imagines herself as a representative of the gentile mainstream, a personification of Saint Lucy whose religion and gaze are dominant enough to determine the affect and identity of the Jews. She is labeling, generalizing, exoticizing, pitying, and judging others for pitying themselves. But Lucy is as tied to shame as her husband; she has formed her own identity from the same spring and the same affective spirits. In "Levitation," Ozick uses the magical realist mode to animate the imaginary space where identity and the dominant gaze are impelled.

For Jews, the past will never go away—they cannot allow it to—and in the essential effort "to remember," an element of difference is kept alive. Shame, more than guilt, is a component of this difference, but it is not alone—does not exist in isolation or as a singular, collective spectacle. The affective bond that Jewish communities share sprouts out of a common history, a repetition of trauma and triumph. But even during better times, there exists a lingering threat and an internalized sense of anguish. Until the spirits of history can carry their descendants into the ether, identifying the contemporary manifestations of difference will remain integral to understanding the complexities and peculiarities of Jewish American communities.

NOTES

1. Alan Dundes, "The J.A.P. and the J.A.M. in American Jokelore," *The Journal of American Folklore* 98.390 (1985): 456–75, 457.
2. Ibid., 459.
3. Joyce Antler, *You Never Call! You Never Write!: A History of the Jewish Mother* (Oxford: OUP, 2007), 137.
4. Ibid., 135–37.
5. Mordecai H. Levine, "Philip Roth and American Judaism," *CLA Journal* 14 (December 1970), 166.
6. Dundes, "The J.A.P. and the J.A.M.," 466.
7. Martha A. Ravits, "The Jewish Mother: Comedy and Controversy in American Popular Culture," *MELUS* 25.1 (2000), 1.
8. Ibid., 6.
9. Philip Roth, *Portnoy's Complaint*, 1967 (New York: Random House, 2002), 3, 11.
10. Ibid., 189.
11. Steven Carr Reuben, *There's An Easter Egg on Your Seder Plate: Surviving Your Child's Interfaith Marriage* (Westport, CT: Praeger, 2008), 39.
12. Calvin Goldscheider, "Judaism, Community, and Jewish Culture in American Life: Continuities and Transformations," in *Religion or Ethnicity?: Jewish Identities in Evolution*, ed. Zvi Gitelman (New Brunswick: Rutgers UP, 2009): 267–85, 278.
13. Donald L. Nathanson, "A Timetable for Shame," in *The Many Faces of Shame*, ed. Donald L. Nathanson (New York: Guilford P, 1987): 1–63, 4–5.
14. June Price Tangney and Ronda L. Dearing, *Shame and Guilt* (New York: Guilford P, 2002), 18, 23.
15. Silvan Tomkins, "Shame-Humiliation and Contempt-Disgust," in *Shame and Its Sisters: A Silvan Tomkins Reader*, ed. Adam Frank, Eve Kosofsky Sedgwick, Irving E. Alexander (Durham, NC: Duke UP, 1995), 133–78, 143.
16. Andrew Morrison, "The Eye Turned Inward: Shame and the Self," in *The Many Faces of Shame*, ed. Donald L. Nathanson (New York: Guilford, 1987): 271–91, 273.
17. Sara Ahmed, "Shame Before Others," *The Cultural Politics of Emotion* (Edinburgh: Edinburgh UP, 2004): 101–21, 103.
18. Tangney and Dearing, *Shame and Guilt*, 21.
19. Matthew Frye Jacobson, *Special Sorrows: The Diasporic Imagination of Irish, Polish, and Jewish Immigrants in the United States* (Berkeley: UCP, 2002), 7,9.
20. Following World War II, when the "Jewish majority" status came to the United States in a sweeping, horrific blow—prior to the Holocaust, the majority of the world's Jews lived in Europe—the responsibility to remember and maintain a connection to Jewish history became even greater for many American Jews. Additional factors range from awareness of national and international anti-Semitism, to the emotions, rituals, media and commercial coverage associated with Christian and Jewish holidays, to the reality of working within a society prone (for practical and not-so-practical reasons) to label its citizens by race, religion, and ethnicity, to the ubiquitous coverage of Israeli and Middle Eastern politics and events, which carries its own pressures regarding Jewish ethnic identity.
21. Dean Franco, "Re-Placing the Border in Ethnic Literature," *Cultural Critique* 50 (2002): 104–34, 114.

22. Victoria Aarons, "The Outsider Within: Women in Contemporary Jewish-American Fiction," *Contemporary Literature* 28.3 (1987): 378–93, 382.

23. Cynthia Ozick, "Toward a New Yiddish: Note," in *Art & Ardor: Essays by Cynthia Ozick* (New York: Knopf, 1985), 152.

24. Aarons, "The Outsider Within," 382–83.

25. Cynthia Ozick, "Levitation," in *Levitation: Five Fictions* (New York: E.P. Dutton, 1983), 3–20, 3–4.

26. Ibid., 3–20.

27. Ahmed, "Shame Before Others," 103.

28. Ibid., 104.

29. Ibid.

30. Ozick, "Levitation," 4.

31. Ibid., 6.

32. In this same regard, the party can be imagined as a metaphor for assimilation itself.

33. Ozick, "Levitation," 10.

34. Ahmed, "Shame Before Others," 103.

35. Ozick, "Levitation," 9–10.

36. Tangney and Dearing, *Shame and Guilt,* 18.

37. Ibid.

38. Roth, *Portnoy's Complaint*, 146.

39. Allen, *Annie Hall.*

40. Ozick, "Levitation," 8, 6.

41. Cynthia Ozick, "Tradition and (or Versus) the Jewish Writer," in *Who We Are: On Being (and Not Being) a Jewish American Writer*, ed. Derek Rubin (New York: Schocken Books, 2005), 19–23, 21–22.

42. Ibid., 22.

43. David Hugh Farmer, *The Oxford Dictionary of Saints*, 4th ed. (Oxford: OUP, 1997), 312.

44. Ahmed, "Shame Before Others," 105.

45. Tomkins, "Shame-Humiliation and Contempt-Disgust," 134.

46. Ozick, "Levitation," 4, 12.

47. Ibid., 7, 9.

48. Ibid., 7–8.

49. Ibid., 8–9.

50. Tangney and Dearing, *Shame and Guilt,* 23.

51. Ozick, "Levitation," 11–12.

52. Melquíades, from Gabriel García Márquez's *One Hundred Years of Solitude*, is a classic example.

53. Richard Bernstein, "Being Nice or Rotten in Writing," *New York Times*, October 3, 1989: C15, C21.

54. Debarati Sanyal, a scholar of violence and trauma who has written on aspects of the Holocaust, is one of many who caution against "conflating the irreducibly distinct subject positions of victim, executioner, accomplice, witness, and secondary witness" (3). Sanyal's warning is raised again in chapter 3, which deals more directly with the Holocaust and various "subject positions."

55. Franco, "Re-Placing the Border in Ethnic Literature," 108.

56. Ozick, "Levitation," 12–13.

57. Ibid., 14.

58. Ibid., 19.

59. Ibid., 14. Although a passing reference here, many have written about the role that movies and the media have played in the dissemination and cultural perception of the Holocaust within the United States. Gary Weissman's *Fantasies of Witnessing: Postwar Efforts to Experience the Holocaust* offers an especially lucid discussion on this subject.

60. Although this chapter focuses on levitation as a manifestation of shame, emphasizing the perceived separation from national soil before a dominant witness, there are well established, Jewish fabulist and mystical sources that feature ascent. Such sources, along with direct references to Ozick's story, are addressed in the conclusion.

61. Ibid., 15.

62. Ibid., 16–18.

63. Ahmed, "Shame Before Others," 103.

64. Feingold's obsession with the Holocaust and death is comparable to Alvy Singer's obsession in *Annie Hall*. In Alvy's case, it manifests in his fixation with Marcel Ophüls's film *The Sorrow and the Pity* and the books that Alvy buys for Annie: Ernest Becker's *The Denial of Death* and Jacques Choron's *Death and Western Thought*. In the book store scene, Alvy admits that he is "obsessed with death" and suggests that "life is divided up into the horrible and the miserable."

65. Ozick, "Levitation," 19.

66. David Biale, Michael Galchinsky, and Susannah Heschel, "Introduction: The Dialectic of Jewish Enlightenment," in *Insider/Outsider: American Jews and Multiculturalism,* ed. David Biale, Michael Galchinsky, and Susannah Heschel (Berkeley: UCP, 1998: 1–13), 5. Related suggestions can be found in Peter Novick's *The Holocaust in American Life* and Gary Weissman's *Fantasies of Witnessing* (among other sources).

THREE

Collecting Pain

Masochism, Identity, and Archiving Trauma Testimony in Melvin Jules Bukiet's "The Library of Moloch"

In chapter 2, the analysis of Cynthia Ozick's short story "Levitation" allows us to look at how shame can be a telling affective lens through which to view the enigma of Jewish American difference. On the surface, chapter 3 engages in a comparable analysis; once again, we are working with a piece of short fiction that has a Holocaust survivor who figures prominently in the story's magical conclusion. While the goals of each story and each analysis are complementary, they are also quite different. The ending of Ozick's story highlights the self-conscious separation that can be imagined for contemporary Jewish Americans who remain "comfortably uncomfortable" in their diasporic homeland. In chapter 3, the magical conclusion of Melvin Jules Bukiet's story speaks more to the pressures and impossibilities that exist for contemporary American Jews who are compelled to "remember" an unlived and potentially unknowable historical atrocity. This effort to "remember," which is tied in with the effort to collect and archive testimonials of trauma, contributes to the enigmatic difference that exists for American Jews. Chapter 3 explores the archiving process and considers the masochistic potential of putting the unknowable Holocaust at the center of an effort to access and understand Jewish American identity.

In the late twentieth century, with the realization that there was not much time before witnesses to the Holocaust would no longer be around, efforts to archive Holocaust testimony and construct museums and memorials to "remember" this monumental atrocity began to grow. The Fortunoff Video Archive for Holocaust Testimonies, which was estab-

lished in 1979 and is housed at Yale University, opens their "Concept"
page with a reminder that "survivors and witnesses of the Holocaust are
diminishing in number. Each year their recollections become more important, but each year moves them farther away from the original experience. This gives special urgency to the effort to collect as many testimonies as possible—now."[1] The urgency not only relates to the need to
maintain an accurate historical record, but also to maintain a record that
can help sustain Jewish identity in the United States. Geoffrey H. Hartman, one of the founders of the Fortunoff archive, writes in *The Longest
Shadow*: "As the eyewitnesses pass from the scene and even the most
faithful memories fade, the question of what sustains Jewish identity is
raised with a new urgency."[2] Walter Benn Michaels contends "the dependence of identity on memory is . . . undeniable," suggesting that efforts to
keep "memories" of the Holocaust alive are indeed efforts "to keep Jewish identity alive."[3] But Benn Michaels addresses the problems and potential impossibilities that exist in terms of representing and recalling
memories of the Holocaust—"its resistance to intelligibility"—and characterizes the effort "to turn history into memory" as cultural mythology.[4]
While there is room to challenge Benn Michaels's characterization, the
effort he identifies has a firm place in contemporary Jewish consciousness, and—as I discuss in this chapter—when the effort is portrayed in
fiction, magical realist means can be used to highlight the complications
cited by Benn Michaels.

Similar to Benn Michaels, contemporary scholars such as Gary Weissman have also noted and discussed the move within Holocaust studies
"from what we know of the event (the providence of historians), to how
to remember it." Expanding on this idea, he posits: "[a]s the last generation of witnesses to the Holocaust passes away, excessive reference to
'memory' may express a denial of this loss, or an effort to compensate for
it by relocating the witnesses' memories of the Holocaust not only in
museums and archives, but also in second-generation and nonwitnesses'
imaginations."[5] In discussions of contemporary Jewish American ethnicity, conversation often touches on the centrality of the Holocaust and its
importance in terms of understanding Jewish identity. Michael L. Morgan has written about how Holocaust "films, poetry, fiction, monuments,
and museums" have "authorized the centrality of the Holocaust in
American Jewish self-consciousness and hence Jewish identity."[6] Deborah Dash Moore notes how "The Holocaust increasingly came to occupy
a central place in the identity politics of American Jews."[7] Related suggestions, discussions, and examinations (some noted in chapter 2) can
also be found in Peter Novick's *The Holocaust in American Life* and Gary
Weissman's *Fantasies of Witnessing*, among many other sources. Similar to
Novick, Morgan touches on the "debate about the role and influence of
the Holocaust on American Jewish identity," but focuses his study on
those who "began to treat the Holocaust as a central and determining

feature of . . . Jewish thinking."[8] This chapter addresses, in part, the complications for contemporary American Jews who are compelled to imagine the Holocaust as *the* "central and determining feature" of their Jewish identities.

Discussing the changing national context for contemporary Jewish Americans, Novick suggests the focus on the Holocaust has led to "the decline in America of an integrationist ethos (which focused on what Americans have in common and what unites us) and its replacement by a particularist ethos (which stresses what differentiates and divides us)."[9] This "particularist ethos" is reinforced by claims of exclusivity and incomprehensibility made by survivors such as Elie Wiesel;[10] it also serves to complicate issues of identity for nonwitnesses and Jews born after World War II. Part of what I am arguing in this chapter is that there is a direct relationship between the importance of the Holocaust for Jewish American identity and the enigma of Jewish American difference. The crux of this relationship, what contributes to the enigma of difference, exists in the Holocaust's "resistance to intelligibility" and its subsequent centrality for many contemporary American Jews. According to Elie Wiesel, "[t]he Holocaust [is] the ultimate event, the ultimate mystery, never to be comprehended or transmitted. Only those who were there know what it was; the others will never know."[11] If this is the case, then what are the consequences for contemporary American Jews who are compelled to look almost-exclusively toward the Holocaust for a sense of ethnic identity? How is "the ultimate mystery, never to be comprehended or transmitted," supposed to be "remembered" by those who were never there? These are some of the concerns that are featured in Melvin Jules Bukiet's short story "The Library of Moloch" and emphasized through the magical conclusion of his story. The goal of this chapter is to demonstrate how the effort to keep the memory of an unknowable atrocity alive, and the portrayal of such an effort—an effort which Benn Michaels links to "cultural mythology"—lends itself to the magical realist depiction found at the end of Bukiet's story. Furthermore, the events that lead up to this end—the effort to access the traumatic memory of Holocaust survivors—contains a potential relationship to masochism.

Through a close examination of "The Library of Moloch," I demonstrate how the portrayal of Dr. Arthur Ricardo—the protagonist and archivist of trauma testimony—provides us with a figure who not only seeks out Holocaust testimony as a means of establishing and understanding his ethnic identity,[12] but the obsessiveness with which he pursues testimonies of trauma (and yearns for the suffering which accompanies these testimonies) can be understood as a form of masochism. The magical ending that concludes this story speaks to the impossibility of truly accessing the Holocaust, while reinforcing the enigmatic difference that exists for Jewish Americans who are compelled toward such an impossible effort.

Melvin Jules Bukiet's short story "The Library of Moloch" focuses on a video archive housed at a university, established to record and preserve testimonies of trauma. It was conceived and is now run by Dr. Arthur Ricardo who has "three hundred faces on file, nearly a thousand hours, tens of thousands of deaths described in ferocious detail." The spark for the library's construction came from a scandal at the university in which an older, respected professor was found to be a "wartime collaborator."[13] When a man affected by the wartime acts of this professor speaks out, and a tape of this man's statements starts to circulate, a "bizarre fascination" emerges in the community. With the institution of the library of video testimony, Ricardo's thirst for testimonies of trauma gains force. He goes out of his way to persuade as many witnesses as possible to testify for the archive. As his desire intensifies, so does his personal suffering. He neglects his wife and his students, and becomes obsessed with his service to the library.[14]

The story settles on an older woman—the final witness—who questions Dr. Ricardo's motives, and questions the library's purpose. She accuses him of being driven by jealousy, and like a "vampire" or a "leech" or a "jackal," he wants to feast on the blood of the past. Ricardo threatens to abandon the session, but the woman's suggestion that he's judging her story based on how she treats him, pushes him to continue his record of her "testimony." After she leaves, Ricardo obsesses over her claim that "'[t]here are two separate inviolate realms,'" one being memory, while the other is never revealed (or at least never heard). Ricardo sits in the woman's chair and lights a cigarette—he has taken up smoking again since opening the library. As he unwinds, he falls asleep, the ash from the cigarette falling onto the arm of the chair where there is exposed stuffing from the anxious scratching of those who have unleashed their testimonies. The chair catches on fire, its flame spreading to the files, climbing the shelves and burning the tapes. It is not until "the guard towers, the barbed wire, the fires blackening the sky, escape . . . into the air along with the smoke" that Dr. Ricardo wakes up. He is surrounded by flames, but instead of fleeing to save himself he blisters his hands on the last tape of testimony and forces it into the video player. On screen, the old woman appears. Talking out of the video screen—magically, in the present—she speaks of the tragic places where God can be found, warning that "those who enter the Holy of Holies are condemned to burn." She states again that there are two inviolate realms. Desperate to know what they are, Ricardo screams through the fire for the answer that concludes the story: memory and theology.[15]

As an avenue into the relationship between "The Library of Moloch" and the characteristics common in tales of masochism, I will begin with ideas about the archiving process that are relevant to the portrayal found in Bukiet's story. Describing the process of being an interviewer responsible for retrieving testimony from Holocaust survivors, Dori Laub emphasizes his involvement in the telling, positioning himself as the object upon whom the horrors are projected. According to Laub, he "actually participates in the reliving and reexperiencing of the event."[16] Shoshannah Felman, Laub's co-author on *Testimony*, makes related claims. After showing films of testimony to her college students, Felman describes the reflective response papers she received, characterizing them as a "profound statement of the trauma they had gone through and of the significance of their assuming the position of the witness."[17]

Although scholars such as Debarati Sanyal warn against "conflating the irreducibly distinct subject positions of victim, executioner, accomplice, witness, and secondary witness,"[18] one cannot completely divorce the impact of traumatic testimony from the individuals who are present for the telling. Saul Friedlander, Dominick LaCapra and others have picked up on Freud's notion of "working through" that, according to Friedlander—whose articulation is described by LaCapra as "especially valuable"[19]—is necessary for "historians of the Shoah, when confronted with the echoes of the traumatic past."[20] For Friedlander, the process requires a conscious balance: "the numbing or distancing effect of intellectual work on the Shoah is unavoidable and necessary; the recurrence of strong emotional impact is also often unforeseeable and necessary."[21] According to LaCapra, "[w]orking-through implies the possibility of judgment that is not apodictic or ad hominem but argumentative, self questioning, and related in mediated ways to action."[22] In "The Library of Moloch," Bukiet portrays a figure whose "insatiable" yearning for testimonies denies him the balance, which Friedlander claims is essential, and blocks him from "the possibility of judgment that is not apodictic or ad hominem." Instead, we are shown a figure whose compulsion and immersion begin to define him: "those who listened to them [testimonials from Holocaust survivors] were devastated. . . . Dr. Ricardo in particular suffered. . . . Yet the more he suffered, the greater his passion for his self-appointed mission."[23] It is Ricardo's "self-appointed" obsession, for which he suffers and yearns for that suffering, that begins to invoke a connection to masochism.

The term masochism is taken from the last name of the Austrian writer Leopold von Sacher-Masoch, whose fiction—most notably the novel *Venus in Furs*—portrays relationships and behaviors which figure prominently in the "perversion" originally described and labeled by the German psychiatrist Richard von Krafft-Ebing in his 1886 book *Psychopathia Sexualis.*[24] The term gained more widespread recognition in 1905, with the publication of Freud's "Three Essays on the Theory of Sexuality," in which he wrote about the unique characteristics of masochism and linked the perversion with sadism.[25] As a psychoanalytic term, masochism has been used to account for a wide range of behaviors, the common element existing in the desire to suffer.[26] While noting this common feature, Victor N. Smirnoff troubles this "basic requirement" by suggesting "that the essential phenomena of masochism may well be not in the suffering but in the position of the masochist in the masochistic relationship." He draws directly from the work of Sacher-Masoch, most specifically from "his best-known novel *Venus in Furs*," and contends "masochism can only be based on a contract that is also an alliance. . . . [T]he executioner must be part of the masochistic position, not an outside figure. Sacher-Masoch does not use the vocabulary of a victim, but that of the director of this play." Ultimately, Smirnoff argues for a rethinking of masochism, "not through the 'pleasure in pain' element, but as the actualization of a contract which must regulate the relationship in the masochistic performance."[27] While I consider how "the relationship in the masochistic performance" is regulated, I am most concerned with how the concept of masochism can be applied to and can function within a literary context, rather than how it figures in the realm of clinical psychoanalysis. Although my aim and argument extend outside of literature to culture and identity, I am working with a concept of masochism derived primarily from Sacher-Masoch's novel *Venus in Furs* and, perhaps more significantly, Gilles Deleuze's analysis of masochism, from *Coldness and Cruelty*, which works closely with characteristics found in *Venus*.

In *Coldness and Cruelty*, Deleuze notes the persuasive use of language as a common feature within tales of masochism.[28] Since the masochistic relationship is so unique—and not always easy to understand and digest upon initial exposure—the masochist must persuade an agent ("executioner," for Smirnoff) to consider and ultimately agree to the roles and conditions of the masochism that he has imagined. In *Venus*, the reader is taken through the process of masochistic persuasion. Severin, the protagonist, employs techniques meant not only to persuade Wanda, his chosen agent, to consent to her role—one in which she agrees to dominate, humiliate, and inflict pain on Severin—but also to allow her to believe, on some level at least, that she is making a choice to play a part for which she is ideal. She acknowledges (and warns) that she has tendencies that can be unleashed if given the opportunity, and Severin does his persuasive best to encourage her, without appearing to make the decision for her.[29] In "Moloch," we are told of the agents whom Ricardo "hunted, begged, cajoled, and, if necessary, bribed into telling their stories,"[30] which he suffers to hear and record. Even Ricardo's threat that he will abandon the recording session with the old woman can be viewed as a persuasive ploy, given that the old woman only agrees to speak after he threatens to take the opportunity away. While there are important differences between the old woman and Wanda—most significant is the fact that the old woman is being persuaded to recount an actual nightmare while Wanda is being persuaded to act out a fantasy—Ricardo's and Severin's strategies, motivations, and experiences are notably similar (Bukiet's portrayal seems intentional here). In each case, Ricardo and Severin are persuading someone to unleash something that she is reluctant to unleash, and from intensely personal and largely selfish perspectives, Ricardo and Severin are both driven by the promise of pain and the prospect of controlling and transforming that pain into an augmented sense of identity.

Deleuze identifies a characteristic coldness in Masoch's novels, represented by frozen images, often covered in furs. He suggests that "the function of the masochistic ideal is to ensure the triumph of ice-cold sentimentality by dint of coldness."[31] This coldness is necessary to achieve the disavowal of reality that allows the ideal to remain suspended in fantasy. Although "Moloch" ends in flames—a conclusion discussed later in this chapter—a comparable coldness is found through a large part of the story, starting with the initial description of the final witness:

> One old lady arrived wearing a large rhinestone brooch on a highly textured brocade dress. Her hair was cut short in a golden helmet. She could have been a dentist's receptionist, or a dentist's mother. When the tape started to roll, and Ricardo began by asking her to tell him "a little about yourself," she said, "Pardon me, but why do you wish to know?"[32]

The first words out of her mouth defer the testimony that Ricardo desires. From a narrative standpoint, the cold images of her rhinestone brooch and golden helmet—one might imagine these accoutrements as substitutions for the fur coat and hat worn by Masoch's Wanda—and the association of dentistry, are complemented by the terse manner of the "old lady," a description that lacks the narrative warmth of a proper name, while adding the association of old age. Moving beyond this opening description, the room in which the testimony takes place is described as "a dental chamber," a sterile environment often associated with pain, which adds to the general frigidity of video archives, in which collections of tapes are stored in dark rooms and identified through numbers and labels. After the session begins, the woman rejects the label *survivor* in favor of the colder, less human "remainders, or the remains." She relates his camera to a gun, but refuses to elaborate when asked what she means.[33]

The video screen through which the old lady makes the final disclosure of the story, and the nature of video archives in general, imply a narrative distance consistent with the layered narrative found in *Venus in Furs*. In *Venus*, the events of the story are not told directly to the reader, but rather contained within a memoir which a guest of the hero, Severin, is encouraged to read. The story, which the nameless guest is reading, tells of the process that Severin undergoes to convince Wanda to become his master and to treat him as a wretched slave. As with the journal, read by Severin's guest, that frames and informs *Venus in Furs*—keeping the actions and events at a certain remove and making them less personal as a result—the conversation with the videotaped testimony of the nameless old woman maintains a similar distance. The narrative distance also draws attention to the writing as artifact, serving as yet another reminder of the frozen art—portraits, statues, texts, and tapes—that hold such value in masochism.[34] But more significantly for "Moloch," the *magical* scene that concludes the story is used to emphasize the *impossible* distance that exists between Ricardo and the events of the Holocaust. Jon Thiem suggests "[t]he magic in magical realism emerges from the interpenetration of irreconcilable worlds."[35] While the conversation represents such an interpenetration, the screen between them reemphasizes the irreconcilability and distance.

Along with the narrative distance and the fantasy of masochism, the changing of names that take place in *Venus* and "Moloch" are also significant. In *Venus*, Severin agrees contractually to become Gregor and take on a new identity and social status. In "Moloch," though more subtle, the old woman—distanced and depersonalized by the absence of a name—attempts to unnerve Ricardo by referring to him as "Herr Doktor Professor," a title he considers an insult;[36] the German title aligns him more with the oppressor than with the noble archivist that he imagines himself to be. These changes/modifications in name and identity contribute to the fantasy and deferral that mark masochistic texts and are enhanced through magical realism in "Moloch."

The contract that is common within tales of masochism—stressed, by Deleuze, as a significant characteristic—represents yet another layer of narrative and a formality to the events and responsibilities of the participants. In *Venus*, the contract between Severin and Wanda is referenced specifically on several occasions, modified during the course of their relationship, and ultimately cited as the barrier that prevents Severin from taking his own life—an important difference between Severin and Ricardo. Although the term contract is never used in "Moloch," the terms and conditions of the library are formally established, Dr. Ricardo's roles and responsibilities are made clear, and the archiving process is laid out for each new agent. The tension only mounts when the final subject—the old lady—challenges the purpose of the archive and Ricardo's motivation for engaging in the archiving process with such lust, leading Ricardo to threaten to terminate the recording.

After the old woman has left, when it is clear that Ricardo is still suffering from the violence of her words—different from the violence she was asked to reference and remember[37]—and the absence of the insight about inviolate realms that he craves, he does not review the tape, but instead wallows in his anguish. After lighting a cigarette, he falls asleep—subconsciously inviting greater suffering and eventual death. Consistent with tales of Masochism—evidenced in *Venus in Furs* and discussed in *Coldness and Cruelty*—the end of "The Library of Moloch" proves anti-climactic after the heightened and prolonged suspense. In

"Moloch," the last word of the story, "Theology," reveals the other inviolate realm, but says nothing more about the library, Ricardo, nor his reaction to this desperately desired knowledge. Even if learning of the second inviolate realm is enough, there is a distance that dampens the reaction. The last realm is not *God*, but the *study* of God. If the *study of God* is inviolate, than God itself is suspended in an even greater impossibility. This also gestures to the equivocal nature of the old lady's "testimony," which seems to challenge the purpose behind and process of archiving testimonies more than it actually participates in the act of testimony. It also asserts "memory" as an inviolate realm, which implicitly challenges the credibility of the archive[38] and the effort "to remember," which plays such an important role for contemporary Jewish Americans. As with the magical conclusion itself, the old woman's meta-testimony—and all she discloses and withholds—reinforces the impossibility of the connection that Ricardo seeks.

Masoch's novel has a comparably anti-climactic ending, which seems to emphasize the impossibility of achieving satisfaction. In *Venus*, there is a cursory, two page conclusion to Severin's lengthy story—a letter from Wanda, a return to the guest who had been reading his tale, an ambiguous moral, and a curious claim about being "cured"—that comes just after he has been whipped by a third party and the suspense has reached a new level. The satisfaction from Wanda that Severin had been seeking—or seemed to be seeking, at least—is now farther away, and the reader is left to assume that this third party put satisfaction out of reach. Severin suffers the whipping by fixing his eyes on a painting of Samson and Delilah, a frozen/suspended image of a man betrayed by the woman he loves. As Deleuze notes, "[i]n Masoch's novels, it is the moments of suspense that are the climactic moments"; this is in part "because the woman torturer freezes into postures that identify her with a statue, a painting or a photograph."[39]

Just as *Venus in Furs* has the painting of Wanda as Venus—along with other related paintings—"The Library of Moloch" has the frozen frame on the video screen where Ricardo's eyes are fixed when the story ends. While *Venus* highlights the suspension of satisfaction through frozen art, "Moloch" makes a similar gesture through frozen history. In each case, satisfaction is deferred and some aspect of fantasy remains. However, in "Moloch," this fantasy is animated—given magical life—to highlight the potentially destructive (in the case of "Moloch," masochistic) quest for understanding that can be imagined when access to the secrets of cultural identity are located within inviolate realms. This magical life represents a turning away from the frozen imagery found in masochistic fantasy into the fiery chamber of Jewish history. Whereas Severin experiences some sort of recovery and tries to convince himself and his guest that he has moved on, Ricardo immolates himself in the effort to get as close as he can—learn as much as he can—from the image of a witness who refuses to divulge the contents of her memory and may not be able to even if she were willing (see note 38).

As Benn Michaels has tried to make clear, the call to remember for nonwitnesses is already problematic. This is particularly true if we subscribe to the idea that "remembering the Holocaust is now understood as the key to preserving Jewish cultural identity,"[40] as Benn Michaels and others have expressed. This "key," and the reality that the number of survivors is dwindling, has led to the urgency to archive Holocaust testimony. However the testimony of trauma is an abstraction/distortion of the original event; the video record of that testimony is yet another copy, diluting and distancing the actual experience. Lawrence L. Langer details some of the problems with oral testimonies. According to Langer,

> Listening to accounts of Holocaust experience, we unearth a mosaic of evidence that constantly vanishes, like Thomas Mann's well of the past, into bottomless layers of incompletion. There is no closure, because the victims who have *not* survived—in many ways, the most important "characters" in these narratives—have left no personal voice behind. They can only be evoked, spoken *about*. We wrestle with the beginnings of a permanently unfinished tale, full of incomplete intervals, faced by the spectacle of a faltering witness often reduced to a distressed silence by the overwhelming solicitations of deep memory.[41]

Despite these problems, there are many important reasons why these testimonies are recorded, archived, and reproduced. However, there are complications that arise when these recordings and reproductions are looked upon as *the* essential artifacts in the effort to sustain Jewish cultural identity—the artifacts meant to stand in for what Jews must never forget. When the Holocaust is given such an exclusive position in the formation and maintenance of Jewish cultural identity, it can act as a barrier in the effort to understand the complexities of contemporary Jewish American difference. As a result, the archive has the potential to contribute to a certain fantasy and violent distortion, yet the rationale behind the archive—"to remember"—gets serialized and repeated more than any other aspect of contemporary Jewish American culture. As shown in "The Library of Moloch," this *repetition* can contribute to a destructive effort to hold on to—conjure or inspirit—what is already gone.

Repetition and reiteration are also common characteristics in tales of masochism. Deleuze speaks of repetition as an independent force that "runs wild." He suggests that there is a "double action of repetition, which on the one hand binds the excitation and on the other tends to eliminate it."[42] This plays itself out in both *Venus* and "Moloch." In *Venus*, Severin anxiously awaits each encounter—each repetition—with Wanda, deriving excitement and being stripped of excitement at the same time. He begs to be whipped and ill-treated, yet in his humiliation, often feels unworthy and jealous, questioning Wanda's love for him. There exists a related process with Dr. Ricardo, who works hard to procure testimony for the archive—excited by the repeated opportunities to receive these experiences of pain and horror—yet suffers deeply as a result of this process: "The more he heard, the more Ricardo needed. He grew insatiable."[43] The story concludes with the replaying of the final recording, a repetition that becomes an independent force, ultimately serving a transgressive function that drives Ricardo to "enter the Holy of Holies."[44] In terms of magical realism, Lois Parkinson Zamora and Wendy B. Faris contend "[m]ind and body, spirit and matter, life and death, real and imaginary, self and other, male and female: these are boundaries to be erased, transgressed, blurred, brought together, or otherwise fundamentally refashioned in magical realist texts."[45] Bukiet uses such magical realist techniques to highlight the connection that is being sought—and emphasize the distance and impossibility—by portraying a conversation with a survivor who is speaking out of a video screen.

Karmen MacKendrick alludes to Deleuze's characterization of masochistic repetition in her description of Masoch—and the masochistic hero—as a "visual aesthetic," suggesting that "in Masochism the running wild of repetition occurs in the realm of the image, which is set, frozen and fetishized, constantly before the gaze of the enraptured Masochist."[46] For Ricardo, his images are on screen, and the tapes of testimony are his fetishized objects: "He ignored his students as he expanded his collection. One hundred, two hundred, three hundred tapes on the wall, a thousand hours of horror, and he knew them all by heart. His wife was eager to have children, but he would not breed. The tapes were his children."[47] MacKendrick suggests that the masochist seeks out "scenes that can be frozen," a movement from "the act to its infinite suspension." For Ricardo, the archive serves as a storage bank for the frozen acts of testimony, for the "arrested movement" characteristic of masochism.[48]

According to Deleuze, "Masoch is animated by a dialectical spirit." He maintains that "[d]ialectic does not simply mean the free interchange of discourse, but implies transpositions or displacements of this kind, resulting in a scene being enacted simultaneously on several levels with reversals and reduplications in the allocation of roles and discourse."[49] As with *Venus*, Ricardo functions as both subject and object; he identifies an agent and persuades him/her to participate. Once the agent has signed on—most literally in *Venus*, with the presence of a contract—then Ricardo, as with Severin, becomes the object of the agent's actions, a receiver of pain, yet one who desires this role. In "Moloch," the "transpositions" extend even further. Ricardo is at once a sympathetic archivist who is working tirelessly for the benefit of humanity, while also acting as an obsessive masochist with an insatiable thirst for the pain of testimony. Asked to explain and defend the purpose of the archive to the old lady, Ricardo responds: "To prevent such a thing from ever happening again."

However the old lady not only rejects the rationale of prevention, but also the "deliberate redundancy . . . 'to remember. Never to forget.'" She identifies a personal motivation behind Ricardo's actions, suggesting that what is driving Ricardo is jealousy: "'Jealous of the Holocaust . . . Jealous of having a reason to hate. Jealous of tragedy.'"[50] Weissman surveys a few sources in which "nonwitnesses" have admitted to feelings of "envy," "resentment," "jealousy," and "obscene regret"[51] at being born after the Holocaust. Although Weissman does not get into the reasons why these feelings might exist within Jewish people born after the war, it is the assertion of this chapter that it relates to an identity-uncertainty that exists for post-Holocaust Jews who can never truly access or understand the atrocity that is central to their ethnic identities. This is fueled, to some degree, by the repeated directives to "never forget" something which one has never lived.

At the end of the "The Library of Moloch," the old woman's accusation of jealousy begs several questions about the character of Dr. Ricardo and the reasons that a "doctor of letters" would take on the task of directing an archive of trauma testimony; it also begs questions about the old lady herself, whose reluctance can suggest a defensiveness about her exclusive identity position as a Holocaust survivor. The search for identity featured in "Moloch" is a product of multiple factors, ranging from survivor's guilt to a reaction to the exclusive terrain, which Holocaust survivors such as Elie Wiesel have claimed for their experiences and the Holocaust itself (see note 10). The compulsion to remember this monumental atrocity contributes to the enigma of difference that exists for contemporary American Jews, and the call to remember something never lived and scarcely attainable lends itself to magical realist portrayals. As mentioned before, Bukiet highlights the inherent inaccessibility and impossibility by depicting a conversation between a nonwitness and the videotaped recording of a survivor unwilling, and potentially unable, to truly testify. Simultaneously, he demonstrates the destructive path down which Holocaust centrality can lead someone who is compelled to understand and establish a more concrete sense of ethnic identity. Through "The Library of Moloch," Bukiet implicitly questions the extremes that one will go to achieve this sense of identity and ethnic connection.

Wendy Brown discusses a comparable quest for identity within a group that has suffered as a result of "social crimes." She examines the idea that one may wish to be punished for "the 'social crimes' of being female, colored, or queer in a sexist, racist, and homophobic social order that also is acutely conscious of and has fashioned a sophisticated set of critical discourses about these injustices." She maintains that

> identity rooted in injury is not achieved through a single act or experience but must be reenacted or reaffirmed over time. Indeed, there is probably no better testimony to this than its apparent counterexample:

identity rooted in a traumatic past. To make . . . [this] into an identity, to make the past into the subjective and objective present, one has to reiterate the injury discursively, emotionally, as bodily and psychic trauma in the present.[52]

For Jewish Americans, the issue of identity is a complex and important one. There are few places in the United States where it would be considered a "social crime" to be Jewish, yet anti-Semitism still exists and still makes news headlines,[53] and so much of Jewish culture calls to mind — consciously, deliberately — a history of persecution, oppression, and even genocide: the "social crime" of being a Jew that was a fatal one for many living in Europe during the first half of the twentieth century. The identity of "Holocaust survivor" — clearly rooted in a traumatic past — gets concretized ("reenacted" and "reaffirmed") through public and private reiterations, news stories, books, films, and testimonial archives.

Witnesses, scholars, critics, and artists have written, spoken, and testified about the guilt experienced by survivors of trauma, as well as the residual guilt experienced by children of survivors. Sanyal discusses how "the circulation of innocence and guilt . . . is now reproduced in current theorizations of the Holocaust, and particularly in approaches indebted to the conceptual apparatuses of deconstruction and trauma theory." She goes on to suggest that within "a generation who did not live through the Holocaust but encountered it as secondary witnesses, as readers and viewers of films and documentaries, a peculiar sense of metaphorical survival and secondhand guilt, has emerged."[54] Aaron Hass posits "[c]hildren of survivors may also inwardly question their entitlement to their abundance, their safety, and even their insecurities."[55] These questions and "peculiar" feelings of "metaphorical survival" contribute to the uncertain sense of identity that exists for some Jewish Americans, even those who are not direct descendants of survivors. For American Jews, many of whom were raised with or around survivors of the Holocaust and are likely aware (at least generally) of the frighteningly consistent history of atrocity that has plagued the Jewish people — many of these reminders are linked to Jewish holidays — an identity-uncertainty can emerge as a byproduct of relative comfort. This combination — comfort with an identity steeped in discomfort — contributes to the enigma of difference discussed throughout *Magical American Jew*.

In writing about the quest for "identity rooted in injury," Wendy Brown contends that the pain must be repeated to maintain a strong sense of identity-in-injury; in place of (as a substitute for) receiving that pain personally and repetitively, one initially seeks out others who are and have been victimized, and links him/herself to their pain: "a certain nonsadistic gratification is thereby obtained through the specter of the victimization of 'one's people.'" She goes on to suggest that "[i]f the staging of punishment against one's peers confirms identity rooted in injury without making the subject suffer the injury directly, then presumably this displacement also spurs guilt that itself must be assuaged or expiated." In the effort to assuage this second round of guilt, there emerges a new desire to experience the suffering more personally, directly, to validate one's identity.[56]

In "The Library of Moloch," it is not until the emergence of the old woman that Ricardo's guilt and identity truly come into question. Although it is clear that Ricardo has neglected his wife and his students, their absence from the story—indicative of his obsession with the library—allows no opportunity for an exploration into his changed behavior, nor the anxieties and desires that have emerged since he began his quest to quench his "insatiable" thirst for the testimonies of trauma. As Ricardo is interrogated about the purpose of the library, the old woman refers to Holocaust Survivors as "remainders, or the remains," further undermining Ricardo's pursuit of, and effort to identify with, this stable identity. Speaking directly to Ricardo she charges: "'Leeches. Vampires. You cannot get more blood from our loved ones, so you're sinking your teeth into us. I do not think you are unsympathetic. I think you are jealous, Herr Doktor Professor.'"[57]

It is useful to consider the use of the plural form in the accusation cited above—"our," "us." Brown claims that there is a "*tendency* toward 'victimization' . . . that leads even those who do not appear overtly victimized to claim victim status."[58] It would seem that the old woman is reacting in response to this tendency. Uncomfortable with more violence being done to her identity, she is protective, territorial. As Weissman discusses about Wiesel most explicitly, many Holocaust survivors have claimed an exclusive position for their traumatic experiences, resisting the idea that others could understand or attempt to describe it.[59] Weissman further notes how "historical knowledge of the Holocaust and lived knowledge of the Holocaust experience may not always complement one another; rather, these two bodies of knowledge may compete with each other in a bid for what has been called 'proprietorship' of the Holocaust." Elaborating on this idea, Weissman suggests that "the question of whether or not the Holocaust is at all understandable is embroiled in a contest over who *really* understands the Holocaust—and must therefore defend it against deformations by those who lack such understanding."[60] As if to instigate this competition, the old lady in "Moloch" asks Ricardo where he was during the war; his response that he was a young child living in suburban Philadelphia leads him to bow his head—whether in shame or reverence is not clear. However it is the old woman's charge of jealousy, gesturing to the reactions which Weissman briefly surveys (mentioned earlier) that resonates most deeply with Ricardo, forcing him to reflect aloud—while the tape is still rolling: "'Jealous of what? Jealous of suffering? Jealous of death?'" Although it is not jealousy *alone* that we should imagine when the narrative tells of the survivors whom Ricardo "hunted, begged, cajoled, and, if necessary, bribed into telling their stories," it is part of what compels him and part of what fuels his obsession.[61]

Brown suggests that a "restaging" of the trauma—"either at the site of our own bodies (masochism) or at the site of another (displaced masochism in which we are split off from that with which we identify as we are 'passively looking on,' to use Freud's phrase)"—elicits an "erotic gratification." She claims "in so doing, it also sustains us in imaginary community with others 'of our kind.'"[62] One could imagine that Ricardo receives an emotionally erotic charge out of his service to the library, especially since he forgoes erotic activity with his wife and indulges a consummating act with his tapes of testimony, his "children." And Ricardo is clearly involved in the staging and restaging of trauma testimony, which can be viewed as involvement in the "reliving and reexperiencing of the event," as well as "in imaginary community with others." Weissman discusses a similar imaginary community, describing the connection and "desire [which] can be satisfied only in fantasy."[63] Indeed, Bukiet gives magical and independent life to the image on screen to emphasize how "desire can be satisfied only in fantasy." Only for Ricardo, he is not satisfied, and he is not "passively looking on." He has not only coordinated the testimonies, but he asks the questions that elicit the responses, and his voice exists on the tapes, fusing and freezing a part of himself with the victims of trauma. His role is very much that of the masochist, *seeming* passive while really enabling the subject to act upon him—in this case, with the violence of testimony. He suffers as a result of his role in these testimonies, yet desires them with increasing intensity.

Ricardo's desire to suffer and to sacrifice himself is suggested by the title of Bukiet's story. "Moloch" is a biblical reference that is mentioned specifically: "Moloch was the fire god to whom children were routinely sacrificed. Moloch, the Lord of Gehenna, lived outside of Jerusalem in what was truly the valley of the damned, forever exiled in sight of the heavenly city." The theme of sacrifice is significant; not only does Ricardo sacrifice his former life for the sake of the library, but in the end, he sacrifices himself, along with his tapes of testimony—"his children"—to satisfy his desire for the inviolate and "enter the Holy of Holies."[64]

Reference to Moloch can also be found in Theodor Reik's *Masochism in Modern Man* in which he describes a patient who "is fully potent sexually only with the aid of varied and different phantasies," one of which relates to the story of Moloch. In this fantasy, young men are stripped and placed on an altar where one by one their genitals are inspected by a high priest—for "weight and form"—and they are either discarded as unworthy, or else castrated and sacrificed. Prior to the sacrifice, each castrated man is placed on a scalding grate from which he will eventually be lifted and thrown into the fire.[65] Kaja Silverman discusses the relevance of the Moloch fantasy for Masochism. Not only does it demonstrate a literal castration, but it is steeped in suspense, as the person who is fantasizing imagines that his turn at the alter is coming at any moment. Silverman also points to the moments on the grate, where the question of whether the castrated man can wait out the scalding pain in order to be ritually thrown into the fire—rather than jumping in on his own for a quicker death—keeps one in suspense. She cites a variation on the Moloch fantasy in which captives are forced to maintain the fire in which they will eventually burn.[66] With the Moloch fantasy in mind, Ricardo's responsibility to maintain the archive where he and "his children" are ultimately burned to death can reinforce the impotency of his desire to establish a genuine connection to the Holocaust.

The suspense in "The Library of Moloch" that aligns most closely to the fundamental suspense of masochism takes place toward the end, when the old woman shares her insight about the two inviolate realms. Ricardo only hears one, memory, in her meta-testimony, and though he ultimately immolates himself in the effort to hear the second, this does not take place until the archive has already caught fire and the forum for his masochistic play is about to collapse. As long as the archive is standing, and he remains true to his desire to suffer along with (and as a result of) the testimonies of trauma, Ricardo willfully allows the second inviolate realm to remain suspended. But, as noted earlier, there is an important difference between the violence that the final witness is referencing and the violence of her words (see note 37). Ricardo acts as if the violence of reference is a way to connect to the violence that she is referencing—the concrete experience of the Holocaust. But just as the conflation is false, the route to this experience is masochistic fantasy—reinforced by the magical reality of the ending.

Although Ricardo does not consciously start the fire that concludes the story, the lighting of his cigarette occurs through the use of fire and the "soporific" act of smoking leads to the initial move out of the physical world and into his own memory; when "the images of his parents' home" go up in flames, he moves out of his own memory and awakens into the inferno of archived memories of the Holocaust. In this blazing scene, one can locate the traumatic repetition of testimonials where fires and burning bodies are described in "ferocious detail,"[67] each description enabled and experienced by Ricardo. One can also make a connection to the "performative speech act"[68] of the witness.

In discussing the breakdown of language that exists for survivors who try to communicate what is arguably incommunicable, Shoshanah Felman describes the "testimony [that] in effect addresses what in history is *action* that exceeds any substantialized significance, and what in happenings is *impact* that dynamically explodes any conceptual reifications and any constative delimitations."[69] The testimony that "exceeds" and "explodes" in "Moloch" is found initially in "the arm of the chair [which] had been scratched clear through to the stuffing, a mixture of straw and compressed fibers." The reader is told of the "supple leather surface" that was "punctured" during survivor testimonies—performative expressions of horror. It is the "exposed stuffing" of the chair that catches fire when Ricardo falls asleep, the ashes from his cigarette falling into this vulnerable area, leading to the flames that ignite the magical connection that concludes the story.[70] In the end, Ricardo merges fantasy with reality; he throws himself into the pit of Moloch's fire, making the ultimate sacrifice to fulfill his desire for "identity rooted in injury."

As with "Levitation"—the story analyzed in chapter 2—the magical moments analyzed in this chapter exist at the end of the story, but are crucial to the effort to understand the central themes and ideas. In "The Library of Moloch," what takes magical life at the end highlights the pursuit to find identity through historical tragedy and the effort to turn history into memory. Ricardo's most personal connection is with the video recording of a survivor, a conversation over a space impossible to traverse. His compulsion to "remember" a traumatic history and to understand how it impacts his present day identity is complicated by the exclusivity and incomprehensibility of the Holocaust. Also illustrated are the extreme lengths that some will go to try and reify the enigma of Jewish American difference. As portrayed in "The Library of Moloch," the effort can reach fantastic and masochistic heights.

NOTES

1. Fortunoff Video Archive for Holocaust Testimonies, May 2005, http://www.library.yale.edu/testimonies/.

2. Geoffrey H. Hartman, *The Longest Shadow* (Bloomington: Indiana UP, 1996), 41.

3. Walter Benn Michaels, "'You Who Was Never There': Slavery and the New Historicism—Deconstruction and the Holocaust," in *The Americanization of the Holocaust*, ed. Hilene Flanzbaum (Baltimore: Johns Hopkins UP, 1999), 181–97, 189–90.

4. Ibid., 193–94, 196.

5. Gary Weissman, *Fantasies of Witnessing: Postwar Efforts to Experience the Holocaust* (Ithaca: Cornell UP, 2004), 101–2.

6. Michael L. Morgan, *Beyond Auschwitz: Post-Holocaust Jewish Thought in America* (Oxford: OUP, 2001), 3.

7. Deborah Dash Moore, "Introduction," in *American Jewish Identity Politics*, ed. Deborah Dash Moore (Ann Arbor: U Michigan P, 2008), 12.

8. Morgan, *Beyond Auschwitz*, 4.

9. Peter Novick, *The Holocaust in American Life* (New York: Mariner, 2000), 6–7.

10. On many occasions, and in various media, Elie Wiesel has expressed sentiments suggesting such exclusivity and incomprehensibility. These statements can be found throughout the three volumes of Wiesel's collected essays: *Against Silence: The Voice and Vision of Elie Wiesel*, edited by Irving Abrahamson (1985).

11. Elie Wiesel, "Trivializing the Holocaust: Semi-Fact and Semi-Fiction," *New York Times*, April 16, 1978, 2, 29.

12. Although Bukiet never states it explicitly, there is evidence that Dr. Arthur Ricardo is Jewish. Beyond directing an archive of Holocaust testimonies, he demonstrates an awareness of Jewish prayers and traditions. Most notably, after the final witness challenges his rationale for directing the archive, she makes a gesture which Ricardo interprets as "the rod of the shepherd who winnows his flock by determining which pass beneath it and which do not. In the Yom Kippur prayer, the U-nisaneth

Tokef, that image is a symbol of God's judgment for the upcoming year, who shall live and who shall die" (191). His knowledge of and reference to this Yom Kippur prayer seems too specific to come from a character who is not meant to be read as Jewish.

13. Bukiet's story was almost certainly influenced by the construction of the Fortun-off Video Archive for Holocaust Testimonies at Yale University. The "wartime collaborator" would be a reference to Paul de Man—Sterling Professor of the Humanities at Yale at the time of his death in 1983—whose wartime journalism revealed Nazi sympathies. In de Man's case, his wartime journalism did not receive widespread attention until after his death, and after Yale's archive had been established, in 1979. Since his death, much has been written about de Man's wartime journalism; many notable essays have been collected in the volume *Responses: On Paul de Man's Wartime Journalism* (1989).

14. Melvin Jules Bukiet, "The Library of Moloch," in *While the Messiah Tarries* (New York: Harcourt Brace, 1995), 184–97, 185–87.

15. Ibid., 191–97.

16. Dori Laub and Shoshana Felman. *Testimony: Crises of Witnessing in Literature, Psychoanalysis, and History* (New York: Routledge, 1992), 76.

17. Ibid., 52.

18. Debarati Sanyal, "A Soccer Match in Auschwitz: Passing Culpability in Holocaust Criticism," *Representations* 79 (2002): 1–27, 3.

19. Dominick LaCapra, *Representing the Holocaust: History, Theory, Trauma* (Ithaca: Cornell UP, 1994), 211.

20. Saul Friedlander, "Trauma, Memory, and Transference," *Holocaust Remembrance: The Shapes of Memory*, ed. Geoffrey H. Hartman (Oxford: Blackwell, 1994): 252–63, 260.

21. Ibid.

22. LaCapra, *Representing the Holocaust*, 210.

23. Bukiet, "The Library of Moloch," 189.

24. Sacha Nacht, "*Le Masochisme*, Introduction," *Essential Papers on Masochism*, ed. Margaret Ann Fitzpatrick Hanly (New York: NYUP, 1995), 18–34, 21.

25. Ibid., 23.

26. Victor N. Smirnoff, "The Masochistic Contract," *Essential Papers on Masochism*, ed. Margaret Ann Fitzpatrick Hanly (New York: NYUP, 1995), 62–73, 62.

27. Ibid., 62–63, 72.

28. Gilles Deleuze and Leopold von Sacher-Masoch, *Masochism: Coldness and Cruelty & Venus in Furs*, trans. Jean McNeil (New York: Zone Books, 1991), 20.

29. Ibid., 170–72.

30. Bukiet, "The Library of Moloch," 188.

31. Deleuze and von Sacher-Masoch, *Masochism*, 53, 52.

32. Bukiet, "The Library of Moloch," 190.

33. Ibid., 185, 191.

34. Deleuze and von Sacher-Masoch, *Masochism*, 69.

35. Jon Thiem, "The Textualization of the Reader in Magical Realist Fiction," in *Magical Realism: Theory, History, Community*, ed. Lois Parkinson Zamora and Wendy B. Faris (Durham, NC: Duke UP, 1995), 235–48, 244.

36. Bukiet, "The Library of Moloch," 191.

37. In *The Longest Shadow*, Geoffrey H. Hartman discusses the potential for a "secondary trauma" (152) that can result from seeing a violent image or hearing a violent story, but he makes a clear distinction between this secondary violence and the violence of direct experience. In "Memorizing Memory," Amy Hungerford discusses Hartman's "secondary trauma," and provides her own articulation, emphasizing the importance "to distinguish this experience of trauma [hearing, viewing, or reading words or images of violence], if one wishes to call it that, from the trauma that the survivor herself has experienced and then represents in her testimony" (264–65).

38. In *Testimony*, Shoshana Felman discusses the problematic nature of Holocaust testimonies, referring to the Holocaust as "an event without a witness" (80). Signifi-

cantly, she discusses the need to separate one's self from the event to function as a reliable witness, and posits this separation as an impossibility for those who experienced the Holocaust. Felman maintains it would be "inconceivable that any historical insider could remove herself sufficiently from the contaminating power of the event so as to remain a fully lucid, unaffected witness, that is, to be sufficiently detached from the inside, so as to stay entirely *outside* of the trapping roles, and the consequent identities, either of the victim or of the executioner" (81). In her discussion of Claude Lanzmann's film *Shoah*, Felman uses the concept of "the Holocaust as the *event-with-out-a-witness* to posit the very "impossibility of testimony" (224). For Felman, "this impossibility of testimony by which the film is traversed, with which it struggles and against which it precisely builds itself is, in effect, the most profound and most crucial subject of the film" (224).

39. Deleuze and von Sacher-Masoch, *Masochism*, 266–71, 33.

40. Benn Michaels, "'You Who Was Never There,'" 195.

41. Lawrence L. Langer, *Holocaust Testimonies: The Ruins of Memory* (New Haven: Yale UP, 1991), 21.

42. Deleuze and von Sacher-Masoch, *Masochism*, 120, 114.

43. Bukiet, "The Library of Moloch," 188.

44. Ibid., 197.

45. Lois Parkinson Zamora and Wendy B. Faris, "Introduction: Daiquiri Birds and Flaubertian Parrot(ie)s," in *Magical Realism: Theory, History, Community*, ed. Lois Parkinson Zamora and Wendy B. Faris (Durham, NC: Duke UP, 1995), 1–11, 6.

46. Karmen MacKendrick, *Counterpleasures* (Albany: SUNY Press, 1999), 57.

47. Bukiet, "The Library of Moloch," 189.

48. MacKendrick, *Counterpleasures*, 57, 62.

49. Deleuze and von Sacher-Masoch, *Masochism*, 22.

50. Bukiet, "The Library of Moloch," 190, 196.

51. Weissman, *Fantasies of Witnessing*, 122. Weissman specifically discusses writings by George Steiner and Henri Raczymow, and interviews with "French Jews born just after the war," conducted by Nadine Fresco (122).

52. Wendy Brown, *Politics Out of History* (Princeton: Princeton UP, 2001), 46, 53.

53. In the first few months of 2017, the Anti-Defamation League and other agencies reported a significant rise in the rates of anti-Semitic acts, some of which have been reported by mainstream news.

54. Sanyal, "A Soccer Match in Auschwitz," 3.

55. Aaron Hass, "Survivor Guilt in Holocaust Survivors and Their Children," in *A Global Perspective on Working with Holocaust Survivors and the Second Generation*, ed. John Lemberger, 163–83, July 1995, http://www.holocaust-trc.org/glbsurv.htm, 176.

56. Brown, *Politics Out of History*, 53–54.

57. Bukiet, "The Library of Moloch," 191.

58. Brown, *Politics Out of History*, 54 (emphasis added).

59. Weissman, *Fantasies of Witnessing*, 48–49.

60. Ibid., 93.

61. Bukiet, "The Library of Moloch," 192, 188.

62. Brown, *Politics Out of History*, 55.

63. Weissman, *Fantasies of Witnessing*, 4.

64. Bukiet, "The Library of Moloch," 196, 189, 197.

65. Theodor Reik, *Masochism in Modern Man* (New York: Grove, 1941), 41.

66. Kaja Silverman, "Masochism and Male Subjectivity," in *Male Subjectivity at the Margins* (New York: Routledge, 1992), 53–53.

67. Bukiet, "The Library of Moloch," 195, 185.

68. Dori Laub and Shoshana Felman. *Testimony: Crises of Witnessing in Literature, Psychoanalysis, and History* (New York: Routledge, 1992), 5.

69. Ibid.

70. Bukiet, "The Library of Moloch," 194, 195.

FOUR

"Jewish, Here in the Back"

Magical and Comical Discord between Religiosity and Ethnicity in Nathan Englander's "The Gilgul of Park Avenue" and Steve Stern's "The Tale of a Kite"

As discussed in previous chapters, there exists an edge of self-consciousness for many contemporary American Jews, a "sense of unease" from "occupying an anomalous status," and from the "very lack of belonging to a recognizable category."[1] In this chapter, I examine how the discord between religiosity and ethnicity contributes to this "sense of unease," demonstrating how magical and comical modes are effective at conveying the enigmatic difference that marks contemporary Jewish American communities. Anchoring my discussion in analyses of Nathan Englander's short story "The Gilgul of Park Avenue" and Steve Stern's short story "The Tale of a Kite"—stories that marry magical and comical modes in comparably effective fashions—I show how the magical and the comical work well together because of their respective correlations with incongruity and the ways in which they are often, if not always, subversive. I also illustrate how tensions between the magical and the real parallel the tensions between religiosity and ethnicity, between Judaism and Jewishness. Together, these stories highlight the fallacy of a stable Jewish American identity—or the equivalently aberrant idea of a purely religious or a purely ethnic Jewish American identity—and shed light on the heterogeneous and continuously changing character of contemporary American Jewry.

Nathan Englander's "The Gilgul of Park Avenue" opens in a New York City taxi, just as the protagonist, Charles Morton Lugar, is imbued with a "Jewish soul." Following the internal metamorphosis that opens

71

the story, which in the magical realist context is related to the reader as a narrative fact—not unlike the external metamorphosis that awaits Gregor Samsa after waking from fitful dreams—we follow Charles as he struggles to feel comfortable with his new-found Jewishness. He never doubts the authenticity of his new Jewish soul, but he does struggle with the best way to share the newest reality of his life with his wife, Sue. Charles enlists the help of Rabbi Zalman Meintz who, we are told, underwent a similarly sudden transformation before moving from Bolinas to Brooklyn. Zalman implores Charles to tell his wife about his new soul as soon as possible. With comical timing, Charles shares the news after Sue has returned from the dentist, her mouth slack with novacaine. The turmoil that follows leads Sue and Charles to agree to host Zalman and Charles's psychiatrist, Dr. Birnbaum, to a kosher dinner. The story ends after Zalman and Dr. Birnbaum have gone home, and Sue and Charles are left alone. Wallowing in the tension of this new situation, Charles longs "to stand without judgment, to be only for Sue, to be wholly seen, wanting her to love him changed."[2]

Steve Stern's story "The Tale of a Kite" is set in the "Pinch" district of Memphis during the early twentieth century.[3] The story is narrated by a secular Jewish businessman named Jacob Zipper who associates with "an enterprising" bunch of Jewish business owners, all of whom are upset when they discover that the Chasidic Rabbi Shmelke "has begun to fly." Zipper's obsession with and distress over Rabbi Shmelke, exacerbated by the enthusiasm displayed by his son Ziggy, becomes the principal concern of the story. Eventually, Zipper is anointed the leader of his band of businessmen—"by virtue of what's perceived as [his] greater indignation"—and is given the task of cutting the rope that has been keeping Rabbi Shmelke connected to the synagogue. The story ends after Zipper severs the connection between the celestial rabbi and the terrestrial world, allowing the rabbi to float away from the synagogue;[4] the rabbi's followers, led by Zipper's son Ziggy, jump onto the end of the rope, becoming a human tail on this ascending kite, which is wafting away to Paradise, leaving Zipper alone to wallow in sadness, regret, and the harsh reality that he is "a stout man and no match for gravity."[5]

Both stories, Englander's "The Gilgul of Park Avenue" and Stern's "The Tale of a Kite," establish their magical realist contexts—featuring authoritative, unquestioning narrative voices—from the outset. In "Gilgul," the magical premise is embedded in the opening details:

> It was then, three stars visible in the Manhattan sky and a new day fallen, that Charles Morton Luger understood he was the bearer of a Jewish soul.
>
> *Ping!* Like that it came. Like a knife against a glass.
>
> Charles Luger knew, as he knew anything at all, that there was a Yiddishe neshama functioning inside.

He was not one to engage taxicab drivers in conversation, but such a thing as this he felt obligated to share. A New York story of the first order, like a woman giving birth in an elevator, or a hot-dog vendor performing open-heart surgery with pocketknife and Bic pen. Was not this a rebirth in itself? It was something, he was sure. So he leaned forward in his seat, raised a fist, and knocked on the Plexiglas divider.

The driver looked into his rearview mirror.

"Jewish," Charles said. "Jewish, here in the back."[6]

The details and the tone that open Englander's story keep our focus on the *consequences* of the magical occurrence, rather than on the nature of the occurrence itself. As we are directed toward the thoughts and actions that follow the magical *"Ping,"* we are struck by the comical analogies — "like a woman giving birth in an elevator, or a hot-dog vendor performing open-heart surgery with pocketknife and Bic pen" — rather than the inclination to interrogate the logic of what has taken place. The location — Manhattan, in this case — also plays a role, as it grounds us in a specific setting that is familiar yet mysterious at the same time — a place where extraordinary things really do occur.

In an interview with Derek Parker Royal, Steve Stern discusses the extraordinary potential of cities, contending that such locations, "by virtue of enduring in time and accumulating history, have roots that extend beyond the confines of the merely mortal. Places can achieve immortality in ways that human beings cannot, although human beings who dwell in such places can partake of eternal and universal elements, thus extending the possibilities of their own lives beyond the bounds of the ordinary." After referencing the extraordinary potential of cities such as London, Dublin, and Odessa, Stern discusses how writers such as "Dickens and Joyce and Babel . . . have distilled real cities into places as fantastical as they are historical and geographical; and by the same token the characters that inhabit these cities may display, beyond the merely terrestrial, celestial and infernal attributes as well. This is the sort of thing I was hoping to do . . . with the Pinch."[7] Such a timeless and magical infusion, grounded in an historical location (notably the Pinch), is evident in several of Stern's short stories and novels.[8] Similar to Stern's Pinch, many of Englander's stories are set in a fictionally named, yet markedly familiar section of Brooklyn called "Royal Hills." Although Englander's work does not bend the boundaries of realism as consistently as Stern's, the "fantastical" potential of The City *is* evident in "The Gilgul of Park Avenue," in which the major magical event is characterized as "[a] New York story of the first order."

For Englander and Stern, the city settings allow the supernatural to be perceived as extraordinarily real, helping to establish the magical realist contexts that are crucial to each story. The ways in which the magical realist narratives subvert conventional notions of realism help to emphasize the ways in which Jewish American identities subvert conventional notions of ethnic and religious classification. Describing how "[m]agical realist texts are subversive," Lois Parkinson Zamora and Wendy B. Faris suggest "their in-betweenness, their all-at-onceness encourages resistance to monologic political and cultural structures."[9] Implicit in such resistance is the inclination to reevaluate and imagine anew. As Shannin Schroeder contends, "[l]iterary modes like magical realism play an important role in the reviewing and revision of our 'selves' . . . resulting in cultural corrections and forcing readers to reconsider reality as they know it."[10] The enigma of difference for contemporary American Jews comes out of the persistent re-evaluations, re-imaginations, and re-articulations that epitomize contemporary Jewish American communities. Just as magical realist narratives subvert stable structures, "humorous incongruity disorders what had been ordered, breaking open the frame and scattering its elements. . . . [I]t takes its character from what it is not—that is, ordered, and therefore expected, experience."[11] In "Gilgul" and "Kite," the comical and magical modes highlight the illusion of stable, often polar classifications (i.e., Jewish as either religion or ethnicity), while demonstrating how Jewish American identities resist efforts to be placed within fixed categories.

In "Gilgul," we see such resistance personified in Rabbi Zalman Meintz who (as mentioned earlier) underwent a transformation similar to Charles's before he moved from Bolinas to Brooklyn and opened "the Royal Hills Mystical Jewish Reclamation Center." This story-fact is significant on many levels. First, the comical details, such as the description of the Center as "a sort of clearinghouse for the Judeo-supernatural," help to normalize the presence of the magical, by coupling the "supernatural" center with the mundane description of a "clearinghouse," casually gesturing beyond the realms of realism. Along similar lines—making the extraordinary ordinary—Zalman's transformation, and the presence of the Reclamation Center where the phone seems to ring incessantly, reinforce the magical realist "co-presence" of the natural and supernatural: what Charles has experienced is not so unique. In fact, it is common enough to establish the center and list it in the Manhattan yellow pages where one can "find anything." It also gives Zalman an opportunity to state most explicitly that what Charles has experienced is "miraculous" but "not unbelievable";[12] the potential for such a transformation was "always already" there. The only question now is how to proceed. Most significantly, however, the Royal Hills Mystical Jewish Reclamation Center speaks to the changing face of contemporary American Judaism—an example of one of the "communal institutions and social and family networks," which bolster (or in this case, reclaim) contemporary American Jewish communities.[13] As Calvin Goldscheider posits, such "institutions" and "networks"—regardless of how secular or non-traditional—help to "sustain the ethnic and religious continuity of American Jews in the absence of overt discrimination and disadvantage," and function as one of the "structural and cultural forces [that] sustain continuity in the face of pressures toward the disintegration of the uniqueness and distinctiveness of their communities."[14] In "Gilgul," Charles's discovery is described as a "small miracle" and "exactly why he'd moved to New York."[15] Once again, the city space helps to normalize the supernatural while highlighting the diversity and continuous transformations that contribute to the constitution of contemporary American Jewry.

Similar to "Gilgul," "The Tale of a Kite" opens with narrative details and a narrative tone that help characterize the protagonist, Jacob Zipper, and establish a comical and magical realist framework: "Boss Crump and his heelers, who gave us a dispensation to stay open on Sundays, have declared more than once in our presence, 'Our sheenies are good sheenies!' So you can imagine how it unsettles us to hear that Rabbi Shmelke, head of that gang of fanatics over on Auction Street, has begun to fly."[16] The magic is embedded within the comical voice and narrative details. By emphasizing his desire to assimilate, we are compelled to consider Zipper's regrettably familiar, yet still comical point of view and less inclined to question the magical flight that drives the actions of the story. It is through the first-person presentation of the circumstances—where the narrator is ostensibly trying to persuade readers of the soundness of his perspective (most evident in his second-person appeal: "you can imagine how it unsettles us")—that, ironically, compels readers to sympathize with Rabbi Shmelke. Zipper comes across as the misguided one, more unsettled by the power and allure of Shmelke and his growing group of followers than by the backhanded and demeaning "compliment" that he and his cohorts are "good sheenies."

In each story, "The Gilgul of Park Avenue" and "The Tale of a Kite," religiosity seems to be pitted against ethnicity, and in each story, this apparent tension is highlighted through magical and comical means. While the religiosity-ethnicity dichotomy is portrayed differently in each piece, the degree of comically discriminatory rhetoric is similar. In "Kite," Zipper and his cohorts share their "apprehensions [about Shmelke and his followers] to the courtly Rabbi Fein, who runs the religious school in the synagogue basement. At . . . [their] urgency he lets it be known from the pulpit that fraternizing with Chasids, who are after all no better than heretics, can be hazardous to the soul. He hints at physical consequences as well, such as warts and blindness."[17] While humor is used to emphasize the perceived divide between the secular and the religious, it also pulls from a history of discriminatory mythology[18]—suggesting the "physical consequences" of interacting with "heretics"—and touches on the reality that certain Jewish stereotypes have been perpetuated by other Jews, some through the prominence and influence of Jewish humor.[19] In "Gilgul," Charles's wife Sue confronts Charles about the mezuzah he has nailed to the frame of their door, anxious to know why it has "'blue paint on it. Where does one buy a used mezuzah?'" she asks him. Charles admits that he "'pried it off eleven-D with a letter opener. They don't use it. Steve Fraiman had me in to see their Christmas tree last year. Their daughter is dating a black man.'"[20] As with "Kite," the humor emphasizes the tensions that can surface over religious and secular practices and values. Of course the irony and humor are not only found in Charles's attempt to discredit Fraiman's Jewishness—as if Charles, who recently and instantaneously became Jewish, is suddenly an authority on Jewishness and would properly "use" this stolen mezuzah—but more significantly that desecration of property and theft of this religious object (not to mention coveting a neighbor's possessions and spreading discriminatory gossip) would be acceptable, even righteous, and somehow more Jewish.

Just as the magical realist narratives found in "Gilgul" and "Kite" subvert conventional notions of reality (as well as "monologic political and cultural structures"), humor can also subvert stable structures, classifications, and categories. Discussing Ben Katchor's graphic narrative *The Jew of New York* and Jewish humor more generally, James Bloom discusses "the commitment among funny Jews both to sustain and discredit nearly three millennia of 'lost tribe' myth making." Bloom contends that "[t]hese two mutually offsetting moves, sustaining and discrediting, require a renunciation of home and identity."[21] Such a renunciation is on display with Charles Lugar's "offsetting" move to steal the mezuzah from someone's home in an effort to make his own home more Jewish. Bloom follows his contention about "sustaining and discrediting" by pulling from a 1955 essay by Irving Kristol who suggests that Jewish humorists maintain "a knife edge between faith and nihilism."[22] Just as the humor in "Gilgul" emphasizes that liminal territory between the sacred and profane, "between faith and nihilism," the humor in "Kite" rises out of that same in-between space.

Describing the march to cut the rope tied to the ankle of Rabbi Shmelke—almost literally applying "a knife edge between faith and nihilism"—Zipper tries to justify his impending actions: "We're all of one mind, I tell myself, though yours truly has been elected to carry the hedge shears—donated for the deed by Hekkie Schatz of Hekkie's Hardware. Ostrow our titular chair, Nussbaum the treasurer, Benny Rosen the whatsit, all have deferred the honor to me, by virtue of what's *perceived* as my greater indignation."[23] Zipper's unwillingness to take ownership of—to fully claim—the "greater indignation" that others have "perceived" betrays his own uncertainties and misgivings about the supernatural occurrence that has taken place and his own uncertainties and misgivings about his identity and responsibility as an American Jew. Stern admits that he's "partial to the idea of the marriage of the ordinary and the extraordinary," suggesting "the union, put that way, remains in the realm of the secular. The wedding that interests me more, in life as well as literature, is the marriage of the sacred and the profane."[24] While the magical realist narrative "remains in the realm of the secular," Zipper is presiding over that wedding "of the sacred and the profane," and his uncertainty about his role in this magical union is featured through his comical narrative, the diversions of which (telling us who donated the hedge shears, grasping for and commenting on committee titles, sharing how he has come to be holding the hedge shears—all while he is en route to cut the rope tied to the ankle of the levitating rabbi) emphasize the ambivalence that characterizes contemporary Jewish American identity.

Although both Englander and Stern incorporate religious figures and events into their stories, the magical realist context keeps their stories outside of the realm of the religious, and away from theological or mythological explanations and interpretations. "The Gilgul of Park Avenue" is not a Kabbalistic reincarnation tale[25] (as the "Gilgul" might suggest), but a "New York story of the first order," which does not rely on religious mythology for its magic. Similarly, "The Tale of a Kite," also grounded in an historical city district, is very much an American story about assimilation and the struggle to discern one's cultural identity, rather than a religious fantasy, allegory, or fable. By incorporating religious aspects into a mode that generally subverts and works outside of any theological or mythological realm, these stories implicitly demonstrate the paradoxical construction that complicates efforts to understand and describe Jewish American identity—a construction that contributes to the enigma of difference for contemporary American Jews.

Despite the discriminatory rhetoric directed toward secular Jews (in "Gilgul") and Chasidic Jews (in "Kite"), neither Charles nor Zipper really understands their own religious and cultural identities. When Zalman asks Charles how he feels, Charles answers "'Jewish and content. Excited. Still excited. The whole thing's ludicrous. I was one thing and now I'm another. But neither holds any real meaning. It's only that when I discovered I was Jewish, I think I also discovered God."[26] In this case, Charles not only demonstrates his inability to express what being Jewish means— he uses "Jewish" as an adjective to describe his state—he also makes the distinction between being Jewish and practicing Judaism, saying that when he became Jewish he *thinks* he "also discovered God." As he describes it, discovering God is more incidental than integral, yet the obvious, if not intrinsic association between Jewishness and God reinforces the conflation of religiosity and ethnicity. When confronting her husband, Sue asks "'if you have to be Jewish, why *so* Jewish? Why not like the Browns in six-K? Their kid goes to Haverford. Why . . . why do people who find religion always have to be so goddamn extreme?'"[27] One way to demonstrate one's Jewishness, especially for someone who did not grow up religious—or even Jewish in Charles's case—is through adherence to *Halacha* (religious law): for Charles it means keeping kosher, wearing "a prayer shawl and phylacteries," reciting the "Eighteen Benedictions," and "making ablutions" (more often than Sue can tolerate).[28]

For Charles, religious observance becomes the most concrete and accessible expression of Jewishness. And yet, Charles is still not certain that he discovered God, only that he has a Jewish soul. Soul, in this case, is the perfect word—the ultimate enigma—as ordinary and extraordinary as almost any human concept, inherently defying concrete definition.

The questions about what makes someone Jewish or how to characterize American Jewishness sprout out of the persistent changes—new and exhausted affiliations, modernized and increasingly personal interpretations, interfaith marriages with integrated holidays and rituals (to mention a few)—that have marked the Jewish experience in the United States. Advocating the use of "multiplicity" over "hybridity" when describing "Jews in the modern period," David Biale suggests that in contemporary times, "intermarriage needs to be seen . . . as creating new forms of identity, including multiple identities, that will reshape what it means to be Jewish in ways we can only begin to imagine."[29] In his study of the "Demographic Revolution in American Jewry," Egon Mayer devotes significant sections to intermarriage and Jewish conversions, finding that "[c]hildren raised in families where the formerly non-Jewish spouse is a 'Jew by choice' are overwhelmingly raised as Jews and identify as Jews. Moreover, the religious affiliations and practices of such families are consistently more identifiably Jewish than is typical for American Jews in general."[30] As noted in chapter 2, Goldscheider makes the argument that "intermarriage cannot have the same meaning in modern context of generations as it did in the former context of rejection and escape." Significantly, "Jewish communities in America have changed and . . . have developed new and creative forms of Jewish culture."[31] These "new and creative forms" have emerged as the number of interfaith marriages has increased and Jewish Americans have become more confident about their national standings and identities. With diminished pressure to marry inside the faith—today, few face the harsh judgments of old when some Jews would suggest an interfaith marriage was a victory for Hitler[32]— Jewish Americans can more freely express their individual and communal characters and embrace the "multiplicity" of their identities.

The continuous changes taking place in American Jewish communities are, ironically, a sign of an increasingly fixed place within American society. As Vivian Klaff notes (following analyses of the National Jewish Population Survey conducted in 2000/2001), "the Jewish population has become much more diverse in terms of culture and religious identification" and the findings are consistent with "the general American population where religious identification is in constant flux."[33] Responding to the tendency to see changing Jewish communities as a sign of the end of Jewish religion, culture, and identity, Goldscheider and others suggest it is rash to "define change as decline . . . or the development of new forms of Jewish culture and religion as secularization"; in the contemporary United States especially, it is prudent to consider "a more dynamic view of change that implies the value of choice, diversity, and creativity in the emergence of new forms."[34] These "new forms" have been enriched and expanded by those who have chosen to become Jewish (or in the case of Charles, been imbued with a Jewish soul).

In an interview with Random House (boldtype), when asked about the sudden transformation that takes place in "Gilgul," Englander responds:

> Religion got a lot more religious while I was growing up. Mostly because we were a bunch of little zealots coming home on the school bus and announcing things, like, "It's a sin to rip toilet paper on Shabbos, there will be no more toilet paper ripping under this roof." We'd out-religious the next guy. And it was the people who came from the least religious homes who often got the most religious the quickest and that is a lot to deal with for the folks in their world. I've watched a lot of people turn very religious very quickly, and it always interests me, this change. And especially having turned very not religious, very slowly, I can obviously empathize with the act of changing.[35]

It is "the act of changing" that lives at the heart of the contemporary Jewish American community. Descriptions and characterizations that try to capture or freeze complex identities, must stay mindful of the consistency of change that is one of the markers of American Jewishness. Goldscheider alleges "that those who have taken snapshots of the community at one survey time period (and not dynamic moving pictures) obtain distorted pictures of ethnic identity and community"; he notes how "[l]ife course transitions, such as when children are not living at home and have not yet started their families, are particularly vulnerable. People's ethnic and religious identity is often in flux, and their communal commitments throughout life are difficult to forecast."[36] Part of what "Gilgul" depicts is the *flux* of "ethnic and religious identity," most significantly the impact of sudden turns toward religiosity, which can be "a lot to deal with for the folks in their world," and "a lot to deal with" for those who try to define or attach stable terms to the contemporary Jewish American community.

Englander can "empathize with the act of changing" since he was raised orthodox and is now secular, but has always been (and will always be) Jewish. The enigmatic difference felt by many American Jews is tied to the fluidity of "ethnic and religious identity" and can be hard to capture and "difficult to forecast"; it is a difference that emerges out of the coexistence (to pull a term often used in discussions of magical realism) of ever-evolving Jewish American factions and individuals, more diverse and complex than "ethnic" and "religious" tags would suggest. Contemporary American Jewishness can accommodate rigid observance but it presents a direct challenge to rigid thinking that refuses to acknowledge the diversity and flexibility of contemporary American Jewry.

For Steve Stern, who grew up in Memphis and later in life (as noted earlier) became fascinated by the city's old Jewish district, the Pinch—setting many of his stories in this southern urban landscape—his own "life course transition" would have been exceedingly "difficult to forecast." In his interview with Derek Parker Royal, Stern describes how a job as Ethnic Heritage Director at "a local folklore center" opened his eyes to a part of the city and the Jewish past that instigated a change in his awareness and involvement in the diverse, contemporary Jewish American community—seen most poignantly in his fiction, so much of which is written in magical and comical modes. According to Stern, his "characters are frequently torn between two worlds—the one they're born into where they tend to feel awkward and uncomfortable, and the one they are trying to enter by means of Rube Goldberg vehicles assembled out of bootlegged myths and dreams."[37] While this complicated dichotomy is notable in many of Stern's stories, a similarly divided trajectory can be identified in Englander's piece. In "Gilgul," Charles moves out of the security of the gentile mainstream and into the "awkward and uncomfortable" world where he has to grapple with his new Jewish soul, leading to his efforts to observe Jewish rituals and laws—trying (one might imagine) to enter a world "by means of Rube Goldberg vehicles assembled out of bootlegged myths and dreams."

Both Stern and Englander draw their material from assorted Jewish American communities, which they have participated in, read about, researched, and observed from the periphery. As James Bloom (via Lenny Bruce) suggests, "[t]o *observe*[38] even religiously . . . involves acknowledging change, usually coupled with a wish for permanence, while to observe perceptually readies observers for change. These lexical ambiguities of *observe*, its meaning at once 'honor,' 'watch carefully,' 'notice,' and 'comment,' make it the foremost imperative of funny Jewishness."[39] Indeed, it is the patience and ability to *observe*, note incongruities, and convey those incongruities on the page (in the case of Englander and Stern) that allows us to see—just a tad more clearly—the changes and tensions that contribute to the enigma of Jewish American difference. Comical and magical modes allow those incongruities—a foundation for much humor and an integral component in magical realism—to become more evident; these modes offer textual space to present and observe the changing face of American Jewry. Describing the world conjured in magical realist stories, Rawdon Wilson suggests "[t]he hybrid nature of this space becomes evident when you observe the ease, the purely natural way in which abnormal, experientially impossible (and empirically unverifiable) events take place." For Wilson, "[i]t is as if they [the supernatural entities and events] had always already been there; their abnormality normalized from the moment that their magical realist worlds were imagined. The narrative voice bridges the gap between ordinary and bizarre, smoothing the discrepancies, making everything seem normal."[40] Established in and sustained by discrepancies, magical realism—especially when coupled with humor—possesses the unique ability to expose and subvert ostensibly stable labels and structures.

In "Gilgul," after Charles undergoes his radical transformation, he is compelled to share the change immediately—in this case, to the New York City taxi driver who is taking him home. What he says after the *"Ping"* of his Jewish soul has reclaimed his identity—"Jewish, here in the back"—has several pertinent meanings. In the context of the story, and for many contemporary American Jews, it demonstrates a desire and an inability to express or define one's Jewishness; it is just a fact: *Somewhere in the back of it all, I'm Jewish.* It also refers to the reality that for many American Jews, Jewishness is always there, but often in the background, occasionally calling out for recognition or emerging from an assortment of disparate ingredients: like a distinct spice in a robust soup. Such calls for recognition—reminders of Jewish identity—are disseminated within public and private documents, asking for religious preference; they stream out of countless news sources, spinning and reporting stories about Israel or national and international anti-Semitism; they are broadcast from entertainment media sources[41]—in movies and on television, in magazines, web zines, and newspapers—they are embedded in holiday decorations and salutations: at department stores, office parties, and public squares. These reminders of difference may leave some contemporary American Jews feeling disconcerted, yet most are just hit with a *Ping,* unsure exactly what it means or how to act, react, or respond.

Of course, deciding how to respond to a fairly innocuous salutation ("Merry Christmas, Mr. Goldberg!") may be a luxury of our contemporary time—here in the United States, at least. In the time period of "Kite," Jewish difference elicits more fears and insecurities for Zipper than it generally would today for most Jews. In Zipper's case, his distress over Rabbi Shmelke stems from fears of a sweeping and discriminatory reaction to the Chasidic group in town—one which would jeopardize his business and overall "good standing." Upon first entering the dark room of the Chasidim, Zipper is unsettled by "all the blind superstition of our ancestors preserved in amber," revealing his paranoia:

> But how did it [the collection of cultural artifacts] manage to follow us over an ocean to such a far-flung outpost as Tennessee? Let the goyim see a room like this, with a ram's horn in place of a clock on the wall, with the *shnorrers* wrapped in their paraphernalia mumbling hocus-pocus instead of being gainfully employed, and right away the rumors start. The Yids are poisoning the water, pishing on the communion wafers, murdering Christian children for their blood. Right away somebody's quoting the *Protocols of Zion.* A room like this, give or take one flying rebbe, can upset the delicate balance of the entire American enterprise.[42]

Zipper's use of the first-person plural ("how did it manage to follow *us*") sets up a crucial irony. On one hand, Zipper links himself to the Chasidic group. The artifacts are a reminder of who he is and where he comes from—a reminder of the Jewish diaspora in the United States and beyond. On the other hand, some of the stereotypes and discriminatory mythology he mentions—most significantly, the reference to the 1903 anti-Semitic text *The Protocols of the Elders of Zion*, which suggests that Jews have a secret plan to rule the world—rival the absurdity of the words that come from Zipper's own Rabbi Fein who warns of "warts and blindness" for those who are "fraternizing with Chasids." In this case, Zipper either wants the religious group to abandon their cultural history (and the accompanying "paraphernalia") and blindly follow his own path toward assimilation, or he wants to imagine that (and proceed as if) there is a genuine divide between the secular and religious, one so evident and irreconcilable that the connection is severed and there is no longer an association. But the "us" gives him away. Indeed, Zipper's distress comes from the deep-seated understanding that the divide he imagines does not exist—secular and religious American Jews are inextricably bound in Jewishness—and despite individual values and behaviors, he may always be subject to the generalizations of an-at-least-partly-imagined anti-Semitic mainstream who tend not to make distinctions when unleashing discriminatory rhetoric. This is not to say that anti-Semitism is the great equalizer, but a Jewish joke or an anti-Semitic slur *does* have the power and potential to offend all Jews equally.

Sensitivity to difference is still a common theme in Jewish American literature. Stern's "Kite" falls into what-has-become, at least since the novels of Abraham Cahan, a Jewish American literary tradition, featuring stories of assimilating or assimilated Jews working hard to downplay cultural and religious differences to "pass" as an equal part of the mainstream—different from the practices and appearances of "greenhorn" and/or more religious Jews. In a brief analysis of Stern's story, Andrew Furman notes the striking similarities between "The Tale of a Kite" and Philip Roth's story "Eli, the Fanatic." As Furman notes, both stories focus on towns where assimilated Jews live in relative harmony with gentiles, and in both stories, the secular Jews are disturbed by the arrival of a religious sect of Jews who—by ritual behaviors and appearance alone—threaten to undermine the relationship between the Jews and the gentiles (at least in the minds of the secular Jewish population). In each story, the secular Jews appoint a representative to try and convince the religious group to leave, and in each case the representative is in some way transformed—or at least affected—by his interaction with the spiritual leader and the commitment of this leader's followers. There are two primary differences. The first difference is in the understood times and places of these stories: "Eli" takes place in Woodenton, NJ, during the second half of the Twentieth century, while "Kite" takes place in Memphis, TN, during (what seems to be) the years just before World War II (see note 3). The second difference is in Stern's magical realist narrative, which portrays a world in which a rabbi can fly. While Furman suggests that the flight of Rabbi Shmelke indicates a "narrative awe in the transcendent powers of the holy,"[43] his discussion does not delve into great detail about the significance of that awe, which is most evident in the concluding fantasy where Zipper imagines he is floating away to Paradise with Rabbi Shmelke and his followers. Part of the argument I have been making here is that the flight of Rabbi Shmelke—and the presence of the magical (whether it is interpreted as "narrative awe" or not)—is used to illustrate and emphasize the ironic tension between religiosity and ethnicity. The taut rope connecting the terrestrial synagogue to the celestial rabbi is a manifestation of that tension, and the characters in "Kite"—Zipper, especially—do not know how to negotiate the space between the magical and the real (between religiosity and ethnicity). It is the illusion that the religious and the ethnic are separate that contributes to the difficulty that Zipper and his associates are having. In "Kite," Zipper tries to sever a part of his own identity, unwilling or unable to see how intertwined he and Rabbi Shmelke and the entire Jewish American community really are. The irony of this illusory tension is reinforced by and consistent with the inherent irony of magical realism where the magical and the real would seem to oppose one another, yet are inextricably bound to the same world—coexisting as integral parts of one complex entity.

In many ways, Rabbi Zalman Meintz—who comes from Bolinas, talks like he's "never been out of Brooklyn" and runs "a . . . clearinghouse for the Judeo-supernatural"[44]—represents just how complex and diverse the contemporary Jewish American community has become; he is an example (along with Charles) of how the comical and the magical are brought together to highlight the enigma of difference for contemporary American Jews. After Zalman experiences his own magical transformation, he becomes a rabbi who is strictly kosher and mindful of Jewish law—encouraging Charles to wear "a prayer shawl and phylacteries," recite the "Eighteen Benedictions," and make "ablutions"—yet has no patience "for the litigious and stiff minded" Jews who put the strict adherence of rituals above "Jewish pride." As a contemporary Jewish American, Zalman does not fit into any stable religious or ethnic category; he embodies and helps others negotiate the complex space between (what appears to be) opposing religious and ethnic—supernatural and natural—worlds. He posits "the sacrifice of Jewish pride" as the "one thing the tender soul can't bear,"[45] but what is meant by "Jewish pride," to say nothing of "the tender soul," is never, and perhaps could never, be expressed explicitly. However his point still comes across: "Jewish pride" embodies all—every variation of Jew. Although cultural and religious calls—the calls of Jewish identity—may get pushed to the background for many Jewish Americans, they cannot be ignored or denied. They have persisted throughout history, and history, along with the fluctuations of contemporary culture, have a way of being heard. Discussing how he came upon the remnants of Memphis's historical Jewish ghetto community—an experience that would profoundly inform his writing—Stern describes how "the past with its ghost population—spooking about empty lots, parking lots, a bridge ramp, a power plant—began to assume more life in my mind than the desolate present. I felt as if I'd tossed my line into the past, expecting to snag a quaint memory or two, and hauled up the lost city of Atlantis." For Stern, "the discovery of the Pinch felt like a homecoming, a place where [his] stories (which had been searching for somewhere to belong) could happen."[46] Part of what I have tried to demonstrate in this chapter is how the coupling of magical realist and comical modes—a combination found in Englander's "Gilgul" and Stern's "Kite" (one of many pieces in Stern's oeuvre where this combination can be found)—can harbor and highlight incongruous conditions, creating complex spaces where the multiplicities and contradictions of Jewish American identities have "somewhere to belong."

Describing the presence of "characters commuting between worlds," Steve Stern suggests "their journeys are not so much between opposing orders of reality as between the present and the past. They often dwell in places where the membrane between the here and now and a yesterday in which the citizens of the Pale of Settlement, both natural and supernatural . . . is quite thin." He goes on to describe how "[a] haunted past invades and occasionally occupies a pedestrian present for good or ill. . . . This is seldom a cozy cohabitation. To pursue a dubious metaphor, the penetration of that aforementioned membrane is often a violent rupture, prompting an abrupt end of innocence and perhaps the beginning of a painful wisdom."[47] For Zipper, the "painful wisdom" comes after he tries to sever the connection between Rabbi Shmelke and followers (including Zipper's own son) and the "enterprising bunch" with whom Zipper associates. It is not until the "violent rupture" of Smelke's rope when Zipper realizes that his actions and outbursts have been in vain, that religious and secular American Jews are inexplicably and inexorably bound in American Jewishness. Efforts to divorce Judaism from the Jewish, or to renounce secular Jews from a Jewishness steeped in Judaism are, comically and fantastically, futile.

In "Kite," Zipper is most distressed by the participation and support of his son Ziggy whom he sees hovering in a crowd around Rabbi Shmelke. "I can hardly believe this is my son," he says. "What did I do wrong that he should chase after moth-eaten *yiddishe* swamis? Did he ever want for anything? Didn't I take him on high holidays to a sensible synagogue, where I showed him how to mouth the prayers nobody remembers the meaning of?"[48] Not only is the criteria for a synagogue *not* based on something spiritual, but knowing "how to mouth . . . prayers" is meant to be more "sensible" than the *actual* prayers of the "moth-eaten *yiddishe* swamis." For Zipper, synagogue is a place to mimic and delude more than to seek any religious identity or connection. Yet, despite the way Zipper's actions are lampooned through the narrative, it is more his judgmental attitude toward his son's interests and actions that warrant scorn, not the ritual "acting" he indulges at his local synagogue. For contemporary American Jews, certain synagogues may serve more as "communal institutions and social and family networks" than houses of worship; while for many others, synagogues remain the center of religious lives: sacred spaces where individuals who do more than just "mouth the prayers"—but know, believe in, and form their identities from and through them—willingly congregate and observe. What should be questioned (by Zipper and others) is not why Ziggy wants to practice his faith, but why Zipper is so threatened by his son's interest and faith, even while he continues to attend a synagogue where he (and presumably others) go through the ritualistic motions. Questions like these, even more than the range of answers, has come to define contemporary American Jewry.

For Zipper, the act of gathering at his synagogue is important for his individual and cultural identity—important for Jewish "continuity" and community—but the purpose for communing has started to shift (or has never stopped shifting for many Jews in the United States). As with many Jewish American communities, there has been some movement toward a more secular perspective; however, religious and ethnic elements still remain linked. Rituals that were once exclusively religious—Passover Seders, for instance—have become cultural for unaffiliated, atheistic, or even some Reform Jews who ritually congregate with family during Jewish holidays and foster cultural identities from these practices and performances. As Goldscheider observes, "Jews have been transformed from an immigrant group defined by a combination of religious and ethnic distinctiveness to an American ethnic community defined by a distinctive cultural construction of Judaism and Jewishness with central, particularly American features."[49] The practices and priorities may be different from congregation to congregation and individual to individual, but each group and each individual contributes to the diverse and fluctuating face of the Jewish American community. Similar to the Royal Hills Mystical Jewish Reclamation Center in Englander's "Gilgul"—one of the "communal institutions and social and family networks" which Goldscheider posits as "the core elements sustaining communal continuity"[50]—Zipper's tenuous affiliation and participation in Stern's "Kite" helps to keep Jewishness alive in the United States.

But just as Zipper represents a faction of the diverse Jewish American population, so does his son Ziggy who perceives something marvelously compelling in Shmelke's more traditional rituals and behavior. Ziggy is taken in by the "magic," claiming his father "'wouldn't know magic if it dumped a load on . . . [his] head!'"[51] In this case, Ziggy's interests are consistent with Marcus Lee Hansen's famous thesis from "The Problem of the Third Generation Immigrant" where he suggests "what the son wishes to forget the grandson wishes to remember."[52] For "Kite," the son refers to the second generation Zipper who wants to distance himself from a religious past and a culture linked to historical persecution; Zipper's son Ziggy, born into a more stable *national* environment—before the atrocities of the Holocaust come to affect the entire world—is more prone to indulge his curiosity, lacking the fear and paranoia of his father who worries that the flying rabbi will undermine the stability and security he has had to earn, in part, by assimilating and shedding the appearance of ethnic and religious difference. The generational tensions highlight the changes indicative of contemporary American Jewishness and expose the problems with conclusions based on "snapshots" rather than "dynamic moving pictures."

Regarding the children who have begun to follow the rabbi, Zipper contends, "[f]or them rebellion is a costume party. They revel in the anomalous touch."[53] The "anomalous touch" is a wonderfully slippery tactile expression marking the point where the divine and the human or the religious and the ethnic come together. It emphasizes the liminal ground on which contemporary Jewish American communities exist and contributes to the enigma of difference for contemporary American Jews. Although we might not all be reveling, Jewish Americans are all aware of that anomalous touch, either nudging from the background, or pushing through the rituals of daily lives. To return to the characterization asserted by Biale, Galchinsky, and Heschel, contemporary Jewish Americans, as a group, hold "an anomalous status" and "represent that boundary case whose very lack of belonging to a recognizable category creates a sense of unease."[54] We can see how a "sense of unease" drives the actions in "Gilgul" and "Kite," and by extension, how this sense has extended through the Twentieth Century and—as evidenced by the rich scholarship of Goldscheider, Biale, Levitt, Kaplan, Kaufman, Furman and many others found throughout *Magical American Jew* and beyond—is prominent even today. But with the "emergence of new forms" of Jewish culture and religion—whether from assimilating into and absorbing aspects of contemporary American society or carrying over traditions and artifacts from the "old world"—"choice, diversity, and creativity" must be recognized as vibrant parts of contemporary American Jewishness. Efforts to deny change or restrict religious or cultural expression will ultimately lead to a "violent rupture," which may, in the most hopeful circumstances, spark "the beginning of a painful wisdom."

In "Kite," Zipper's efforts to deny change are stated most explicitly. Describing his response to the flight of Rabbi Shmelke and the "antics" of his followers, Zipper declares: "those of us with any self-respect have stopped looking up."[55] But such abstinence can only last so long before a consummating confrontation becomes unavoidable. As mentioned earlier, Zipper's perceived indignation earns him the right to cut Shmelke's rope. Once the line has been severed, Zipper imagines joining his son and the others who have latched on to the tail of the ascending rabbi. "Across the river the sunset is more radiant than a red flare over a herring barrel, dripping sparks—all the brighter as it's soon to be extinguished by dark clouds swollen with history rolling in from the east."[56] History, the impending Holocaust in this case, acts as one of the most significant—unavoidable and undeniable—aspects that melds Jewish religiosity and ethnicity together, and demands that Jewish identity remain alive to combat the cycles of death that took away religious rights and inflicted shame, as well as resilient pride, in Jewish communities throughout the world. This is particularly prescient in the time period of "Kite," just before the most profound atrocity in Jewish history, one which shifted the concentration of the world's Jews from Europe—where the greatest majority of Jews lived before World War II—to the United States, where the majority of the world's Jews have lived since. This shift changed the dynamic for Jewish Americans. Nazi laws made no distinction between religious and secular Jews; Jews were a race who needed to be exterminated. While the racial suggestions do not hold up (in any convincing way), the continuity of a diverse and evolving Jewish American identity remains.

It is a failure or unwillingness to see the Jewish American community as a multifarious and modulating entity, where religious and secular concerns are "intertwined," that leads to the tensions and comically futile efforts featured in "The Gilgul of Park Avenue" and "The Tale of a Kite." Englander and Stern themselves have each experienced and observed ethnic and religious transformations that are characteristic of the range of Jewish American identity. With these transformations in mind, it is worth considering the contrasting sympathies they project in their stories. In Stern's "Kite," Zipper's zealous, secular perspective broaches the absurd, while in Englander's "Gilgul," the religious efforts advocated by Rabbi Zalman Meintz and attempted by Charles are comparably absurd. I cite these examples not to suggest that being raised religious (as Englander was) makes one more sympathetic to the secular and vice versa, but rather to demonstrate further how both sides can be depicted as extreme and absurd, yet neither side can exist in isolation from the other—each a part of the diversity and flux of the contemporary Jewish American community.

Jewish identity in the United States involves a complex mixture of secular and religious concerns. Examining the role of Judaism in Jewish American identity, Kaufman notes how "studies framed to gauge more or less and better or worse, cannot, for the most part, capture the many complex, sometimes contradictory, if not ambivalent, expressions of religious identity among American Jews today."[57] Yet many American Jews—some who consider themselves more secular, others more religious—continue to imagine themselves as worlds apart from each other, at

times, articulating their thoughts on the other in the elitist and discriminatory terms of superiority and inferiority. As Adam Chalom notes,
Chasidim have been known to refer to secular Jews as "apikorsim," or
Jewish goys, and "[v]ersions of secular Judaism have . . . defined themselves by their rejections of Jewish law, rabbinic authority, and the constraints and theology of traditional Judaism." Chalom discusses how
some secular Jews have been "determined to scandalize Orthodox Jews,
particularly on Yom Kippur."[58] Addressing the challenge of "differentiating between expressions of ethnic and religious identity,"[59] Herbert
Gans suggests "that Jews not only 'share elements of a common past or
present non-American culture,' but that the 'sacred and secular elements
of the culture are strongly intertwined.'"[60] As Goldscheider illustrates
quite well, "the secular activities of Jewish life reinforce the religious and
vice versa, because so many Jews participate in them. The intensities
often go together because they lead to the same place—the Jewish community."[61] Among other things, what we see in the stories by Englander
and Stern is just how diverse the "Jewish community" has become and
how magical and comical modes can be used to highlight the tensions
and contradictions that make Jewish identity so hard to define.

While few would condone the divisive actions and rhetoric of the
more extreme factions of religious and secular American Jews—despite
the compelling fiction it can inspire—Zvi Gitelman puts a positive spin
on the tension between religiosity and ethnicity, suggesting that "[a]s
long as significant numbers of people debate the issue, the survival of
Jewishness is assured."[62] What is also assured, despite the well cited and
vigorously challenged claims of Irving Howe about the dearth of worthy
experience for contemporary Jewish American literature,[63] is that the evolution and array of Jewish American individuals and communities leave
a substantial amount of material about which to write. Significantly, the
well documented use of humor and the creative use of the magical realist
mode—to portray aspects of the enigmatic difference that has led to, and
is a product of, classification challenges, feelings of unease, and continuous debates—are just two of many angles (literary and otherwise)
through which to consider contemporary Jewish American literature and
contemporary Jewish American communities. No matter how dead the
literature may be deemed, or how assimilated the communities may become, the Jewish community is not going away. One does not have to
listen too hard to hear it, calling across the amorphous membranes of
past and present, sacred and profane: "Jewish, here in the back."

NOTES

1. David Biale, Michael Galchinsky, and Susannah Heschel, "Introduction: The
Dialectic of Jewish Enlightenment," in *Insider/Outsider: American Jews and Multicultu-*

ralism, ed. David Biale, Michael Galchinsky, and Susannah Heschel (Berkeley: UCP, 1998), 1–13, 5.

2. Nathan Englander, "The Gilgul of Park Avenue," in *For the Relief of Unbearable Urges* (New York: Vintage Books, 1999), 109–37, 109, 137. A comparable change exists in Aimee Bender's short story "Dreaming in Polish," which can be read as a work of Jewish American magical realism. In Bender's story, the central character, Celia, is drawn to the center of her hometown, while her mother walks from Connecticut to the Holocaust museum in Washington, D.C., and her ill father takes a train to meet her. The story closes with Celia embracing the statue of a Greek god—that "seemed to have simply grown up from the earth" (148)—"wait[ing] for something to change" (161). In Englander's story, Charles has already "changed" (137) and is hoping his wife will accept that.

3. Although the exact year is never mentioned, there are details that suggest the time period, including references to "the wreck of the Titanic" (17) and "the chrome-plated Belgian Minerva" (only manufactured from 1902–1938), which is driven by a powerful political boss (8). In his own discussion of Stern's story, Andrew Furman also suggests that the story takes place "just prior to the Holocaust" (149), and toward the end of "Kite," the narrative mentions how the radiant sunset is "soon to be extinguished by dark clouds swollen with history rolling in from the east," which can be read as a reference to the Holocaust.

4. Although this chapter argues that Rabbi Shmelke's flight is used to illustrate and emphasize the ironic tension between religiosity and ethnicity, there are well established, Jewish fabulist and mystical sources that feature ascent. Such sources, along with direct references to Stern's story, are addressed in the conclusion.

5. Steve Stern, "The Tale of a Kite," in *The Wedding Jester* (Saint Paul: Graywolf, 1999), 3–20, 3, 18, 20.

6. Englander, "The Gilgul of Park Avenue," 109.

7. Derek Parker Royal, "Tugging at Jewish Weeds: An Interview with Steve Stern," *MELUS* 32.1 (2007): 139–61, 152–53.

8. The majority of Stern's published fiction incorporates magical realist or fabulist elements, and much of his work—including several stories from *The Wedding Jester,* where "The Tale of a Kite" comes—are set in, or reference in some way, Memphis's old Jewish district known as the Pinch.

9. Lois Parkinson Zamora and Wendy B. Faris, "Introduction: Daiquiri Birds and Flaubertian Parrot(ie)s," in *Magical Realism: Theory, History, Community,* eds. Lois Parkinson Zamora and Wendy B. Faris (Durham, NC: Duke UP, 1995), 1–11, 6.

10. Shannin Schroeder, *Rediscovering Magical Realism in the Americas* (Westport, CT: Praeger, 2004), 64.

11. Murray Davis, "Wit's Weapons: Incongruity and Ambiguity," in *Laughing Matters,* ed. Marvin Diogenes (New York: Pearson, 2009), 13–36, 16.

12. Englander, "The Gilgul of Park Avenue," 112, 114.

13. Calvin Goldscheider, "Judaism, Community, and Jewish Culture in American Life: Continuities and Transformations," in *Religion or Ethnicity?: Jewish Identities in Evolution,* ed. Zvi Gitelman (New Brunswick: Rutgers UP, 2009), 267–85, 269.

14. Ibid.

15. Englander, "The Gilgul of Park Avenue," 112.

16. Stern, "The Tale of a Kite," 3.

17. Ibid., 6–7.

18. Sander Gilman's *The Jew's Body* is one of several sources that offers an account of such mythology.

19. As discussed in greater detail in chapter 2, two of the most prominent stereotypes remain the Jewish American Mother and the Jewish American Princess stereotypes. Alan Dundes's essay "The J.A.P. and the J.A.M. in American Jokelore" traces the presence of and relationship between these staples of "American Jokelore." In "The Jewish Mother: Comedy and Controversy in American Popular Culture," Martha A. Ravits argues that "[t]he comic stereotype of the Jewish mother . . . is a cultural

construct developed by male writers in the United States in the 1960s" (1). According to Ravits, *Portnoy's Complaint* provides "[t]he most memorable and fully elaborated caricature of the Jewish mother" (6). In *You Never Call! You Never Write!: A History of the Jewish Mother,* Joyce Antler also points to the 1960s and suggests that the breadth of the Jewish mother stereotype can be linked to the widespread commercial success of three books: Dan Greenberg's guidebook *How to Be a Jewish Mother,* Bruce Jay Friedman's novel *A Mother's Kisses,* and Philip Roth's novel *Portnoy's Complaint* (135–37). Lawrence Epstein's *The Haunted Smile: the Story of Jewish Comedians in America* does a good job of tracing the perceptions and portrayals of Jewish women in the United States. Starting in the late nineteenth century and sweeping through the twentieth century, Epstein discusses the various transitions and transformations to which Jewish comedians—male and female—have perpetuated and reacted.

20. Englander, "The Gilgul of Park Avenue," 127.

21. James D. Bloom, *Gravity Fails: The Comic Jewish Shaping of Modern America* (Westport, CT: Praeger, 2003), 157.

22. Irving Kristol, "Is Jewish Humor Dead?" *Midcentury,* ed. H. Ribalow (New York: Beechurst, 1955): 428–37, 436.

23. Stern, "The Tale of a Kite," 17–18 (emphasis added).

24. Parker Royal, "An Interview with Steve Stern," 149.

25. Although this chapter treats Englander's story as a work of magical realism—a "New York story of the first order"—rather than a modernized retelling of a Kabbalistic tale, I do address the origin of the "gilgul" more directly in the Conclusion.

26. Englander, "The Gilgul of Park Avenue," 119.

27. Ibid., 122.

28. Ibid.

29. David Biale, "The Melting Pot and Beyond: Jews and the Politics of American Identity," in *Insider/Outsider: American Jews and Multiculturalism,* ed. David Biale, Michael Galchinsky, and Susannah Heschel (Berkeley: UCP, 1998), 17–33, 31–32.

30. Egon Mayer, "A Demographic Revolution in American Jewry," in *American Jewish Identity Politics,* ed. Deborah Dash Moore (Ann Arbor: U Michigan P, 2008): 267–99, 281.

31. Goldscheider, "Judaism, Community, and Jewish Culture," 278, 281.

32. Steven Carr Reuben and many others have written about the view of some (even secular) Jews who maintain that intermarriage leads to the erasure of Jewish lineage and Jewish identity, and should be seen as a victory for Hitler who tried to eliminate the Jews from the earth (39). Although I discuss the guilt that can accompany intermarriage in chapter 2, I have tried to show throughout this chapter that there are many—such as Goldscheider and Kaplan—who effectively counter this extreme view and provide new ways of thinking about intermarriage and its impact on Jewish identity and community.

33. Vivian Klaff, "Defining American Jewry from Religious and Ethnic Perspectives: The Transitions to Greater Heterogeneity," *Sociology of Religion* 67.4 (2006): 415–38, 418.

34. Goldscheider, "Judaism, Community, and Jewish Culture," 278, 281.

35. Boldtype, "An Interview with Nathan Englander," RandomHouse.com, April 1, 2010.

36. Goldscheider, "Judaism, Community, and Jewish Culture," 282.

37. Parker Royal, "An Interview with Steve Stern," 141, 146.

38. In Lenny Bruce's famous "Jewish and Goyish" routine, Bruce suggests that "observe" is a Jewish word.

39. Bloom, *Gravity Fails,* 159.

40. Rawdon Wilson, "The Metamorphoses of Fictional Space: Magical Realism," in *Magical Realism: Theory, History, Community,* eds. Lois Parkinson Zamora and Wendy B. Faris (Durham, NC: Duke UP, 1995), 209–34, 220.

41. Henry Bial's *Acting Jewish: Negotiating Ethnicity on the American Stage and Screen* and James Bloom's *Gravity Fails: The Comic Jewish Shaping of Modern America* are two

sources that discuss the influence of entertainment media on Jewish American identity and behavior.

42. Stern, "The Tale of a Kite," 11.

43. Andrew Furman, *Contemporary Jewish American Writers and the Multicultural Dilemma: Return of the Exiled* (Syracuse: Syracuse UP, 2000), 148.

44. Englander, "The Gilgul of Park Avenue," 116, 111.

45. Ibid., 116.

46. Parker Royal, "An Interview with Steve Stern," 142.

47. Ibid., 153–54.

48. Stern, "The Tale of a Kite," 12.

49. Goldscheider, "Judaism, Community, and Jewish Culture," 269.

50. Ibid.

51. Stern, "The Tale of a Kite," 16.

52. Marcus Lee Hansen, "The Problem of the Third Generation Immigrant," in *American Immigrants and Their Generations: Studies and Commentaries on the Hansen Thesis after Fifty Years*, ed. Dag Blanck and Peter Kivisto (Urbana: U Illinois P, 1990), 195.

53. Stern, "The Tale of a Kite," 13.

54. Biale, Galchinsky, and Heschel, "Introduction," 5.

55. Stern, "The Tale of a Kite," 14.

56. Ibid., 20.

57. Debra Renee Kaufman, "The Place of Judaism in American Jewish Identity," in *The Cambridge Companion to American Judaism*, ed. Dana Evan Kaplan (Cambridge: Cambridge UP, 2005), 169–85, 170.

58. Adam Chalom, "Beyond *Apikorsut*: A Judaism for Secular Jews," in *Religion or Ethnicity?: Jewish Identities in Evolution*, ed. Zvi Gitelman (New Brunswick: Rutgers UP, 2009), 286–302, 286.

59. Kaufman, "The Place of Judaism," 172.

60. Ibid. and Herbert J. Gans, "Symbolic Ethnicity: The Future of Ethnic Groups and Cultures in America," *Ethnic and Racial Studies* 2 (1979): 1–20, 7.

61. Goldscheider, "Judaism, Community, and Jewish Culture," 281.

62. Zvi Gitelman, "Conclusion: The Nature and Viability of Jewish Religious and Secular Identities," in *Religion or Ethnicity?: Jewish Identities in Evolution*, ed. Zvi Gitelman (New Brunswick: Rutgers UP, 2009), 303–22, 319.

63. See Howe's "Introduction" from *Jewish American Stories* (New York: Mentor, 1977).

FIVE

"Through the Rube Goldberg Crazy Straw"

Ethnic Mobility and Narcissistic Fantasy in
Sarah Silverman: Jesus Is Magic

In the "melting pot" of the United States, there are vibrant, often public negotiations between the roots of ancestral traditions and the shoots of contemporary practices and sensibilities. Werner Sollors posits "the conflict between contractual and hereditary, self-made and ancestral, definitions of American identity—between *consent* and *descent*—as the central drama in American culture." He elaborates on the crucial terms of this "drama," explaining that "[d]escent language emphasizes our positions as heirs, our hereditary qualities, liabilities, and entitlements; consent language stresses our abilities as mature free agents and 'architects of our fates' to choose our spouses, our destinies, and our political systems."[1] In the twenty-first century, media and other tools of exposure, abstraction, and self-indulgence play an influential role in the individual sense of entitlement and destiny. The childish propensity to consider one's own drama as the only drama can get prolonged in this atmosphere, and the capacity to understand conflicts of culture can get reduced along with the reductions and abstractions that saturate the American cultural landscape. In the performance film *Jesus Is Magic*, comedian Sarah Silverman portrays a Jewish American character who has been nurtured by contemporary American media. This chapter demonstrates how Silverman's comic satire—specifically in *Jesus Is Magic*—exposes and exploits the enigmatic space of her Jewish American identity and allows a line to be traced from ethnicity, through the "central drama" between consent and descent, to a realm of narcissistic fantasy, reflective of an American generation nurtured within a pervasive media culture. Silverman uses magical realist techniques to highlight the slippery space where she fashions her identity and to accentuate the narcissism of her character.

Sarah Silverman is one of the most provocative comedians/comic actors working today. A beneficiary of our digital age, she can be found in an assortment of "viral" internet videos, including roasts of Pamela Anderson, Hugh Hefner, James Franco and others (most airing originally on *Comedy Central*), an enormously popular music video spoof ("I'm Fucking Matt Damon"), which first aired on *Jimmy Kimmel Live!* and earned her two Creative Arts Emmys, a comic political advertisement ("The Great Schlep"), ostensibly written to persuade younger Jewish Americans to travel to Florida to convince their grandparents to vote for Barack Obama, and a controversial video highlighting gender-based wage disparity in which she claims to be adding a penis to avoid the enormous "vagina tax." Silverman also stared in her own *Comedy Central* sitcom from 2007–2010, "The Sarah Silverman Program," in which she played a narcissistic character named Sarah Silverman; in 2013, she released a stand-up comedy special on HBO, titled *Sarah Silverman: We Are Miracles*, and in 2017, she released another stand-up comedy special on Netflix, titled *Sarah Silverman: A Speck of Dust.*[2] While her show, her stand-up specials, and the videos that have circulated on the web have contributed to her popularity, they do not speak to the controversy that is most responsible for Silverman's notoriety. What is most intriguing and controversial about Sarah Silverman relates to her edgy and satirical persona through which she elicits laughs and provokes minds by performing an outrageous and ironic insensitivity. Sam Anderson, in his Slate.com essay on Silverman, suggests she is "an important member of a guerrilla vanguard in the culture wars that we might call the 'meta-bigots.'" Including Sacha Baron Cohen and Dave Chappelle in this group, Anderson describes how "[t]he meta-bigots work at social problems indirectly; instead of discussing race, rape, abortion, incest, or mass starvation, they parody our discussions of them. They manipulate stereotypes about stereotypes. It's a dangerous game: If you're humorless, distracted, or even just inordinately history-conscious, meta-bigotry can look suspiciously like actual bigotry."[3] Since Silverman does her best to blur the line between the "real" Sarah Silverman and her persona, the potential for misinterpretation is indeed great.

In *Jesus Is Magic*, Silverman's persona is striving to make sense of, and comment on, some of the most significant and controversial issues to date. While doing so, she tramples over taboos that pervade discussions of the Holocaust, the events of September 11, 2001, racism, rape, religion, sexual orientation, AIDS, death, and an assortment of equivalently loaded subjects. She appears too consumed with herself to tread lightly or sensitively, or to soften the comically absurd conclusions, which she draws from her meanderings and explorations. As I discuss in this chapter, the result is at turns shocking and hilarious. But it is how she gets us there—the magical route she takes—and what she reveals about contemporary American culture and identity more broadly and Jewish American culture and identity more specifically that speak to the innovation and importance of Silverman's work.

The film opens with a vignette: Silverman is in an apartment living room, sitting in a flowery chair across from two friends who are sharing their stories of commercial success. The male friend has just released an album and is publishing a book, an accomplishment that led to an appearance on *The Oprah Winfrey Show*; the female friend has just procured a part in a television pilot—even her dog filled a role for a scene—and has sold a script to *Comedy Central*. While these achievements are being related, the camera stays mostly on Silverman's face, allowing the viewers to read her awkwardness, jealousy, and vulnerability—most evident in her tense smile and forced words of congratulations and support. When it is her turn to share, she embellishes a story about a show she has written, scheduled to premiere that night—sold out, of course. Asked about the content, she describes an elaborate project, alleging that "it's about . . . the Holocaust . . . and AIDS . . . but it's funny . . . and . . . a musical," characterizing it as "a real opus." When she leaves the apartment, her distress is made explicit in the lyrics of a song—"I Can Write a Show"—set as a music video in which Silverman drives off in a convertible, lamenting her lie as she attempts to sort through the logistics that would be necessary to realize her fabrication. When the car elevates into the ether, we are faced with the first move into the magical air of Silverman's film.[4]

The convertible ride into the clouds is more than a simple fantasy and more than a dream from "the unreliable imagination of a character," which would "relegate the supernatural to a secondary mode of being."[5] As discussed in various part of *Magical American Jew*, works of magical realism must maintain a "co-presence" of the natural and the supernatural that is treated as normal by the narrative. The proportion of supernatural to natural events does not necessarily matter, but the narrative *treatment* does.[6] If the supernatural is *explained* as the dream, vision, or delusion of a character, then, as Amaryll Chanady[7] and others have suggested, it would establish a "hierarchy" rather than an integration of "two mutually exclusive logical codes."[8] In the context of the film, the fantasy acts as a magical vehicle into the "reality" of the stage. The song—"I Can Write a Show"—and the determined movement of events serve as the "narrative voice [that] bridges the gap between ordinary and bizarre, smoothing the discrepancies, making everything seem normal."[9]

During the third movement of the song, Silverman makes a subtle yet crucial connection between the magical and the enigmatic—less subtle, perhaps, for the writer of this study. In a brusque but unremitting transition, her car emerges in a sound studio where she slides off the hood and struts across the studio floor, singing about the type of star she would need for her show. After concluding that this star has "gotta have that thing that you just can't define," Silverman makes a pivotal discovery before her vanity mirror (reinforced by a bridge in the song): *she* is the enigmatic star "that you just can't define." She reworks this cliché to set us up for the anomaly of her show and the enigma of her Jewish American identity, which she exposes and exploits in her effort to satirize aspects of contemporary American culture.[10]

As I demonstrate in this chapter, Silverman takes advantage of this uncertain space to perform a familiar and uniquely flexible American character who portrays herself in a multitude of ways and comments on a multitude of issues without slipping out of her singular persona. Her self-discovery (before her vanity mirror) also sets us up for the narcissism that is crucial to the magical and satirical framing of her film. Drawn in by the idea of herself as star—and the accompanying image of her own reflected face—she advances toward the mirror, stopping just short of consummating the decision with her own reflection. When she eventually does take the stage—a "reality" posited as fantasy in the opening chapters of the film—the space seems natural, as if it had "always already" been there.[11]

As suggested above, the video and opening vignette help to define Silverman's persona as one steeped in narcissistic fantasy, compensating for the vulnerabilities and insecurities that led her to lie[12] to her friends. "Compensatory narcissistic self-inflation is among the most conspicuous forms of pathological self-esteem regulation,"[13] writes Annie Reich, one of the most influential psychoanalysts to focus on narcissism. While Carolyn C. Morf and Frederick Rhodewalt note similar tendencies, they also point out that since "narcissists are insensitive to others' concerns and social constraints and view others as inferior, their self-regulatory efforts often are counterproductive and ultimately prevent the positive feedback that they seek—thus undermining the self they are trying to create and maintain."[14] We see this insensitivity in various segments throughout the film, particularly at the end when her "friends" from the opening scene return, only to be snubbed and uncomfortably urged to leave Silverman's dressing room. This final scene represents a return to the "realism" of the opening vignette. While this return exposes the magically real space where events take place, the film never offers explanations, and it successfully thwarts the urge to question this conflation because of the determined narrative movement and the focus on the awkward social interaction. But long before we get to this point, the opening vignette and video establish the initial inflation-regulation, allowing the film audience to commiserate with this exaggerated figure and her unbridled display of narcissism, while acknowledging how the stage performance (chapter 3 in the film) sprouts out of this narcissistic fantasy and becomes an extension of a manufactured "reality." The near-sexual encounter with the vanity mirror not only reinforces the narcissism of Silverman's character, but highlights the excess and absurdity that are markers of Silverman's satire.

On the heels of the vignette and video, Silverman's stage performance establishes "a unique contextual tone" which Neil Schaeffer, in "Lenny Bruce and Extreme Comedy," calls the "ludicrous context." [15] Many who have written about Silverman and her work have referenced Lenny Bruce,[16] often citing the shocking nature of their routines. While both comedians employ vernacular from their Jewish American backgrounds, it is the extended performances of satiric characters that have proven most affective and controversial. Bruce was known for playing several characters, often in dialogue with each other. In one of his most famous routines titled "Religions Inc.," Bruce equates religion to corporate practice, enacting a scene in which the hypocrisies and contradictions that exist in seemingly pious figures and institutions are amplified to establish an exaggerated world where religions are portrayed as rising and falling stocks and the public is manipulated by a version of corporate spin. In discussing "Religions Inc.," Edward Azlant notes how "the bit works on the juxtaposition of the conventions of the melodrama of business success and media evangelism, both of which flowered in the Fifties." Azlant suggests that within this routine "we see the arrival of perhaps the most widely celebrated aspect of Bruce's work, as fully formed satire. Here the juxtapositions or counterpoints of frames or idioms are not just for novel or incongruous effect, but rather serve to expose or uncover some underlying and widespread folly or vice." [17]

In a discussion of September 11th, Silverman's stage persona takes the relationship between religion and corporate practice to another level by addressing the religious extremism behind the terrorist attacks and merging this extremism with the potentially exploitative extremes employed by corporate America. Suggesting "what we should steal from corporate America" is "positive spin," Silverman asserts that "if American Airlines were smart, their slogan would be: 'American Airlines: first through the towers!'" [18] This receives a mixed reaction from the crowd; it is a provocative and potentially uncomfortable joke that does not exploit ethnic distinctions to establish tension, but strikes at the sensitivities and vulnerabilities of Americans as a whole, something Lenny Bruce did with threatening success. Silverman only "gets away" with this joke (elicits some laughs and does not lose many to the exits) because of the *framing* that she has established, which is satirical, magical, comedic, and "ludicrous." Although Bruce was forced to fight legal battles as a result of his "subversive" comedy, he successfully "broadened the range of material that audiences had been accustomed to find humorous," [19] opening the door for a satiric comedian such as Silverman who makes similar efforts to shed light on the duplicities and malignant trends that are taking place in the twenty-first century United States.

While Schaeffer makes a compelling case for the importance and uniqueness of some of Bruce's routines, he is divergently compelled to draw out distinctions between comedy and satire, suggesting "[s]atirists are only incidentally funny, by choice, for they sense that the laugh unbarbs the anger."[20] His claims are not only curious and a bit confusing, but his efforts detract from his richer discussion on the contextual framing that Bruce employs and seem to discount the value of humor as a conscious and effective satiric tool—one which is not used "incidentally"—while placing strangely singular emphasis on *anger* as the emotion that drives all satire.[21] With an eye on the twenty-first century, we can look to Silverman's stage persona and to any number of television or silver-screen characters, most notably, perhaps, the television-to-silver-screen emergence of Sacha Baron Cohen's Borat, who brought his own brand of satiric comedy to a notable extreme in the film *Borat: Cultural Learnings of America for Make Benefit Glorious Nation of Kazakhstan* (2006). While much can be said about the boundaries that are blurred in Cohen's film, the point here is to note what is so uniquely affective about these acts and to acknowledge what makes Silverman and Bruce *satiric comedians*: they are doing more than simply telling jokes and more than ridiculing elements of society out of anger or some other emotion, but *performing characters* over extended periods, and drawing their audiences into ludicrous contexts, whereby "the individual's framing of activity establishes its meaningfulness."[22] For Silverman and Bruce, the framing is crucial to understanding the satire and acknowledging the humor. Each comedian performs and extends his/her stage routines in a comparable way, working with similarly sensitive themes.

Beyond the time periods in which Bruce and Silverman were/are performing, one of the differences between them—and one of the more dangerous aspects to Silverman's comic satire—exists in her commitment to one character with one name (Sarah Silverman), rarely if ever breaking out of her singularly naïve and narcissistic persona.[23] Her determination to stay in one voice not only allows a "ludicrous" quality to emerge and grow—leaving the audience to grapple with the tension and startling humor of her often incendiary insights—but it provokes reflection about what is real, who is real, and how we are meant to take her routine. It is this tension that is most striking about Silverman's widely discussed role in Paul Provenza and Penn Jillette's film *The Aristocrats*, in which one hundred comedians discuss and retell the "dirty joke" from which the film gets its name. For her small but memorable performance in this film, Silverman received a great deal of attention. Lounging on her living room couch, she describes her role as a child performer in "The Aristocrats." Beyond the graphic extremes to which she takes the description of her family's act (the description *is* the joke, which is told more for graphic extremes then for the punch line), she reveals that she was raped by the legendary television and radio personality Joe Franklin. Although he considered suing her, at the end of the DVD release, as the credits are rolling, Franklin appears in a small box on screen and suggests that "Sarah Silverman is a young lady to watch," but that he has never actually met her.[24]

One could argue that the fiction of Silverman's performance in *The Aristocrats* should have been evident from the graphic description of her role as an Aristocrat, as well as the nature of the joke and of the film. But once she suggests something seemingly outside the bounds of the joke — but still inside the bounds of the ludicrous context — we start to wonder whether she might be serious. This is how Silverman works. She is determined to blur the lines between fantasy and reality, between confession and performance. This tension is crucial to her satire because it provokes and demands attention and reaction. Why is her "revelation" about Joe Franklin so much more shocking (and seemingly more real) than the idea that her brother with Down's syndrome was sexually exploited on stage for profit, as she suggests in her description of her family's act? Perhaps the answer is obvious: remarks about Joe Franklin could have real life consequences. But as Sam Anderson puts it, "Silverman was the only comic in the film who met the challenge of the joke: She pushed it too far."[25]

In terms of *Jesus Is Magic*, there is a startlingly recognizable nature to Silverman's performance; her statements and concerns are so entrenched in a contemporary American context that they are relatable in a curiously slanted way. Before the stage performance has even begun, Silverman's audience is grounded in familiar elements of American culture: self-promoting talk of TV pilots and *The Oprah Winfrey Show*, a music video as a representation of stardust fantasies and imagined retribution. As Schaeffer contends, "[t]he ludicrous context functions best in jokes when it is simply taken for granted. But a work of extended comedy may be said ultimately to be about the exploration and articulation of the ludicrous context itself — about the way the ludicrous context is created to confine the subject matter within the bounds of humor."[26] For Silverman, "the exploration and articulation" is about the problematic nature of cultural, national, and artistic designations; it is about capitalism, religion, racism, narcissism, terrorism, and the internet, and it is about the slippery terrain on which her own "ethnicity" stands.

The "bounds" for Silverman are established through her performance of an exaggerated but uniquely American stereotype — the "Jewish American Princess" (JAP) — whose narcissism is a product of contemporary American culture and the enigmatic nature of Jewish American difference that allows the modulations and re-imaginings of identity to maintain some consistency and coherence. Silverman cultivates the indefinable territory — the territory that resists taxonomy ("that thing that you just can't define") — portraying herself in a multitude of ways, depending on the landscape: as Jewish, as white, as cute, as straight, as thin. She uses stereotypes of her Jewish American identity to indulge a conversation about extreme materialism; she uses the ethnic connotation of Jewish American to feign sensitivity to accusations made by an Asian American watchdog group; she uses religious mythology to claim a "chosen" privilege; she uses a connection to historical atrocity to perform self-righteous indignation; she uses her fair complexion to deny any ethnic association. Her observations and conclusions shed light on the environments that can produce such a character. The more she extends her performance, the more recognizably ludicrous—and potentially poignant—her satire becomes. While the music video and the opening vignette introduce this magically real world, the stage performance is where the audience is truly challenged to negotiate between the provocative material and the persona.[27]

At the start of the stage portion of the film, the audience is witness to Silverman slipping into character. Reminded that she is a comedian—"That's what I *do*"—the audience is led to an initial query about how one *becomes* whatever it is s/he becomes. According to Silverman, the formula for comedians often includes some past humiliation. By acknowledging the process of becoming, Silverman reminds the audience that she has become (or is in the process of becoming) something for them, while also reminding them that she has a job with a purpose: ostensibly, to make people laugh. In the context of the film, her questions about *becoming* are indicative of a greater mobility that runs between her occupation (her focus here) and her "ethnicity": a *becoming* steeped in the *consent* part of Sollors's central drama. But in this early moment on stage, her statement helps her audience make the distinction between the comedian and her persona, allowing her satire to become easier to detect. Her admission of past humiliation provides some background on the character whom she is performing: one whose outlook on life has been informed by a certain discomfiture; in her case, she admits to teenage bed-wetting, excessive hair, and rape at the hands of a doctor, described as "so bitter-sweet for a Jewish girl."[28]

The brazen nature of Silverman's humor—relatable to her brief performance in *The Aristocrats*—is coupled at the outset with an acknowledgement of her "ethnicity." In her opening joke, she characterizes herself as Jewish, employing a signifier grounded in stereotype. By making the first jab at "herself" and the "ethnicity" from which she descends, Silverman allows the initial shock of her stage performance to be at her own expense and the expense of her heritage.[29] Given the complications regarding ethnicity, the stereotype might seem more stable than the signifier itself. In *Gravity Fails: The Comic Jewish Shaping of Modern American,* James D. Bloom devotes over half of his "Preface" to a discussion of the complicated nature of the term "Jew," which (according to Bloom) is neither a race nor a religion and any effort to call it an ethnicity or a culture "leads to a semantic evasion that allows more leeway for confusion rather than clarity." For the sake of his book, Bloom decides to "set-tle . . . on Jewish as an American cultural designation . . . [marked by] observable patterns whereby Jews identify and differentiate themselves." He focuses on Jewish Americans who "seem to make the most of Jewish-ness as a discursive resource and an aesthetic opportunity," (suggesting that his study can, in part at least, be described as "mediations between Jewishness and Americanness, between funniness and reflection."[30] For the purposes of satire, Silverman does indeed "make the most of Jewish-ness as a discursive resource and an aesthetic opportunity," and she in-vites her audience to engage in "mediations" similar to those described by Bloom. In a comic sense, Silverman's early reference to her Jewish identity can be seen as a strategy meant to give her humor an ethnic tint, establishing an avenue through which to address other ethnicities,[31] while giving the audience an early glimpse at the terrain on which she intends to travel: where rape and the Jewish American woman are only the beginning.

In her opening joke, Silverman is working implicitly with the stereo-type of the doting Jewish mother who wants little more than for her daughter to marry a doctor. With this image in mind, other stereotypical associations of "the Jewish mother" (discussed in chapters 2 and 4) are invited to come forward;[32] most useful (for this discussion) is the mother who engenders the chosen-child syndrome. Lois Leveen characterizes this and other Jewish stereotypes through the retelling of a joke: "'How do we know that Jesus was Jewish? Because he lived at home with his mother until he was thirty; he went into his father's business; and he had a mother who thought he was God.'"[33] An allusion to the chosen-child idea follows Silverman's opening lines, when she acknowledges that she has a Catholic boyfriend—a mark of assimilation and a nod to the "con-sent" side of Sollors's "central drama"—and if they had children togeth-er, they "would be honest . . . and just say . . . mommy is one of the chosen people . . . and daddy believes that Jesus is magic." She adds that "Jesus is magic . . . because he turned water into wine . . . And I think he made the Statue of Liberty disappear, in the eighties."[34] The reductions of "chosen" and "magic" are telling when considering the narcissistic perso-na and the magical realist realm that emerge throughout the film, as well as the national and ethnic cultures that contribute to the development of this persona—the cultures which this persona is meant to satirize.

Silverman's performance asks her public to consider what is retained and processed by individuals who are raised in an environment saturat-ed with reductions—sounds bites, cable news clips, tag lines scrolling across the bottom of television screens and stacked on the side of web pages (framed by the shuffling of tabloid photos): so fantastic, yet so real. Are they memories of convenience, such as "chosen" and "magic"? Or descriptions that are heard ("somewhere"), echoed in another context, and subsequently misapplied? The latter takes place consistently throughout *Jesus Is Magic*. One example comes in a discussion of pornography. Silverman claims that if she "did" porn, it would be "purely . . . for political reasons, because . . . [she does not] think there are enough Jewish women represented in porn." The film then provides supplemental imagery—a magical extension, similar to the adjuncts of discourse discussed in chapter 1, found in Woody Allen's *Annie Hall*; in this case we are shown a pornographic clip of a disheveled-looking Silverman demanding: "Fuck my tuchas! Fuck my tuchas!"[35] Within this deceptively loaded bit, there are gestures to narcissism and magical realism—the magical portrayal of this sexualized fantasy—as well as misapplied notions of political activism and ethnic service, while also playing on and defying stereotypes of prudish Jewish women.[36] When the camera cuts back to the stage, Silverman calls herself a "bad Jew . . . a dirty Jew," returning to more stereotypically familiar ground: guilt. She rounds out her routine by calling out another generalization and perpetuating it through physical performance: "People think Jewish women aren't sexy," she says. "That's such bullshit!" Prompting the audience to imagine a Jewish woman putting on a "sexy negligee," she exclaims "Yidle-didle-didle!" as she enacts a campy, comic dance. Even when performing ethnically informed slapstick, Silverman remains rooted to the current American cultural context, wedging this segment between an exposition about strippers, pornography, and the American "pornographic thespian," Ron Jeremy.[37]

Silverman's persona is simultaneously in touch and out of touch with the global world, drowning in abstractions and opportunities for self-indulgence. Once again, it is useful to consider her response to the events of September 11th. Silverman discloses that this day was particularly devastating for *her*, as it was the exact day she discovered "that the soy chai latte was like 900 calories." When she does move on to the terrorist attacks, she proudly reveals her response: "Domain names." She claims to have purchased "OsamaBinLaden.com, OsamaBinLaden.net, Osama-BinLaden.org," to send a message: "Looks like you're gonna have to be Osama1. And then who's laughing last? America."[38] Through the absurdity, one can recognize the landscape that abets the narcissism and global misunderstanding found in Silverman's character who is product of a corporate environment that places inordinate emphasis—money, media exposure—on calorie counting, exotic coffee drinks, and catchy internet addresses. And yet the internet and corporate environments are only part of this landscape. In "The Turn Within: The Irony of Technology in a Globalized World," Susan Douglas discusses the trend on network and cable television to reduce the number of international stories and increase the number of "celebrity and lifestyle news." She argues that "the proliferation, especially after 9/11, of nonscripted television has brought viewers into private realms—apartments, houses, resorts, or made-for-TV camps set up on remote islands—where dramas about relationships, personal behavior, and people's 'confessions' urge viewers to look inward, not outward." For Douglas, twenty-first century television news and entertainment (categories that are becoming increasingly blurred) have made significant contributions to what she sees as a "turn" toward narcissistic behavior.[39]

Silverman reflects the trend discussed by Douglas and others; her humor is "connected to the cultural code[s] of society." As Joseph Boskin contends, "[t]he culture code is perhaps the elemental aspect in the structure of social humor. . . . This does not mean that humor is constantly appreciated or comprehended but that it must relate, in an intimate way, to the scope and direction of society."[40] Just as Lenny Bruce's comedy touched such a raw nerve because of its unswerving commentary on the contradictions and hypocrisies that permeated American society during the mid-twentieth century,[41] Silverman's satire and the magical realist techniques used in *Jesus Is Magic* magnify the "scope and direction" of her era—early twenty-first century United States—where increasingly, serious matters, as grave as war and terrorism, are disseminated through web sites and processed in startlingly short intervals, bound to be trivialized and misunderstood. Silverman performs this trivialization and misunderstanding, becoming the narcissistic princess whose "central drama" is entangled in American media culture where the space between what is real and what is not real has already begun to collapse. As Silverman's audience wrestles with the audacity of her September 11th material, they are pushed to consider what they have already been laughing at: jokes about rape, the crucifixion of Christ, AIDS, homosexuality, child-rearing, extreme materialism (enough to "debone" an Ethiopian baby)—all within the first eleven minutes of the stage performance.[42]

Although her satire is primarily about American culture and the conditions that can lead someone to make the connection between "positive spin" and September 11th, as important is the road she takes to get there: en route to the stage, she takes a magical mode of transport, establishing a psychic foundation for her character and a contextual frame for her narrative; once the forum for her voice is established, she mobilizes the enigmatic position of her Jewish American identity and moves through the central drama of consent and descent (again, the title joke speaks to this drama), settling into a narcissistic realm where terrorism has united with positive spin. As mentioned above, her response to the September 11th terrorist attacks was to acquire domain names, which she would defiantly refuse to sell to Osama Bin Laden. By merging sales with terrorism, and tying it all in with the internet—which *is* a medium used by terrorists—she has exposed something real while extending the "ludicrous context," and casting light back on the cultures (Jewish American and mainstream American) that have engendered her persona.

Even when discussing personal issues, such as the death of her nana, society looms behind the narcissism and comic emotion. Silverman opens

this personal reflection by dedicating the forthcoming musical performance to her nana who (the audience is told) died a year prior, at the age
of ninety-six; of course, she suspects "foul play." According to Silverman,
her nana had always supported her, unlike her parents who "never"
have, evidenced most recently in their failure to back her effort to ex-
hume her grandmother's body and pay for a full rape exam. The scene
concludes with a sustained period of silence, during which Silverman
appears on the verge of tears, finally mustering up the strength to pray:
"Oh God, please let them find semen in my dead grandmother's vagina!"
The bit is broken up by several moments of affected emotion, but what is
welling inside her are not feelings derived from the loss of her nana, but
rather emotions relating to her personal quest to prove her parents
wrong.[43] Her act is dramatized in such a way that tension is deliberately
sustained,[44] the release coming with the narcissistic pay-off where the
audience laughs at the character and the absurdity of her concerns.

Within the outrageous persona that Silverman has created, there is a
consistency that allows the audience to recognize and relate to—without
having to agree with—her astonishing thought process, and to identify
the presence of narcissistic tendencies and characteristics. Annie Reich
identifies the tendency for the narcissist to inflate the danger or catas-
trophic nature of an event from the past, claiming that

> The only possible defense . . . consists in methods which were available
> to the infantile ego, particularly in *magical denial*: "It is not so. I am not
> helpless, bleeding, destroyed. On the contrary, I am bigger and better
> than anyone else. I am the greatest, the most grandiose." Thus, to a
> large extent, the psychic interest must center on a compensatory narcis-
> sistic fantasy whose grandiose character affirms the denial.[45]

Roy F. Baumeister and Kathleen D. Vohs posit similar tendencies, relating narcissism to addiction and suggesting that "a narcissist's life may be
characterized not by a stable sense of inflated self-regard, but rather by
periods of relative normality punctuated by phases of self-aggrandizing
inflation, possibly leading to destructive consequences that may occasionally cause the person to revert to a more normal, balanced view of
self."[46] While Baumeister and Vohs offer a more hopeful characterization, their discussion is consistent with Reich's in terms of the compensatory moves common to the narcissist—moves that are performed by Silverman, highlighted by magical moments in her film, and reflective of
trends in twenty-first century American culture. As the title of her essay
indicates, Susan Douglas describes the narcissistic trend as a "turn within," arguing that "in the United States . . . new communications technologies have not created a global village[47] but have, ironically, led to a fusion
of ethnocentrism and narcissism."[48] As suggested earlier, Silverman performs a character who embodies the "fusion" discussed by Douglas, only
her ethnocentric view is mobile: when convenient, she's "one of the cho-

sen people," while at other times, her superiority complex comes from being white or straight or smart or thin.

In their survey of research on narcissism, Morf and Rhodewalt identify the common view that "narcissists are preoccupied with dreams of success, power, beauty, and brilliance. They live on an interpersonal stage with exhibitionistic behavior and demands for attention and admiration but respond to threats to self-esteem with feelings of rage, defiance, shame, and humiliation."[49] Accordingly, it seems appropriate that Silverman brings her character to life (largely) on stage. She is performing an extreme version of this character type, one "rooted in magical denial and characterized by primitive features of an early ego state [in which] the compensatory narcissistic fantasies often are poorly integrated into realistic, adult thinking."[50] Although she does not address the impact that the internet has had on "realistic, adult thinking," Douglas's research on the consequences of the contemporary "televisual experience" is thorough and compelling, and the persona she imagines as a product of this experience is, as noted earlier, closely aligned to the character portrayed by Silverman. According to Douglas, "as we move between news and reality TV, we are invited to distance ourselves from people abroad and, instead, to insert ourselves deeply into the interpersonal relations of a group of preselected, mostly young, mostly white people whose major concerns are staged as highly narcissistic and vapid."[51]

The conclusions drawn by Silverman in the "Nana" scene, as well as the emotions projected to the audience and the manner in which her suspicions are "integrated," are most certainly "staged as highly narcissistic," though not exactly "vapid"; they do, however, adhere to Reich's characterization of how "the narcissistic fantasy is [often] expressed in the form of sexualized and concrete images."[52] Following Reich, it is significant that rape is the suspected cause of Silverman's nana's death, which becomes sexualized and misappropriated much as the ethnically-tinged "Fuck my tuchas!" fantasy does earlier. Only here, the conspiracy theory is also indicative of the rumors and speculations of "foul play" that accompany so many reports of death—on the news, on the internet, on television, and in film—which are often sexualized in the effort to "sell" these stories. Douglas suggests "[t]he mass media pander to all of this and offer fare obsessed with sex, relationships, self-surveillance, physical challenges, voyeurism, the humiliation of others, and incessant celebrity psychodramas."[53] Silverman pushes this idea to a fantastic extreme, offering a magical display of "sexualized" and voyeuristic obsession. When discussing her own extraordinary sensitivity, Silverman flicks a tear from her face; the camera follows the tear backstage where it is caught by a peeping technician who uses it for sexual self-gratification. Once again, her narcissism is reinforced through magical realism.[54]

Whether on film, stage, or television, Silverman rarely (if ever) breaks out of the act, and when/if she does, it is only partial; she flirts with the audience's desire for an explanation of her satire (and an abatement of tension). She owns the awkwardness and manufactures silence, using her control to enhance her performance and enforce the absurd humor inherent in her satirical figure. Again, part of the strength of her act is that she never offers an absolute escape from her persona, never steps completely outside her character to make it plain that she is only performing—that the "real" Sarah Silverman would never draw such absurd and offensive conclusions. As she relates to Dana Goodyear in a 2005 profile published in *The New Yorker*, "'I'm interested in that kind of person, but I'm not that kind of person. It's an unreliable narrator. I do consciously do that. . . . I tend to say the opposite of what I think. You hope that the absolute power of that transcends, and reaches the audience.'"[55] Although some critics have tried to paint Silverman as "mean-spirited and rarely witty"[56] or have found it difficult to get past her "colossal insensitivity,"[57] the critical reception of *Jesus Is Magic* was largely positive.[58] As Carina Chocano notes in her *Los Angeles Times* review, "[i]t's easy to misunderstand Silverman (if you're inclined to)," going on to acknowledge what most reviewers seem to get, that Silverman "makes fun of bigotry by pretending to be a bigot; hypocrisy by pretending to be a hypocrite; and stupidity by pretending to be dumb."[59] But Silverman never overtly gives her act away. The most explicit she ever gets on stage or on film about the satirical nature of her performance exists in the commentary—available on DVD—where Liam Lynch, the director of *Jesus Is Magic*, asks about the origin of one of her more shocking bits about the singular jewel that is "only found on the tip of the tailbone of Ethiopian babies," who have to be "deboned" to extract the stone. She responds to Lynch's astonished laughter by acknowledging "it's just the basic idea that . . . diamond miners die all the time. But still women love those diamonds." Lynch follows: "Yeah, who cares if a million men died to get me this tiny piece of rock?"[60]

Silverman's diamond routine is worth reflecting on for reasons that extend beyond the commentary, as it is one of the more extreme bits offered in the film—deboning Ethiopian babies for materialistic gratification—and the satire uses ethnicity as an entryway into a troubling national trend. In the process of introducing this remarkable jewel, Silverman concedes that she is going to "sound like such a JAP."[61] Until this point, the "Jewish-American Princess" (JAP) stereotype had only been performed, but not mentioned explicitly. Through this basic utterance, her persona becomes shaded just a bit more—a touch more ethnic texture. In this case, she mobilizes her "ethnicity" to help sell a routine meant to satirize the absurd lengths that portions of the American public will go for material goods. Her act not only comments on stereotypes of Jews, but American Jews, and American society as well. Part of what makes Jewish American difference enigmatic is that it is never clear where the lines are drawn.

In his discussion of the connection between comedy and U.S. culture, John Lowe suggests "[h]umor has played and continues to play a role in the process of Americanization. Ethnic comedians, especially blacks and Jews, have in many ways created the national sense of humor . . . paralleling changes both in the general culture and in the ethnic groups themselves."[62] A "Jewish joke" that speaks as much about American society as Jews themselves is cited in Joseph Telushkin's book *Jewish Humor: What the Best Jewish Jokes Say About the Jew*: "A Jewish woman is wheeling her grandson in a baby carriage. A woman stops her. 'What a beautiful baby,' she says. 'Ah, this is nothing! You should see his pictures.'" As Telushkin suggests in his discussion of this joke, "[w]hat matters is not who we truly are, but what image we wish to project."[63] We see this angle played out in Silverman's exposition of the rare jewel that she covets, but it comes up more explicitly later in her performance. In a discussion about labeling, she says "I just want people to . . . look at me and . . . see *me*, you know, as white." On the heels of this declaration, in which she tries to align herself with the dominant majority rather than with her ethnicity—exercising a consent by convenience—she discusses her "half-black" exboyfriend, who apparently broke up with her after she paid him the "compliment" that "he probably would have made . . . a really expensive slave." The obvious insensitivity is meant to be beyond Silverman's (stage persona's) ability to recognize. Instead, she suggests that her innocent remark traveled "through the . . . Rube Goldberg . . . crazy straw of his low self esteem," causing him to get offended.[64]

What's interesting in the example above, is that the crazy straw metaphor, which relates to the convoluted path that makes the otherwise simple and direct more complicated—depicted in the comic and satiric drawings of Rube Goldberg (the "self-operating napkin" and "self-operating toothpaste" being two popular examples)—is more apt for how information is being diverted, reduced, abstracted, and half-processed by Silverman herself. Instead of a direct line from experience to understanding, information travels a convoluted course, particularly when channeled through the network of contemporary media sources, condensed and filtered for young minds with limited attention or interest (or more attention and interest in themselves and their own social spheres/networks). In this sense, the crazy straw metaphor is related to the "irony of technology" discussed by Susan Douglas who argues "that just when a globe-encircling grid of communications systems indeed makes it possible for Americans to see and learn more than ever about the rest of the world, Americans have been more isolated and less informed about global politics."[65] Silverman performs such a character in her satiric comedy, demonstrating an exaggerated isolation, insensitivity, and ignorance for the purposes of reflection and ridicule. She follows her remarks about her exboyfriend by revealing: "I don't care if you think I'm racist, I just want you to think I'm thin."[66] These statements underscore the image-obsession that exists within factions of American society, mimetic of the image-saturated media that accounts for so much of how Americans view and understand the world and their place within it. It also gestures to the magical realities and narcissistic fantasies that are part of our everyday lives.

The irrational conclusions and distorted priorities that are performed by Silverman are products of a persona who employs a type of humor that Freud has termed "naïve." In "Wit and the Various Forms of the Comic," Freud suggests that "[t]he naïve originates . . . outside of inhibition. . . . What conditions the function of the naïve is the fact that we are aware that the person does not possess this inhibition, otherwise we should not call it naïve but impudent, and instead of laughing we should be indignant." [67] Of course the "real" Sarah Silverman knows the difference—and (as noted earlier) has been called "mean-spirited and rarely witty." But her awareness, as expressed to Dana Goodyear and others, and the largely effective portrayal of her naïve persona (her unapologetic, unrestrained callowness) is why the shocking nature of her material should be understood as satire—the naïve narcissist produced by American media culture—rather than as racist or offensive, a charge she raises herself.

In one of the few moments when Silverman steps beside her persona, she relates an incident in which a figure from an Asian American advocacy group accused her of being racist for using the word "Chink" on a talk show. Although she claims that it was embedded in a joke, and makes a joke out of it, employing a Jewish American stereotype—"as a member of the Jewish community . . . I was really *concerned* that we were losing control of the media"—she uses this anecdote as an opportunity to address the topic of racism within humor. Silverman suggests that people are only comfortable making jokes about those they are not afraid of—citing "midgets" and Asians as easy targets. Then she discloses another story in which she declined to tell a joke that used the word "nigger" because of a table of African Americans who were in the front row. This leads her to raise the question most explicitly: "Is that an edgy joke or is that a racist joke?" [68] Although Silverman does not answer her question in explicit terms, the seed has been planted, allowing her stage persona to return to the topic later in the show, in a futile attempt to defend herself against the charge.

In addition to a discussion of racism, the above example speaks to the comical and satirical *framing*, and the importance of establishing this frame, or "ludicrous context" to use Schaeffer's terminology, for satiric comedians such as Silverman. In the setting of a talk show—the forum out of which her "racist" joke was criticized—there is typically not enough time to establish such a context; as a result, it is much easier for casual or reactionary viewers to misinterpret a joke and/or fail to identify the frame within which the material is grounded. In other words, it can be difficult to distinguish a racist joke from a joke about racism. What is important to consider for Silverman is that she wants her audience to recognize the racism in her character—she brings it up most pointedly. What she refuses to do is indulge in a discussion that would exist outside the boundaries of the ludicrous context. While she is more than willing to extend the frame into the magical, the sexually explicit, and/or the absurd, she is not going to define and explain what she does; such a move would cause the magical realist realm and the comedic tension so important for her satire to collapse.

It is ultimately her rejection of the label "racist," and the defensive discussion in which she engages, that indicates the racism inherent within the narcissistic figure that Silverman is performing. With each attempt to assert her innocence, she exposes another unsavory layer, until finally she admits that if she "based [her] material on stereotypes, that would be messed up." Instead, she maintains that she bases it on "facts." She proceeds to list a few "facts," the most telling is presented first. She proclaims that the "SAT test . . . is culturally biased towards Caucasians," following her statement with the affirmation: "That's a fact; I heard that somewhere." [69] In this final clause, important elements of her character are being exposed and satirized: the inclination to found arguments on "facts" that have no identifiable sources; the propensity to confuse fact and rumor; the frightening reality that in contemporary American society, many develop an understanding of significant, worldly events based on statements heard at uncertain times, delivered by uncertain sources—information that traveled through the Rube Goldberg crazy straw before being processed.

Silverman closes her stage performance with a provocative segment and a telling final line. After addressing charges of racism, and turning each charge into a race-based joke, she gives the impression that she is finally going to reveal her secret. She makes it clear that what she is doing is telling jokes, implicitly bringing the audience back to the opening of her stage performance when she establishes that she is a comedian— "That's what I *do*." Now at the end, she relates a story of a Mexican woman who confronted her after a show to address the charge that Mexican people smell. Employing her acting talents, Silverman suggests that it is difficult to get her point across in this type of situation. The audience is led to believe that she is talking about satire, but instead of indulging an explanation of what she has been doing, she stays true to character: "I had to explain to her that . . . you can't smell yourself." [70] This final line is presented as yet another one-liner delivered for comedic effect, once again rebuffing the audience's desire to be put at ease: the principal tantalization of her performance. However, when analyzing this last line, it reveals itself as more loaded than her delivery would indicate. "You can't smell yourself" can be viewed in a few important ways. More than a simple odor issue, it is the inability to look at one's self and to identify the tendencies and implications of one's statements and actions. What racist thinks s/he's a racist? Seeing/smelling yourself is a much greater feat than most would like to believe. It is because of this difficulty that satire holds such value, particularly in contemporary American society, where one can get lost so easily in images and abstractions—magical projections in the realm of the real—losing sight of the sensitivities of others, indulging too entirely in the resources designed (quite profitably) to encourage self absorption. Furthermore, "you can't smell yourself" or (as suggested above) you will give yourself away and the framing—be it magical realist or satirical—will fall apart.

Silverman accentuates and dramatizes the connection between narcissism and magical realism, punctuating her performance with two different sexual encounters with her vanity mirror. In her portrayal of an assimilated, narcissistic Jewish American woman, Silverman sheds light on a movement in American culture, one that affects the development of the budding American persona. She is satirizing the "MySpace" generation, where the projection of and consumption with the self has reached new levels. It is a generation of consent by convenience, where issues of ethnicity and culture are played up or down based solely on how they affect the self. It is how wide Silverman is able to extend her performative space that speaks most poignantly to the enigma of Jewish American difference. The world she creates in *Jesus Is Magic* exists outside of taxonomy, but inside the persona of the *Magical American Jew*.

NOTES

1. Werner Sollors, *Beyond Ethnicity: Consent and Descent in American Culture* (Oxford: OUP, 1986), 6.

2. Silverman's *We Are Miracles* and *A Speck of Dust* both have edgy and outrageous moments, but they are more conventional stand-up acts (for Silverman); in either special, she does not mobilize her ethnicity in quite the same way as she does in *Jesus Is Magic*, and she does not incorporate any magical devices.

3. Sam Anderson, "Irony Maiden: How Sarah Silverman Is Raping American Comedy," *Slate.com*, November 15, 2005.

4. Sarah Silverman, *Sarah Silverman: Jesus Is Magic*, DVD, dir. Liam Lynch, Roadside Attractions, 2006.

5. Amaryll Beatrice Chanady, *Magical Realism and the Fantastic: Resolved Versus Unresolved Antinomy* (New York: Garland, 1985), 30.

6. I discuss this issue of magical proportion or duration in the conclusion. Specifically, I address claims made by Lyn Di Iorio Sandín and Richard Perez, editors of the anthology *Moments of Magical Realism in U.S. Ethnic Literatures,* that "often texts are erroneously categorized as 'magical realist' when, in fact, what they mainly display are momentary yet very significant *irruptions* of nonrealist tendencies into a realist text" (3).

7. Many contemporary scholars of magical realism, including Shannin Schroeder, Rawdon Wilson, and Phil McCluskey privilege Chanady's definition of magical realism. As Schroeder explains in her book *Rediscovering Magical Realism in the Americas*, "Over the countless versions of the 'definitive' definition of magical realism, Chana-

dy's proves to be not only the most persuasive but also the most easily applicable" (14).

8. Chanady, *Magical Realism and the Fantastic*, 30.

9. Rawdon Wilson, "The Metamorphoses of Fictional Space: Magical Realism," in *Magical Realism: Theory, History, Community*, ed. Lois Parkinson Zamora and Wendy B. Faris (Durham, NC: Duke UP, 1995), 209–34, 220.

10. Silverman, *Jesus Is Magic*.

11. Ibid.

12. Although Silverman does eventually put on the show she describes in the opening vignette, the lyrics in the first movement of the song—including "I'm so full of shit, man. What was I thinking?"—as well as the title, "I Can Write a Show," make it evident that at the time of the telling, she was lying about her preexisting show. The (fantastic) conclusion that one is meant to draw is that she found the theater space, wrote and performed her show after leaving her friend's apartment.

13. Annie Reich, "Pathological Forms of Self-Esteem Regulation," in *Essential Papers on Narcissism*, ed. Andrew P. Morrison, M.D. (New York: NYUP, 1986), 47.

14. Carolyn C. Morf and Frederick Rhodewalt, "Unraveling the Paradoxes of Narcissism: A Dynamic Self-Regulatory Processing Model," *Psychological Inquiry* 12.4 (2001): 177–96, 177.

15. Neil Schaeffer, "Lenny Bruce and Extreme Comedy," in *The Art of Laughter* (New York: Columbia UP, 1981), 59.

16. Dana Goodyear's profile, "Quiet Depravity," published in *The New Yorker* (October 24, 2005), identifies a Bruce routine, which Silverman has "reprised with a harder edge." A.O. Scott's review, "A Comic in Search of the Discomfort Zone," *New York Times*, November 11, 2005, cites the "tradition" of Lenny Bruce and Richard Pryor in discussing Silverman's material.

17. Edward Azlant, "Lenny Bruce Again: 'Gestapo? You asshole, I'm the mailman!'" *Studies in American Humor* 15 (2007): 75–99, 78–79.

18. Silverman, *Jesus Is Magic*.

19. Schaeffer, "Lenny Bruce and Extreme Comedy," 80.

20. Ibid., 72.

21. In a response to the original publication of Schaeffer's essay (*College English*, February 1976), George A. Test makes a similar point about Schaeffer's curious claims (*College English*, January 1977), noting Schaeffer's "lack of understanding of satire [as] the most distressing aspect of his essay" (518); but Test makes an equally perplexing, and no less sweeping, statement about Schaeffer's "failure to understand that character has very little place in either comedy or satire" (518). In the same issue, Schaeffer answers Test's response by listing a number of satiric characters, including "Saint Joan, Huckleberry Finn, Tom Jones, Falstaff, Lemuel Gulliver, Emma, Don Quixote" (520).

22. Erving Goffman, *Frame Analysis: An Essay on the Organization of Experience* (Cambridge: Harvard UP, 1974), 345.

23. Again, there is a similarity to Sacha Baron Cohen's Borat, but for Silverman, the distinction between the comedian and the character is far more subtle, since, as mentioned in the body of the chapter, her name is the same (Sarah Silverman), and she is not wearing a disguise or affecting an accent, as Cohen has done with Borat and others.

24. Paul Provenza, dir. *The Aristocrats*, DVD, Mighty Cheese Productions, 2005.

25. Anderson, "Irony Maiden."

26. Schaeffer, "Lenny Bruce and Extreme Comedy," 59.

27. Silverman, *Jesus Is Magic*.

28. Ibid.

29. Ibid.

30. James D. Bloom, *Gravity Fails: The Comic Jewish Shaping of Modern America* (Westport, CT: Praeger, 2003), xii–xv.

31. John Lowe's "Theories of Ethnic Humor: How to Enter, Laughing" is a valuable, brief survey of ethnic humor, addressing (among other things) the various tracks of humor that run around and between "out-groups" and "in-groups."

32. As noted in chapters 2 and 4, Alan Dundes's essay "The J.A.P. and the J.A.M. in American Jokelore" traces the presence of and relationship between the Jewish American Mother and the Jewish American Princess stereotypes that have become staples of "American Jokelore." In "The Jewish Mother: Comedy and Controversy in American Popular Culture," Martha A. Ravits argues that "The comic stereotype of the Jewish mother . . . is a cultural construct developed by male writers in the United States in the 1960s" (1). According to Ravits, *Portnoy's Complaint* provides "The most memorable and fully elaborated caricature of the Jewish mother" (6). In *You Never Call! You Never Write!: A History of the Jewish Mother* (2007), Joyce Antler also points to the 1960s and suggests that the breadth of the Jewish mother stereotype can be linked to the widespread commercial success of three books: Dan Greenberg's guidebook *How to Be a Jewish Mother*, Bruce Jay Friedman's novel *A Mother's Kisses*, and Philip Roth's novel *Portnoy's Complaint* (135–37).

33. Lois Leveen, "Only When I Laugh: Textual Dynamics of Ethnic Humor," *MELUS* 21.4 (1996): 29–55, 37.

34. Silverman, *Jesus Is Magic*.

35. Ibid.

36. Lawrence Epstein's *The Haunted Smile: the Story of Jewish Comedians in America* (2001) does a good job of tracing the perceptions and portrayals of Jewish women in the United States. Starting in the late nineteenth century and sweeping through the twentieth century, Epstein discusses the various transitions and transformations that Jewish comedians—male and female—have both perpetuated and reacted to. Alan Dundes's essay (noted above) also spells out various stereotypical incarnations, in many cases, allowing the jokes that perpetuate these stereotypes to speak for themselves.

37. Silverman, *Jesus Is Magic*.

38. Ibid.

39. Susan J. Douglas, "The Turn Within: The Irony of Technology in a Globalized World," *American Quarterly* 58.3 (2006): 619–38, 619–20.

40. Joseph Boskin, "The Ethics of Laughter and Humor," in *The Philosophy of Laughter and Humor*, ed. John Morreall (Albany: SUNY P, 1987), 254.

41. Much has been written about the charges of "public profanity" with which Bruce had to contend as a result of his provocative humor. His autobiography *How to Talk Dirty and Influence People* and *The Lenny Bruce Performance Film* are two sources in which he directly addresses these charges. In both cases, he allows the audience to view some of the transcripts, in an effort to acknowledge the absurdity of the charges and interrogations.

42. Silverman, *Jesus Is Magic*.

43. Ibid.

44. This is just one of many tensions that is sustained through her performance; also prominent are the tensions between what is real and what is not (fantasy and reality), who is real and who is not (comedian and character), and what is serious and what is satire.

45. Reich, "Pathological Forms of Self-Esteem Regulation," 49.

46. Roy F. Baumeister and Kathleen D. Vohs, "Narcissism as Addiction to Esteem," *Psychological Inquiry* 12.4 (2001): 206–10, 206.

47. The term "global village" comes from Marshall McLuhan who, in *Understanding Media* (1964), suggested that the development of new communications technologies would give easier and greater access to different parts of the world and would effectively bring the world together. Douglas's essay is, in part, a response to McLuhan's idea.

48. Douglas, "The Turn Within," 620.

49. Carolyn C. Morf and Frederick Rhodewalt, "Unraveling the Paradoxes of Narcissism: A Dynamic Self-Regulatory Processing Model," *Psychological Inquiry* 12.4 (2001): 177–96, 177.

50. Reich, "Pathological Forms of Self-Esteem Regulation," 49.

51. Douglas, "The Turn Within," 633.

52. Reich, "Pathological Forms of Self-Esteem Regulation," 48.

53. Douglas, "The Turn Within," 636.

54. Silverman, *Jesus Is Magic*.

55. Dana Goodyear, "Quiet Depravity: The Demure Outrages of a Standup Comic," *New Yorker*, October 24, 2005: 50–55, 53.

56. Bruce Westbrook, "There Are No Miracles in Silverman's Stage Show," *Houston Chronicle*, December 9, 2005, Chron.com, August 20, 2008, http://www.chron.com/disp/story.mpl/ent/movies/reviews/3503740.html.

57. Jean Lowerison, "*Sarah Silverman: Jesus Is Magic*: Not Funny," *San Diego Metropolitan*, December 6, 2005, SanDiegoMetro.com, August 20, 2008, http://www.sandiegometro.com/reel/index.php?reelID=887.

58. One indication of the critical reception can be found in the summation of reviews compiled by the online resource *Rotten Tomatoes*, which noted 65 percent positive reviews, out of 96 total reviews collected from newspapers, magazines, and online sources.

59. Carina Chocano, "Silverman Will Make You Cringe while Making You Laugh," *Los Angeles Times*, November 11, 2005, E6.

60. Silverman, *Jesus Is Magic*.

61. Ibid.

62. John Lowe, "Theories of Ethnic Humor: How to Enter, Laughing," *American Quarterly* 38.3 (1986): 439–60, 452–53.

63. Joseph Telushkin, *Jewish Humor: What the Best Jewish Jokes Say about the Jews* (New York: Quill, 1998), 56.

64. Silverman, *Jesus Is Magic*.

65. Douglas, "The Turn Within," 625–26.

66. Silverman, *Jesus Is Magic*.

67. Sigmund Freud, "Wit and the Various Forms of the Comic," *The Basic Writings of Sigmund Freud* (New York: Modern Library, 1938), 763.

68. Silverman, *Jesus Is Magic*.

69. Ibid.

70. Ibid.

Conclusion

Portraying the Impossible: Franz Kafka and the Magical Influence of an Enigmatic Artist

In distinct yet overlapping ways, the chapters of *Magical American Jew* have highlighted some of the indefinite positions and paradoxical descriptions of contemporary Jewish Americans. As central has been the felicitous way in which the magical realist mode aligns with and helps to animate—and often elevate—complex identities and enigmatic differences. Among other things, these chapters have shown how the challenges of defining and describing American Jewish culture and identity have evolved more than resolved over time. Discussing his own efforts to address the progressive classification challenges, Vincent Brook references David Biale's claim, made in *Cultures of the Jews*, that "[w]hat may be the most defining characteristic of modern Jewish culture is the question of *how* to define it." [1] Brook follows Biale's suggestion with a related contention: "[w]hat may be the most defining characteristic of *post*modern American Jewish culture and identity is the increasing inability, yet persistent necessity, to define it." [2] Beyond taking Biale's claim from the modern to the postmodern, Brook locates and further complicates the challenges by turning "Jewish culture" into "American Jewish culture and identity," and perhaps more importantly, turning Biale's "question" about definition into an "increasing inability, yet persistent necessity." The works that are examined most closely in *Magical American Jew* exemplify the persistence and challenge of cultural classification for contemporary Jewish Americans. These works also demonstrate postmodern efforts to illustrate particular aspects of difference—methods that aim to make the questions, needs, positions, and struggles more evident to the eye and to the mind. As discussed in this concluding chapter, these methods, each deploying the magical realist mode, are also pulling from a rich history of biblical and secular storytelling.

Although it is beyond the scope of this study to trace all potential origins and inspirations for Jewish magical realism, there is a substantial foundation of mystical, magical, and fabulist Jewish writing and performance. While this chapter delves into some of that tradition, as suggested in the Introduction, few artists have absorbed those influences as uniquely and been more impactful in bringing the magical and the marginalized

115

together as Franz Kafka. Along with the bewildering realities of everyday life, Kafka found inspiration in the expressions of Jewish culture that he saw at low budget theaters in Prague. According to Walter H. Sokel, the Yiddish theater "came to Kafka as a revelation and prepared him for the breakthrough in his writing."[3] Kafka's enthusiasm for Yiddish theater led to an intensive study of Jewish history and Jewish texts, including the Talmud, the Kabbalah, and other sources that use fabulist means to raise and respond to religious, cultural, political, and existential concerns. This concluding chapter casts more light on Kafka's Jewish identity, as well as his awareness of and interest in historical and cultural Jewish expressions. Linking Kafka's writing with his own anomalous cultural position, this chapter connects his fiction, and the long tradition of fantastical Jewish writing, to the fiction and film in this study, as well as to works from significant Jewish American artists not addressed in great depth in previous chapters. This concluding chapter closes with a discussion of the ways that the magical realist mode has been and can be used to examine U.S. ethnic literatures more broadly.

Not unlike his fiction, Kafka's Jewish identity is difficult to quantify. As Arnold J. Band notes, "If . . . one was not committed to a traditional religious style of life and was yet deeply interested in a variety of Jewish concerns—as Kafka was—being Jewish was a nagging identification problem. . . . You knew you were categorized as an 'assimilated' Jew, that you lived on the margins of several societies, but at the heart of none."[4] We see Kafka grappling with the significance and challenge of being Jewish most directly in his letters and in his diary. In *Dearest Father,* he laments his inability to escape from or connect with his father in Judaism, identifying the challenge of trying to interpret the "version of Judaism" that was being modeled for him. He acknowledges the guilt he felt for showing the same "negligible commitment to Judaism" that his father displayed, suggesting that his father "resembled more . . . the indifferent throng than the few who took it seriously."[5] In this case, it is not simply the fluid concept of Judaism and the complex set of emotions he felt regarding his father's curiously rigid stance that his son somehow intuit the appropriate relationship to Judaism—what to observe and what to ignore—but Kafka's characterization of the "throng" of Jews who were indifferent, yet apparently still compelled to attend synagogue on select occasions. We can glean from this passage, and from letters to family and friends, that Kafka, his father, and the "throng" of Jews in Prague were constantly negotiating their relationship with both Judaism and Jewishness, but could never escape their identity as Jews, despite an inability to define in concrete terms what it meant, exactly. As Band suggests, "For Kafka as for most of his friends in Prague, being Jewish was an ineluctable fact of existence. You could live with it; you could try to escape it; you could try to repress it. But you could never ignore or forget it."[6] The "ineluctable fact" of an ambiguous Jewishness could be made for many secular American Jews—the very population featured in *Magical American Jew*. Complicating the "ineluctable fact" are the social, political, religious, and even educational pressures for cultural identification that exist. Kafka, of course, faced more extreme circumstances, and the discomfort that he felt in the present and sensed about the future was far more dire than what most Jewish Americans experience today, despite some troubling circumstances that continue to pop up in the United States and around the world.

Although explicitly Jewish content and characters are largely absent from Kafka's fiction, the themes are quite present, and "from 1911 on, when Kafka was twenty-eight . . . he began to be intensely occupied with Jewish history, Jewish tradition, Jewish lore, and Jewish culture—an interest which was not only sustained but constantly grew until his death in 1924 at the age of forty."[7] Kafka was raised and educated with largely German speaking Jews in Prague, and his "Jewishness . . . was not traditional, learned from childhood through ritual observance and study, but situational, an amalgam of the varied responses to historical forces."[8] What was utterly perplexing about Judaism and the observance of the Jewish religion as "taught" to him by his father and carried out by many in his synagogue, became fascinating and relatable through art and the vibrant and varied expressions of Jewish culture. Among other sources, Kafka's "consciousness of the richness of the Jewish past was awakened by his reading of Graetz's *History of the Jews* and his attending the performances of Itzik Löwy's travelling Yiddish theatre."[9] Despite his interest and enjoyment in the history and performance of Jewish culture, he never stopped wrestling with and straining to convey the complexities and contradictions of his Jewish upbringing and the complex cultural position he and other Jews found themselves in.

In one of his oft cited letters to Max Brod, written in 1921, Kafka addresses some of his most personal and profound struggles: his Jewish identity, his father, his father's ambivalence to Jewishness, and his own writing in German while living as a Jew in Prague. Kafka begins by offering an alternative to the "father-complex" he associates with psychoanalysis,

> prefer[ing] another version, where the issue revolves not around the innocent father but around the father's Jewishness. Most young Jews who began to write German wanted to leave Jewishness behind them, and their fathers approved of this, but vaguely (this vagueness was what was outrageous to them). But with their posterior legs they were still glued to their father's Jewishness and with their waving anterior legs they found no new ground. The ensuing despair became their inspiration.[10]

The image that he conjures in this passage is one that readers of Kafka will find familiar. In this letter, written six years after the publication of

"The Metamorphosis," Kafka is clearly referencing and perhaps even interpreting his story. At the very least, he's offering another angle from which to consider the central metaphor. He also seems to be suggesting why he was compelled to take this approach when writing his most iconic piece. Relating from a contemporary American context, the "inspiration" he mentions at the end calls to mind the "increasing inability, yet persistent necessity" to define Jewish culture that Brook discusses.

Elaborating on the inspirational despair he mentions at the end of the passage above, Kafka introduces, what he calls, "linguistic impossibilities," including:

> The impossibility of not writing, the impossibility of writing in German, the impossibility of writing differently. One might also add a fourth impossibility, the impossibility of writing (since the despair could not be assuaged by writing, was hostile to both life and writing; writing is only an expedient, as for someone who is writing his will shortly before he hangs himself—an expedient that may well last a whole life). Thus what resulted was a literature impossible in all respects, a gypsy literature which had stolen the German child out of its cradle and in great haste put it through some kind of training, for someone has to dance on the tightrope.[11]

What we see is Kafka firmly grounding himself and his literature in the impossible. As much clarity of himself and his surroundings as he might divulge through his writing, he is simultaneously erasing these elements, deeming the writing "impossible in all respects, a gypsy literature" void of any stable or concrete home. However, in a paradox fitting of Kafka and relevant to the contradictions that comprise efforts to articulate contemporary Jewish American identity—the enigma of difference addressed in *Magical American Jew*—he is deploying a mode of expression that helps to illustrate the impossible positions of his cultural identity, casting light into the darkness of his and his readers' understanding. And perhaps the greatest paradox of all is that in his own fiction, he is highlighting some of the most complex aspects of Jewish cultural identity without any explicit portrayals of Jewish characters or events.

Few have experienced anomalous cultural positions quite like Kafka, and his works of fiction, written in "cool, objective narration [that] provides no explanation" for any fantastical circumstances or events[12]—an essential feature of the magical realist mode—became the foundation for many of the magical realist texts that came after. The paradoxes and impossibilities are captured in a number of his pieces, some more magical than others—"The Metamorphosis," "The Judgment," "In the Penal Colony," *The Trial*, to name a few—but his short story "A Report to an Academy" might be the most explicit example of the impossibilities of assimilation: the performances and barriers inherent in the effort to convince some faceless "academy"—a group most assuredly free of any current or former apes, in this case—that he is fully assimilated, enough to deliver a report of the life he "formerly led as an ape."[13] In this story, Kafka uses comical and magical realist means to portray "that form of difference that is mimicry—*almost the same but not quite*," which Homi Bhabha discusses in considerable depth in his essay "Of Mimicry and Man," turning the phrase into *"almost the same but not white"* or "not quite/not white" to highlight "the ambivalent world . . . on the margins of metropolitan desire."[14] The impossible efforts at assimilation are consistent with those of Kafka's family and many Jews in Prague in the early twentieth-century, "strenuously assimilating, but not yet fully assimilated."[15] In such a characterization, we also see a primary contributor of the excess, the "just like everyone else, only more so," that manifests through magical and postmodern extensions in *Annie Hall*,[16] and in varied other ways in Jewish American fiction and film. Furthermore, the "gypsy literature" cited in the passage above fuels the compulsion to assimilate—to accept and even embrace the "training . . . to dance on the tightrope"—that exists for many who associate with a diasporic identity: a common and comparable theme in Jewish American and U.S. ethnic literatures, illustrated in dynamic configurations through magical realist means.

In many ways, Kafka laid the foundation for the magical realist depictions of the enigmatic difference discussed in this book. However, mystical and magical portrayals have a long history in biblical and secular Jewish literature, and these works influenced Kafka as well as those artists featured in this study, some tapping into these sources more directly and explicitly than others. Caroline Rody suggests that since the 1800s, "modern Jewish fiction has drawn on the 'magical' strands of the Jewish textual heritage: the miraculous supernaturalism pervading the holy texts, from Genesis to the . . . midrash and aggadot; the mystical beliefs and practices of late medieval kabbalism, and the tales of miracles produced by seventeenth-century Eastern European Hasidism." She goes on to note the influence of "a large, varied oral folklore that is as full of magic as any such literature in the world."[17] As much as I might argue for particular, contemporary readings of the works in *Magical American Jew*, the artists are not creating in a void, or simply working from the distinctive flooring that Kafka laid down, but pulling from and adding to a living, historical and literary context.

In his overview of the magical and miraculous events that have existed in Jewish literature throughout time, Daniel M. Jaffe identifies the many "fabulist" occurrences that are present in the bible: from the very creation of the universe to the story of Jonah getting "swallowed by a great fish and liv[ing] to tell of it." Once he establishes how much "biblical storytelling relies . . . on the fabulist," Jaffe brings up the texts created to interpret the events of the bible, from the Talmud and the Midrash, to the Zohar and the Kabbalah more broadly.[18] His discussion not only helps us see how the stories from these texts have influenced the literature that has come after, but it demonstrates how integral fantastical modes have been in our efforts to convey and to understand the complexities of our world and our places within it.

Howard Schwartz points specifically to the significance of the story in the Talmud about the four sages who entered Paradise, one losing his mind, another his life, a third his religion, while the fourth sage, Rabbi Akiba, ascending and returning in peace. According to Schwartz, rabbis have argued for ages over "what caused the downfall of the three sages," and this talmudic story "represents a kind of tale . . . found in every phase of Jewish literature." In setting up the stories in *Gabriel's Palace: Jewish Mystical Tales*, Schwartz describes the variety of circumstances featured in the collection, suggesting that "despite these disparate themes, virtually all of them have in common some kind of revelation or interaction with the Divine realm, and as such can be properly defined as mystical."[19] Although the works featured in *Magical American Jew* are not mystical tales but stories and films in the magical realist mode, and as such do not contain the same sort of revelation or interaction with the Divine realm, there are common themes with many mystical stories.

Perhaps the most notable similarity in the pieces addressed in *Magical American Jew* would be the existence of ascension or levitation. This theme is found most explicitly in Cynthia Ozick's story "Levitation" and Steve Stern's story "The Tale of a Kite," but it can also be found in Sarah Silverman's *Jesus Is Magic*, as Silverman's character rides a red convertible into the sky, winding up in a studio where she discovers herself as the star who has "that thing that you just can't define,"[20] bridging the magical ascension with the enigmatic, indefinable description discussed in chapter 5. Howard Schwartz addresses how "the myth of ascent," derived "from Ezekiel's vision," contains an ascending chariot and "represents the longing to come into the Divine presence. . . . This longing, then, consists of a yearning for personal experience of the Divine." Schwartz suggests that "[t]his myth of ascent finds expression both in the tale of the four sages who entered Paradise and in many accounts of heavenly journeys found in the Hekhaloth texts."[21] While Silverman's red convertible, featured in what is arguably the most secular of the ascent stories mentioned above, might be the closest approximation to Ezekiel's chariot, various chariot-like vehicles can be imagined in the other stories too. In Stern's "The Tale of a Kite," Rabbi Shmelke functions as a rising kite, his followers grabbing onto the rope that was used to hold him down, trailing him as a human tail; in Ozick's story, it is the living room itself that serves as the chariot, ascending with a floor full of Jews into the ether. But more than the ascent, it is the longing in Schwartz's description that stands out. The "yearning for personal experience of the Divine . . . rather than to remain outside the palace and hear rumors of the King."[22] In the secular, magical realist tales, the longing and desire are most evident; the wish to be included and to have a place in the palace, along with the manifestations of the corresponding projections, perceptions, and desires, are often on display.

Although ascension figures prominently in works discussed in this study, other allusions and appropriations from Jewish mystical texts exist. Nathan Englander's "Gilgul of Park Avenue," discussed along with Stern's story, draws from the *gigul*, or "transmigration of souls," that is introduced in the Zohar.[23] According to Schwartz, "*gilgul* . . . was one of the most influential mystical doctrines in sixteenth-century Safed. Drawing on this doctrine, it was common to assert that one rabbi was a reincarnation of another or that one rabbi had sparks of the souls of several great figures."[24] While Englander uses this to comic affect—the transmigration occurs in a NYC taxi cab, in this case—he enables the *gilgul* concept to highlight the tension between religiosity and ethnicity that exists for many contemporary American Jews.

In Melvin Jules Bukiet's "The Library of Moloch," the central character, Dr. Arthur Ricardo, experiences a "revelation," which is one of the common features in the mystical tales included in Schwartz's book. However, in Bukiet's story, the revelation is about "two inviolate realms"— memory and theology—and as discussed in chapter 3, this illustrates the impossibility of Divine connection more than any connection itself.[25] Once again, the impossible desire for connection takes us back to Kaka's descriptions, specifically his Metamorphosis-like analogy of an insect stuck to some cryptic concept of Jewishness and unable to find concrete ground. In the circumstances addressed in Bukiet's story, we see the impossible effort to locate a stable sense of identity by forging connections to witnesses of historical atrocities.

In most of the works in *Magical American Jew*, the influence of fabulist or mystical Jewish literature can be tracked, but these stories and films— and works of magical realism most commonly, if not by definition—are secular texts, the magical components normalized, not explained away by religious or hallucinatory elements. The specific pieces addressed in *Magical American Jew* have more contemporary, cultural aims—at least as read and discussed within this book. Despite Divine aspects present in particular narratives—Ozick, Stern, and Englander, most notably—the works resist any "*interaction* with the Divine realm" (my emphasis), which Schwartz identifies as the constant theme among the 150 mystical tales in his collection. Although the aims and constructions are different, the pieces in *Magical American Jew* do help to reinforce Jaffe's claim that "[f]abulist forms of storytelling can accommodate a broad range of investigations and express varied imaginations."[26] Kafka exemplified this claim, and the works that have followed further display "investigations" and "imaginations" of impossible positions between worlds, ethnic designations, nationalistic loyalties, and terrestrial and Divine pressures.

According to Jaffe, "all fiction is an answer to 'what if?,' [whereas] fabulist fiction takes the questioning even farther by challenging the assumed premises, by starting with the premise 'if only. . .'"[27] While Jaffe's claim may play out in the stories anthologized in his collection, the works addressed in *Magical American Jew* do not work with the premise "*if only . . .*" as much as "*it's as if . . .*" The position of the "if" in each construction is important. What is given in Jaffe's "*if only . . .*" phrase is that the works are exactly *not* real: *if only* these magical elements *were* real. But in magical realism, the magical is treated as real—never questioned or interrogated or otherwise acknowledged as a product of dream, hallucination, Divine intervention, or anything out of the realm of the natural, hybrid world—and the aim of the work is more to illustrate a condition, represent a circumstance, or strike an analogy.

Looking back at Kafka's description of the relationships that he and other young Jews in Prague had with their fathers, we see such an analogy: it's *as if* "their posterior legs . . . were still glued to their father's Jewishness and with their waving anterior legs they found no new ground." In similar fashion, each work in *Magical American Jew* can help us imagine some aspect of the enigmatic. It's *as if* the excessive self-consciousness over perceived difference were evident to the eye, or the alienation and feelings of secondary status could trigger a physical separation—levitation—into the ether before a dominant witness, or the manifestations of an identity founded too centrally on an historical atrocity could lead to masochistic tendencies and a survivor's lecture through the impenetrable lens of a media screen as an archive of testimonies is enveloped in flames, or the tension between religiosity and ethnicity could force a terrestrial split, or the slippery nature of Jewish American identity could slip into a materialized fantasy of stardom.

In this last example, characterizing the portrayal found in Sarah Silverman's *Jesus Is Magic*, we see a circumstance that threads through most if not all works of contemporary Jewish American magical realism. It's *as if* a "sleight of identity" exists for contemporary American Jews, both consciously and unconsciously displaying the "capacity to duck and merge into whatever culture one happens to inhabit." As Daniel Itzkovitz contends, contemporary Jewish American identity "has been defiantly elusive, rebuffing all attempts to pin it down, to the point that the Jewish presence has the potential to complicate the project of identity-making entirely."[28] For Jewish Americans, this process has been going on for a long time and has taken many forms. The depictions of the Jewish presence in the United States—the immigration and assimilation stories of Abraham Cahan, Mary Antin, Henry Roth, and many others—became foundational narratives for immigrant and early U.S. ethnic literatures. As the methods moved through realism and modernism, the postmodern and magical realist depictions of second and third generation Jewish Americans began to emerge, influenced by and influencing a new, more contemporary group of artists.

Although this study focuses on a select set of short stories and films, the magical realist mode can be found in many more works of Jewish American fiction and film, illustrating aspects of Jewish and American identity that extend beyond or expose differing aspects of the enigma of difference. As discussed earlier, Kafka brought the magical and the marginalized together in an unprecedented way; after Kafka, one of the first major writers to incorporate magical elements in both Jewish and Jewish American contexts was Isaac Beshevis Singer, who wrote in Yiddish and in English and set his magical tales in Europe and in the United States. Caroline Rody characterizes Singer as "[t]he key transitional figure in the career of Jewish magical realism." She describes how he "was steeped in the scriptural and folkloric supernaturalism of traditional Jewish culture, especially Kabbalah, but was exposed in youth to the rationalist intellectual ferment of continental philosophy as well as literature."[29] Along with Yiddish stories with European settings—"Gimpel the Fool," "The Dead Fiddler," "The Last Demon," to name a few—Singer has fantastical tales, both magical and mystical, that are set in New York City and other urban environments. Singer's stories "The Letter Writer," "The Cafeteria," and "A Tale of Two Sisters" are a few that feature "modern city dwellers [who] . . . accept psychic phenomena as part of their lives."[30] As discussed in chapter 4, in Englander's and Stern's stories in particular, the confluence of cultures, spiritual practices, and social eccentricities make city settings ripe for fantastical representations.

In terms of magical incorporation into more contemporary and secular Jewish American short stories, Bernard Malamud may be the most well-known writer not addressed in great depth in the previous chapters of *Magical American Jew*. Although not quite as contemporary as the works in this study, Malamud grapples with similar themes and provides valuable illustrations of the ways that the magical realist mode can highlight cultural contradictions and ambiguities. Caroline Rody suggests that "Malamud frequently centered his tales on an ordinary, often assimilated American Jew's encounter with a surprising, archetypal figure of Old World Judaism or Jewish culture."[31] We see similar circumstances in Steve Stern's "The Tale of a Kite," discussed in chapter 4, as the secular Jewish businessman Jacob Zipper is obsessed by the sudden arrival and swiftly swelling influence of Rabbi Shmelke who seems to have come from another time and place.

Malamud's most well-known Jewish magical realist *short story* is most likely "The Jewbird." First published in *The Reporter* in 1963, Malamud's story famously features a talking, dovening bird named Schwartz who kvetches about "Anti-Semeets" and is anxious for some shelter and good Jewish food.[32] Malamud brings humor and magic together in this piece — a feature present in many of Kafka's stories and in the majority of works in *Magical American Jew*—and exposes the tension of assimilation, a common theme in many works of twentieth-century Jewish American literature, in a manner that "set the stage" for the Jewish magical realist works that came after (the stage literally set in Silverman's *Jesus Is Magic*). Among other characteristics, the strains of self-consciousness and even self-hatred that some writers have attributed to "The Jewbird"[33] can also be found in Ozick's story "Levitation," featured in chapter 2. In "Levitation," self-hatred can be linked to the manifestations of shame that are prominent in Ozick's story. Without question, Malamud's work holds an important place in Jewish American and American literature. A number of contemporary Jewish American writers, including Steve Stern, have acknowledged Malamud's influence, specifically his ability to "veer into fantasy, and occupy a mythic and a perfectly psychologically realistic milieu simultaneously."[34] We see comparably complex dimensions in much of Stern's own fiction, including "The Tale of a Kite," which is featured in chapter 4.

Similar to Kafka and Isaac Bashevis Singer, Malamud's fiction was inspired by fantastical works in Yiddish. According to Julian Levinson, "Bernard Malamud was by his own account moved to write his story 'The Magic Barrel' directly after reading through a series of Yiddish folk tales." Levinson notes how "Malamud's development in this and subsequent works of a symbolic mode—akin to what we might call 'magical realism'—also comes out of his engagement with Yiddish texts."[35] Mark Athitakis distinguishes Malamud from Saul Bellow and Philip Roth, the other two Jewish literary giants who are at the center of what Andrew Furman calls the "golden age of Jewish American fiction."[36] While "Bellow and Roth sought to balance their Jewish backgrounds with a commitment to the larger American scene. . . . Malamud . . . stuck with Yiddish folklore and continued to bear witness to its strange magic."[37]

Of course, Philip Roth is another important Jewish American writer who has used and continues to use magical techniques in his writing. Roth does factor into *Magical American Jew*, but more for the influence of his non-magical works. A discussion of *Portnoy's Complaint* and the association with guilt, and the presence and perpetuation of certain Jewish American stereotypes—overbearing Jewish mother and guilt ridden son, primarily—are addressed in chapter 2 and referenced in other chapters, and his story "Eli, the Fanatic" is discussed in chapter 4, as it provides a story line that is echoed in Stern's "The Tale of a Kite." Roth's magical realist works are more present in his novels—*The Counterlife* being one notable example that features magical realist and postmodern elements. The layers of narrative and metanarrative featured in *The Counterlife* are comparable to those found in Woody Allen's *Annie Hall*, a film discussed in chapter 1. In both cases, a narrative excess reflects the self-consciousness and desire to amend or augment the circumstances of daily life.[38]

In addition to Singer, Malamud, and Roth, many contemporary Jewish American writers have worked and continue to work with the magical realist mode. Caroline Rody provides probing, analytical discussions of Joseph Skibell's novel *A Blessing on the Moon* and Jonathan Safran Foer's novel *Everything Is Illuminated*. Other authors who have been or could be examined in subsequent or alternate studies include Michael Chabon, Pearl Abraham, Rebecca Goldstein, Aimee Bender, Judy Budnitz, Allegra Goodman, Nicole Krauss, Dara Horn, Myla Goldberg, and many others. In nearly all cases, these writers are grappling with and reanimating periods in history, and negotiating with enigmatic aspects of their contemporary American identities. Along with the writers who have deployed the magical realist mode, there are filmmakers who are not included in *Magical American Jew*, but could hold an important place in a study of Jewish American magical realist cinema. Joel and Ethan Coen (the Coen Brothers) have two films, *Barton Fink* and the more mystical *A Serious Man*, that address aspects of assimilation and the influence of Jewish legend that inform concepts of Jewish identity and methods of Jewish storytelling. Woody Allen's *Zelig* provides a physical manifestation of Itzkovitz's "sleight of identity," offering a comic depiction of a character who physically changes based on the culture of his surroundings. And the adaptation of Myla Goldberg's *Bee Season*, directed by Scott McGehee and David Siegel, is another example that pulls from Jewish fabulist history, particularly regarding the sacred magic of words. One might also write about how the magical realist elements are left out of the adaptation of Jonathan Safran Foer's novel *Everything Is Illuminated*, directed by Liev Schreiber. Caroline Rody writes with great depth about the derivation and importance of the magical storyline in Foer's novel, delving into what it raises about post-Holocaust storytelling. It would be valuable to consider how the absence of the magical affects the story and its overall impact.

Although *Magical American Jew* focuses on contemporary Jewish American short fiction and film, the magical realist mode provides a revealing lens through which to examine works of U.S. ethnic fiction and film on a wider scale. There have been two recent books that have taken up this task on the fictive end: *Uncertain Mirrors: Magical Realisms in U.S. Ethnic Literatures*, by Jesús Benito, Ana Mª Manzanas, and Begoña Simal, and the anthology *Moments of Magical Realism in U.S. Ethnic Literatures*, edited by Lyn Di Iorio Sandín and Richard Perez. According to Benito, Manzanas, and Simal, *Uncertain Mirrors* addresses how "magical realism performs a wide profound cultural and ideological work. It yanks us out of the comfortable complacency that assesses the real as an either-or kind of argument, placing us in an alternative intellectual landscape, one where the real is neither stable not static nor subject to rigorous determination and measurement." Although the book does not offer close readings of a wide variety of U.S. ethnic magical realist texts, *Uncertain Mirrors* provides an important and evocative examination of the theoretical lenses through which magical realist works have been and can be viewed, addressing the "changing critical landscape, from Aristotelian mimesis to a vast array of critical '-isms' to finish with Adorno's concept of negative dialectics." The writers contend that "U.S. ethnic magical realist writing offers complex aesthetic artifacts that dialogue with and participate in distinctive cultural contexts."[39] In many ways, that dialogue and those "distinctive cultural contexts" are central concerns in *Magical American Jew* and the means by which the fictions and films featured in this study enter into conversation with other works of U.S. ethnic magical realism.

Moments of Magical Realism delves more deeply and directly into various U.S. ethnic literatures that incorporate "irruptions" of magic into their stories. As an anthology, the book offers a diverse array of critical perspectives, covering a rich selection of U.S. ethnic fiction. The editors, Lyn Di Iorio Sandín and Richard Perez, take mild issue with the liberal application of the magical realist label, suggesting that the mere existence of a magical or supernatural element does not make something a work of magical realism. They argue that "often such texts are erroneously categorized as 'magical realist' when, in fact, what they mainly display are momentary yet very significant *irruptions* of nonrealist tendencies into a realist text."[40] Since not all texts that incorporate supernatural elements are works of magical realism, it is fair to question classifications and note distinctions. Where I differ from Di Iorio Sandín and Perez is in how to categorize works that only incorporate brief moments of magic. If works are not fantasy or science fiction or a genre that exists on a singular, fantastical plane, rather than a hybrid plane, and the presence of the supernatural, no matter how brief, is pivotal to the story and treated as natural by the narrator—not explained away or acknowledged as abnormal—then the duration of magical incorporation should not matter. Furthermore, if an examination of how the magical realist mode is deployed—how and why it has been used—yield substantive and fruitful discussions about language, literature, film, culture, identity, or any number of features that the mode might help to highlight, then classification debates become more a sideline distraction than a worthy pursuit.

Fortunately, Di Iorio Sandín and Perez's suggestion of "erroneously categorized" texts does not seem intended to instigate an extended classification debate, but rather a means to introduce the notion of magical "irruptions," a word which is both meaningful and intentional. It not only conjures the momentary emergence of the magical, suggested in the title of their anthology, but also something violent and shocking. They specifically note that "the magical irruptions . . . help [the writers] decipher the traumatic traces and symbols that have been veiled from social and historical view." They identify the moments of magical realism as "an imaginative response to brutal social and historical marginalization."[41] Indeed, the works addressed in the anthology grapple with various aspects of brutality and violence—current and historical—but I would contend that magical realist incorporation can also be used to highlight, animate, and expose cultural anomalies, paradoxical identities, and liminal cultural positions that are not direct consequences of "brutal social and historical marginalization."

There is no shortage of violence, brutality, and marginalization in Jewish history, and many works of contemporary Jewish American fiction and film engage with such history. Caroline Rody suggests that the magical incorporation "in contemporary American Jewish post-Holocaust fiction joins the magical realism of the postcolonial world in articulating a traumatic, modern collision and fissure of realities."[42] And we see such aims at work in the novels that are examined most closely in Rody's essay, Joseph Skibell's *A Blessing on the Moon* and Jonathan Safran Foer's *Everything Is Illuminated*, as well as in the stories by Ozick and Bukiet that are analyzed in *Magical American Jew*. However, I see the use of the magical realist mode in contemporary Jewish American fiction and film as enabling a fuller, more complex depiction of an enigmatic difference; an opportunity to portray and examine the self-conscious excesses, slippery ethnic signifiers, and other aspects of difference that exist on the margins of the mainstream, but are not always "rendered ghostly by violent and systemic exclusions."[43]

In terms of cultural characteristics—something with which *Magical American Jew* is directly engaged—U.S. ethnic cultures and literatures, quite obviously, contain significant similarities and differences; the particular ways that the magical realist mode has been used to highlight the idiosyncrasies and commonalities of individuals and groups, enables writers, filmmakers, readers, and viewers to consider themselves and each other from wider, richer vantage points. Magical realism helps us see and consider what might otherwise be buried or blurred. Dean Franco writes of how "popular U.S. history assimilates the histories of ethnic groups into a single history, often divesting plural histories of their particularity."[44] The myth of the "melting pot" encapsulates this mythical singularity. However, despite the difficulty of expressing one's own cultural uniqueness, to say nothing of the ways in which cultures are similar to and different from other groups, U.S. ethnic artists have deployed innovative approaches—magical realist and postmodern techniques being uniquely potent—to expose the important ways that individuals and groups are comparable and distinct. Yet the challenge persists, and comparisons among cultural groups and the methods that artists have used to portray the various complexities of those groups can help both artists and their audiences imagine, comprehend, and articulate some of the defining positions and characteristics of particular cultural identities.

In a 2005 interview with Åse Nygren, published in *MELUS*, Sherman Alexie addresses the challenge of portraying Native American identities, suggesting the "strongest parallel . . . has always been the Jewish people and the Holocaust." According to Alexie, both Jewish Americans and Native Americans have identities that are linked to histories of pain.[45]

While there are many differences between Native American and Jewish American cultures, Alexie's claim enables us to consider the important ways that cultural identities overlap and how they are understood by those inside and outside of those cultures. For the purposes of *Magical American Jew* and a consideration of how the magical realist mode can be used to examine U.S. ethnic identities and literatures, Alexie is a pertinent author to consider. Not only a talented and prolific writer, but Alexie has used magical realist techniques to illustrate the collective memories and cultural impacts of history that have influenced the realities and perceptions of contemporary Native American identities.

In Alexie's novel *Flight,* for example, the narrator and central character—a boy named Michael who refers to himself as Zits until the very last page—embodies various individuals throughout history. These magical embodiments expose him to differing perspectives, realities, and impossibilities, enabling him to gain a clearer sense of self, in his case as a Native American and Irish American teenager who is victim of profoundly unfortunate familial circumstances, as well as his own self-contempt and a poorly implemented foster care system.[46] Initial consideration of the magical realist role in the novel might start with three basic questions: What does the magical realist mode make possible in Alexie's *Flight*? How is the magical in conversation with the real?[47] In what ways are the magical realist elements in *Flight* comparable to works of magical realism by other U.S. ethnic authors or, for the purposes of this study, with other works of contemporary Jewish American magical realism?

Although a true examination of the questions raised above would require comprehensive analyses, we can begin to sketch out some general responses here. For example, the magical elements in *Flight* allow the central character to inhabit the bodies of various figures throughout history—each pivotal to his own conceptions of the present—providing him with more enlightened personal, national, and cultural perspectives. The magical components work in conjunction with the more realistic displacement that the narrator experiences as a child who has "lived in twenty different foster homes and attended twenty-two different schools,"[48] emphasizing his lack of home and perceived lack of citizenship and identity. Although the magical realism is incorporated differently, we see comparable concerns played out in Melvin Jules Bukiet's "The Library of Moloch" discussed in chapter 3. In this case, the protagonist, Dr. Arthur Ricardo, is not embodying different individuals in a magical sense, but losing himself and trying to find himself in the testimonies of witnesses to historical atrocities and is comparably self-destructive in his effort to locate a more concrete sense of cultural and personal identity. It's *as if* the pressures to claim a definitive identity are fueling and igniting his obsession.

Part of what *Magical American Jew* is arguing is that when the natural and supernatural coexist—as they do in magical realism—a unique, hybrid space opens up, enabling cogent representations and portrayals of the dichotomies of ethnic identities. Concentrating on ethnicity and magical realism provides the opportunity to consider the diverse, multicultural composition of the United States, while examining the boundaries of fiction, film, or any genre that uses magical realism to illustrate cultural circumstances and concerns. Fortunately, there are many examples of U.S. ethnic artists who have deployed the magical realist mode, and there are a few sustained critical sources—*Uncertain Mirrors* and *Moments of Magical Realism* most notably—that provide avenues into thinking about the significance of the mode in regard to understanding U.S. ethnic identities.

Magical American Jew does not examine an exhaustive list of Jewish American magical realist sources, but aims to provide substantive analyses of select works that reveal aspects of the enigmatic difference that shapes contemporary Jewish American identity. The central chapters of this book are framed by discussions of Woody Allen's *Annie Hall* and Sarah Silverman's *Jesus Is Magic,* films that encapsulate particular, Jewish American types that have embedded themselves into the cultural consciousness: the Jewish American neurotic and the Jewish American narcissist. Both real and fabricated, these constructs emerge from and shed light on the enigmatic difference discussed in *Magical American Jew;* both works illustrate excess, circulate and satirize stereotypes, and inform national and self-perceptions in a sweeping way. Closing with a discussion of *Jesus Is Magic* puts the increasingly slippery terrain on which Jewish American identity stands on full display. As demonstrated in this final body chapter, Silverman uses that shifting identity for her own convenience. She is able to claim her place inside and outside the mainstream of American culture—the ultimate "insider-outsider"—doing so with the "sleight of identity" discussed by Daniel Itzkovitz. However, as much as she tries to use her ambiguous identity to her advantage, she will always be Jewish—as with Kafka and all Jews, it is an "ineluctable fact of existence"—and as a result, will always face reminders of difference, some more subtle than others. It is the portrayals of difference, and the ways in which the magical realist mode helps to illustrate that difference, that make the fictions and films featured in this book, and many outside of this discussion, worthy of our reflection and discussion.

NOTES

1. David Biale, *Cultures of the Jews: A New History,* ed. David Biale (New York: Schocken Books, 2002), 726.

2. Vincent Brook, *You Should See Yourself: Jewish Identity in Postmodern American Culture,* ed. Vincent Brook (New Brunswick: Rutgers UP, 2006), 6.

3. Walter H. Sokel, "Kafka as a Jew," *New Literary History* 30.4, Case Studies (Autumn, 1999): 837–53, 845.

4. Arnold J. Band, "Kafka: The Margins of Assimilation," *Modern Judaism* 8.2 (May 1988): 139–55, 139.

5. Franz Kafka, *Dearest Father*, trans. Hannah and Richard Stokes (London: Oneworld Classics, 2008), 56–57.

6. Band, "Kafka: The Margins of Assimilation," 141–42.

7. Sokel, "Kafka as a Jew," 837.

8. Band, "Kafka: The Margins of Assimilation," 143.

9. Ibid.

10. Franz Kafka, *Letters to Friends, Family, and Editors*, trans. Richard and Clara Winston (New York: Schocken Books, 1977), 288–89.

11. Ibid., 289.

12. Sokel, "Kafka as a Jew," 849.

13. Franz Kafka, *The Complete Stories*, ed. Nahum N. Glatzer (New York: Schocken Books, 1971), 250.

14. Homi K. Bhabha, *The Location of Culture* (New York: Routledge Classics, 2004), 127, 128, 131.

15. Sokel, "Kafka as a Jew," 838.

16. Woody Allen, *Annie Hall*, DVD, dir. Woody Allen, Metro-Goldwyn-Mayer Studios Inc., 1977.

17. Caroline Rody, "Jewish Post-Holocaust Fiction and the Magical Realist Turn," in *Moments of Magical Realism in U.S. Ethnic Literatures*, ed. Lyn Di Iorio Sandín and Richard Perez (New York: Palgrave Macmillan, 2012), 39–63, 42.

18. Daniel M. Jaffe, *With Signs and Wonders: An International Anthology of Jewish Fabulist Fiction*, ed. Daniel M. Jaffe (Montpelier, VT: Invisible Cities Press, 2001), xiii.

19. Howard Schwartz, *Gabriel's Palace: Jewish Mystical Tales* (Oxford: Oxford University Press, 1993), 3–4.

20. Cynthia Ozick, "Levitation," in *Levitation: Five Fictions* (New York: E.P. Dutton, Inc., 1983), 3–20, Steve Stern, "The Tale of a Kite," in *The Wedding Jester* (Saint Paul: Graywolf, 1999), 3–20, Sarah Silverman, *Sarah Silverman: Jesus Is Magic*, DVD, dir. Liam Lynch, Roadside Attractions, 2006.

21. Schwartz, *Gabriel's Palace*, 18.

22. Ibid.

23. Nathan Englander, "The Gilgul of Park Avenue," in *For the Relief of Unbearable Urges* (New York: Vintage Books, 1999): 109–37.

24. Schwartz, *Gabriel's Palace*, 9.

25. Melvin Jules Bukiet, "The Library of Moloch," in *While the Messiah Tarries* (New York: Harcourt Brace, 1995), 184–97.

26. Jaffe, *With Signs and Wonders*, xx.

27. Ibid., xx–xxi.

28. Daniel Itzkovitz, "They All Are Jews," in *You Should See Yourself: Jewish Identity in Postmodern American Culture*, ed. Vincent Brook (New Brunswick: Rutgers UP, 2006): 230–51, 239–40.

29. Rody, "Jewish Post-Holocaust Fiction," 42–43.

30. Tracy Mishkin, "Magical Realism in the Short Fiction of Isaac Bashevis Singer," *Studies in American Jewish Literature (1981–)*, Vol. 22, The Emerging Landscape: Tradition and Innovation (2003): 1–10, 3.

31. Rody, "Jewish Post-Holocaust Fiction," 44–45.

32. Bernard Malamud, "The Jewbird," in *Idiots First* (New York: Farrar Straus & Giroux, 1963), 101–14.

33. See Eileen H. Watts's "Jewish Self-Hatred in Malamud's 'The Jewbird,'" *MELUS* 21.2, Varieties of Ethnic Criticism (Summer, 1996): 157–63.

34. John Maher, "EXCLUSIVE: Steve Stern on *The Pinch*, Pogroms, Enclaves, and 'Yiddishkeit Lite,'" *Outcryer*, June 2, 2015, http://www.outcryer.com/daily/steve-stern-the-pinch-interview-yiddishkeit-lite/.

35. Julian Levinson, *Exiles on Main Street: Jewish American Writers and American Literary Culture* (Bloomington: Indiana UP, 2008), 189.

36. Andrew Furman, *Contemporary Jewish American Writers and the Multicultural Dilemma: Return of the Exiled* (Syracuse: Syracuse UP, 2000), 4.

37. Mark Athitakis, "The Otherworldly Malamud," National Endowment for the Humanities, March/April 2014, www.neh.gov.

38. Philip Roth, *The Counterlife* (New York: Penguin, 1986).

39. Jesús Benito, Ana Mª Manzanas, and Begoña Simal, *Uncertain Mirrors: Magical Realisms in US Ethnic Literatures* (Amsterdam: Rodopi, 2009), 3–4.

40. Lyn Di Iorio Sandín and Richard Perez, *Moments of Magical Realism in U.S. Ethnic Literatures*, ed. Lyn Di Iorio Sandín and Richard Perez (New York: Palgrave Macmillan, 2012), 3.

41. Ibid., 3–4.

42. Rody, "Jewish Post-Holocaust Fiction," 56.

43. Sandín and Perez, *Moments of Magical Realism*, 4.

44. Dean Franco, *Ethnic American Literature: Comparing Chicano, Jewish, and African American Writing* (Charlottesville: University of Virginia Press, 2006), 31.

45. Åse Nygren, "A World of Story Smoke: A Conversation with Sherman Alexie," *MELUS* 30.4 (Winter 2005): 149–69, 157.

46. Sherman Alexie, *Flight* (New York: Black Cat, 2007).

47. Caroline Rody raises a similar question, citing Christopher Warnes's essay "Naturalizing the Supernatural: Faith, Irreverence, and Magical Realism," from *Literature Compass* 2 (2005): 1–16.

48. Alexie, *Flight*, 7.

Bibliography

Aarons, Victoria. "The Outsider Within: Women in Contemporary Jewish-American Fiction." *Contemporary Literature* 28.3 (1987): 378–93.

Ahmed, Sara. "Shame Before Others." In *The Cultural Politics of Emotion*. Edinburgh: Edinburgh UP, 2004, 101–21.

Alexie, Sherman. *Flight*. New York: Black Cat, 2007.

Allen, Woody. *Annie Hall*. Directed by Woody Allen. Metro-Goldwyn-Mayer Studios Inc., 1977.

———. *Hannah and Her Sisters*. Directed by Woody Allen. Orion Pictures Corporation, 1986.

Anderson, Sam. "Irony Maiden: How Sarah Silverman Is Raping American Comedy." *Slate.com*. Slate. 15 Nov. 2005. Web. 29 June 2009.

Antler, Joyce. *You Never Call! You Never Write!: A History of the Jewish Mother*. Oxford: OUP, 2007.

Athitakis, Mark. "The Otherworldly Malamud," National Endowment for the Humanities, March/April 2014, www.neh.gov.

Azlant, Edward. "Lenny Bruce Again: 'Gestapo? You asshole, I'm the mailman!'" *Studies in American Humor* 15 (2007): 75–99.

Band, Arnold J. "Kafka: The Margins of Assimilation." *Modern Judaism* 8.2 (May 1988): 139–55.

Banta, Marta. "Of What Language, Pray, Is 'The American Mind'?" In *Jewish in America*. Edited by Sara Blair and Jonathan Freedman. Ann Arbor: UMP, 2004. 48–57.

Baumeister, Roy F., and Kathleen D. Vohs. "Narcissism as Addiction to Esteem." *Psychological Inquiry* 12.4 (2001): 206–10.

Bender, Aimee. "Dreaming in Polish." In *The Girl in the Flammable Skirt*. New York: Anchor, 1999.

Benito, Jesús, Ana Ma Manzanas, and Begoña Simal. *Uncertain Mirrors: Magical Realisms in U.S. Ethnic Literatures*. Amsterdam: Rodopi, 2009.

Bernstein, Richard. "Being Nice or Rotten in Writing." *New York Times* October 3, 1989, C15, C21.

Bhabha, Homi K. *The Location of Culture*. New York: Routledge Classics, 2004.

Bial, Henry. *Acting Jewish: Negotiating Ethnicity on the American Stage and Screen*. Ann Arbor: U Michigan P, 2005.

Biale, David. "The Melting Pot and Beyond: Jews and the Politics of American Identity." In *Insider/Outsider: American Jews and Multiculturalism*. Edited by David Biale, Michael Galchinsky, and Susannah Heschel. Berkeley: UCP, 1998. 17–33.

———. *Cultures of the Jews: A New History*. Edited by David Biale, New York: Schocken Books, 2002.

Biale, David, Michael Galchinsky and Susannah Heschel. "Introduction: The Dialectic of Jewish Enlightenment." In *Insider/Outsider: American Jews and Multiculturalism*. Edited by David Biale, Michael Galchinsky, and Susannah Heschel. Berkeley: UCP, 1998. 1–13.

Blair, Sara, and Jonathan Freedman. *Jewish in America*. Edited by Sara Blair and Jonathan Freedman. Ann Arbor: UMP, 2004.

Bloom, James D. *Gravity Fails: The Comic Jewish Shaping of Modern America*. Westport, CT: Praeger, 2003.

Boldtype. "An Interview with Nathan Englander." RandomHouse.com. April 1, 2010.

Boskin, Joseph. "The Ethics of Laughter and Humor." In *The Philosophy of Laughter and Humor*. Edited by John Morreall. Albany: SUNY Press, 1987.

———. *Rebellious Laughter: People's Humor in American Culture*. Syracuse: Syracuse UP, 1997.

Boskin, Joseph, and Joseph Dorinson. "Ethnic Humor: Subversion and Survival." *American Quarterly* 37.1 (1985): 81–97.

Brook, Vincent. *You Should See Yourself: Jewish Identity in Postmodern American Culture*. Edited by Vincent Brook. New Brunswick: Rutgers UP, 2006.

Brown, Wendy. *Politics Out of History*. Princeton: Princeton UP, 2001.

Bruce, Lenny. *How to Talk Dirty and Influence People*. New York: Fireside, 1963.

———. *The Lenny Bruce Performance Film*. Directed by John Magnuson. John Magnuson Associates, 1967. DVD.

Bukiet, Melvin Jules. *While the Messiah Tarries*. New York: Harcourt Brace, 1995.

Butler, Judith. *Gender Trouble: Feminism and the Subversion of Identity*. New York: Routledge, 1990.

Caruth, Cathy. *Unclaimed Experience: Trauma, Narrative, and History*. Baltimore: Johns Hopkins UP, 1996.

Castillo, Ana. *So Far from God*. New York: W. W. Norton, 1993.

Chalom, Adam. "Beyond *Apikorsut*: A Judaism for Secular Jews." In *Religion or Ethnicity?:*

Jewish Identities in Evolution. Edited by Zvi Gitelman. New Brunswick: Rutgers UP, 2009. 286–302.

Chanady, Amaryll Beatrice. *Magical Realism and the Fantastic: Resolved Versus Unresolved Antinomy*. New York: Garland, 1985.

Chocano, Carina. "Silverman Will Make You Cringe while Making You Laugh." *Los Angeles Times*. November 11, 2005: E6.

Cohen, Sacha Baron, and Anthony Hines. *Borat: Cultural Learnings of America for Make Benefit Glorious Nation of Kazakhstan*. Directed by Larry Charles. Twentieth Century Fox, 2006.

Conners, C. Keith. "Symptom Patterns in Hyperkinetic, Neurotic, and Normal Children." *Child Development* 41.3 (1970): 667–82.

Corrigan, Timothy, and Patricia White, *The Film Experience: An Introduction*. 3rd ed. Boston: Bedford/St. Martin's, 2012.

Cutter, Martha J. *Lost & Found in Translation: Contemporary Ethnic American Writing and the Politics of Language Diversity*. Chapel Hill: UNC Press, 2005.

Davis, Murray. "Wit's Weapons: Incongruity and Ambiguity." In *Laughing Matters*. Edited by Marvin Diogenes. New York: Pearson, 2009. 13–36.

Delbaere-Garant, Jeanne. "Psychic Realism, Mythic Realism, Grotesque Realism: Variations on Magic Realism in Contemporary Literature in English." In *Magical Realism: Theory, History, Community*. Edited by Lois Parkinson Zamora and Wendy B. Faris. Durham, NC: Duke UP, 1995. 249–66.

Deleuze, Gilles, and Leopold von Sacher-Masoch. *Masochism: Coldness and Cruelty & Venus in Furs*. Translated by Jean McNeil. New York: Zone Books, 1991.

Douglas, Susan J. "The Turn Within: The Irony of Technology in a Globalized World." *American Quarterly* 58.3 (2006): 619–38.

Du Bois, W.E.B. *The Souls of Black Folk*. New York: Simon & Schuster, 2005.

Dundes, Alan. "The J.A.P. and the J.A.M. in American Jokelore." *The Journal of American Folklore* 98.390 (1985): 456–75.

Englander, Nathan. *For the Relief of Unbearable Urges*. New York: Vintage Books, 1999.

Epstein, Lawrence. *The Haunted Smile: the Story of Jewish Comedians in America*. New York: PublicAffairs, 2001.

Farmer, David Hugh. *The Oxford Dictionary of Saints*. 4th ed. Oxford: OUP, 1997.

Flores, Angel. "Magical Realism in Spanish American Fiction." In *Magical Realism: Theory, History, Community*. Edited by Lois Parkinson Zamora and Wendy B. Faris. Durham, NC: Duke UP, 1995. 109–18.

Fortunoff Video Archive for Holocaust Testimonies. May 2005. http://www.library. yale.edu/testimonies/.

Foster, Thomas. *The Souls of Cyberfolk: Posthumanism as Vernacular Theory*. Minneapolis: UMP, 2005.

Franco, Dean. *Ethnic American Literature: Comparing Chicano, Jewish, and African American Writing*. Charlottesville: UVP, 2006.

———. "Re-Placing the Border in Ethnic Literature." *Cultural Critique* 50 (2002): 104–34.

Freedman, Jonathan. *The Temple of Culture: Assimilation and Anti-Semitism in Literary Anglo America*. Oxford: OUP, 2000.

Freud, Sigmund. *Beyond the Pleasure Principle*. Translated by James Strachey. New York: Norton, 1961.

———. *Totem and Taboo*. Translated by James Strachey. New York: Norton, 1950.

———. "Wit and the Various Forms of the Comic." In *The Basic Writings of Sigmund Freud*. New York: The Modern Library, 1938.

Friedlander, Saul. "Trauma, Memory, and Transference." In *Holocaust Remembrance: The Shapes of Memory*. Edited by Geoffrey H. Hartman. Oxford: Blackwell, 1994. 252–63.

Furman, Andrew. *Contemporary Jewish American Writers and the Multicultural Dilemma: Return of the Exiled*. Syracuse: Syracuse UP, 2000.

Gans, Herbert J. "Symbolic Ethnicity: The Future of Ethnic Groups and Cultures in America." *Ethnic and Racial Studies* 2 (1979): 1–20.

Genette, Gérard. *Figures of Literary Discourse*. Translated by Alan Sheridan. New York: Columbia UP, 1982.

Gilman, Sander. *The Jew's Body*. New York: Routledge, 1991.

Gitelman, Zvi. "Conclusion: The Nature and Viability of Jewish Religious and Secular Identities." In *Religion or Ethnicity?: Jewish Identities in Evolution*. Edited by Zvi Gitelman. New Brunswick: Rutgers UP, 2009. 303–22.

Goffman, Erving. *Frame Analysis: An Essay on the Organization of Experience*. Cambridge: Harvard UP, 1974.

Goldscheider, Calvin. "Judaism, Community, and Jewish Culture in American Life: Continuities and Transformations." In *Religion or Ethnicity?: Jewish Identities in Evolution*. Edited by Zvi Gitelman. New Brunswick: Rutgers UP, 2009. 267–85.

Goodyear, Dana. "Quiet Depravity: The Demure Outrages of a Standup Comic." *The New Yorker*, October 24, 2005: 50–55.

Halberstam, Judith, and Ira Livingston, eds. *Posthuman Bodies*. Bloomington: Indiana UP, 1995.

Hansen, Marcus Lee. "The Problem of the Third Generation Immigrant." In *American Immigrants and Their Generations: Studies and Commentaries on the Hansen Thesis after Fifty Years*. Edited by Dag Blanck and Peter Kivisto. Urbana: U Illinois P, 1990.

Hartman, Geoffrey H. *The Longest Shadow*. Bloomington: Indiana UP, 1996.

Hass, Aaron. "Survivor Guilt in Holocaust Survivors and Their Children." In *A Global Perspective on Working with Holocaust Survivors and the Second Generation*. Edited by John Lemberger, 163–83. July 1995. http://www.holocaust-trc.org/glbsurv.htm.

Hayles, N. Katherine. *How We Became Posthuman*. Chicago: University of Chicago Press, 1999.

Howe, Irving. "Introduction." In *Jewish American Stories*. Edited by Irving Howe. New York: Mentor, 1977.

Hungerford, Amy. "Memorizing Memory." In *Literature of the Holocaust*. Edited by Harold Bloom. Philadelphia: Chelsea House Publishers, 2004. 257–87.

Hutcheon, Linda. "The Politics of Postmodernism: Parody and History." *Cultural Critique* 5 (1986–1987): 179–207.

Itzkovitz, Daniel. "They All Are Jews." In *You Should See Yourself: Jewish Identity in Postmodern American Culture*. Edited by Vincent Brook. New Brunswick: Rutgers UP, 2006. 230–51.

Jacobson, Matthew Frye. *Special Sorrows: The Diasporic Imagination of Irish, Polish, and Jewish Immigrants in the United States.* Berkeley: UCP, 2002.

Jaffe, Daniel M. *With Signs and Wonders: An International Anthology of Jewish Fabulist Fiction.* Edited by Daniel M. Jaffe. Montpelier: Invisible Cities Press, 2001.

Jameson, Frederic. "On Magic Realism in Film." *Critical Inquiry* 12.2 (1986): 301–25.

Johnston, Ruth D. "Joke-Work: The Construction of Jewish Postmodern Identity in Contemporary Theory and American Film." In *You Should See Yourself: Jewish Identity in Postmodern American Culture.* Edited by Vincent Brook. New Brunswick: Rutgers UP, 2006. 207–29.

Kafka, Franz. *The Complete Stories.* Edited by Nahum N. Glatzer. New York: Schocken Books, 1971.

———. *Dearest Father.* Translated by Hannah and Richard Stokes. London: Oneworld Classics, 2008.

———. *Letters to Friends, Family, and Editors.* Translated by Richard and Clara Winston. New York: Schocken Books, 1977.

Kaplan, Dana Evan. *Contemporary American Judaism: Transformation and Renewal.* New York: Columbia UP, 2009.

Kaufman, Debra Renee. "The Place of Judaism in American Jewish Identity." In *The Cambridge Companion to American Judaism.* Edited by Dana Evan Kaplan. Cambridge: Cambridge UP, 2005. 169–85.

Kestner, Joseph A. *The Spatiality of the Novel.* Detroit: Wayne State UP, 1978.

Klaff, Vivian. "Defining American Jewry from Religious and Ethnic Perspectives: The Transitions to Greater Heterogeneity." *Sociology of Religion* 67.4 (2006): 415–38.

Kristol, Irving. "Is Jewish Humor Dead?" In *Midcentury.* Edited by H. Ribalow. New York: Beechurst, 1955. 428–37.

LaCapra, Dominick. *Representing the Holocaust: History, Theory, Trauma.* Ithaca: Cornell UP, 1994.

Langer, Lawrence L. *Holocaust Testimonies: The Ruins of Memory.* New Haven: Yale UP, 1991.

Laub, Dori, and Shoshana Felman. *Testimony: Crises of Witnessing in Literature, Psychoanalysis, and History.* New York: Routledge, 1992.

Leveen, Lois. "Only When I Laugh: Textual Dynamics of Ethnic Humor." *MELUS* 21.4 (1996): 29–55.

Levine, Mordecai H. "Philip Roth and American Judaism." *CLA Journal* 14 (December 1970): 163–70.

Levinson, Julian. *Exiles on Main Street: Jewish American Writers and American Literary Culture.* Bloomington: Indiana UP, 2008.

Levitt, Laura. "Impossible Assimilations, American Liberalism, and Jewish Difference: Revisiting Jewish Secularism." *American Quarterly* 59.3 (2007): 807–32.

Lowe, John. "Theories of Ethnic Humor: How to Enter, Laughing." *American Quarterly* 38.3 (1986): 439–60.

Lowerison, Jean. "*Sarah Silverman: Jesus Is Magic*: Not Funny." San Diego Metropolitan. SanDiegoMetro.com. August 20, 2008. http://www.sandiegometro.com/reel/index.php?reelID=887.

MacKendrick, Karmen. *Counterpleasures.* Albany: SUNY Press, 1999.

Maguire, James H. "Fictions of the West." In *The Columbia History of the American Novel.* Ed. Emory Elliott. New York: Columbia UP, 1991. 437–64.

Maher, John. "EXCLUSIVE: Steve Stern on *The Pinch*, Pogroms, Enclaves, and 'Yiddishkeit Lite.'" *Outcryer*, June 2, 2015. http://www.outcryer.com/daily/steve-stern-the-pinch-interview-yiddishkeit-lite/.

Malamud, Bernard. "The Jewbird." In *Idiots First.* New York: Farrar Straus & Giroux, 1963. 101–14.

Márquez, Gabriel García. *One Hundred Years of Solitude.* Translated by Gregory Rabassa. New York: Perennial Classics, 1998.

Mayer, Egon. "A Demographic Revolution in American Jewry." In *American Jewish Identity Politics*. Edited by Deborah Dash Moore. Ann Arbor: U Michigan P, 2008. 267–99.

———. "From an External to an Internal Agenda." In *The Americanization of the Jews*. Edited by Robert M. Seltzer and Norman J. Cohen. New York: NYUP, 1995. 432.

McLuhan, Marshall. *Understanding Media: The Extensions of Man*. New York: Signet, 1964.

Michaels, Walter Benn. "'You Who Was Never There': Slavery and the New Historicism—Deconstruction and the Holocaust." In *The Americanization of the Holocaust*. Edited by Hilene Flanzbaum. Baltimore: Johns Hopkins UP, 1999. 181–97.

Mishkin, Tracy. "Magical Realism in the Short Fiction of Isaac Bashevis Singer." *Studies in American Jewish Literature (1981–)*. Vol. 22: *The Emerging Landscape: Tradition and Innovation* (2003): 1–10.

Moore, Deborah Dash. "Introduction." In *American Jewish Identity Politics*. Edited by Deborah Dash Moore. Ann Arbor: U Michigan P, 2008.

Moraru, Christian. *Memorious Discourse: Reprise and Representation in Postmodernism*. Madison: Fairleigh Dickinson UP, 2005.

Morf, Carolyn C., and Frederick Rhodewalt. "Unraveling the Paradoxes of Narcissism: A Dynamic Self-Regulatory Processing Model." *Psychological Inquiry* 12.4 (2001): 177–96.

Morgan, Michael L. *Beyond Auschwitz: Post-Holocaust Jewish Thought in America*. Oxford: OUP, 2001.

Morrison, Andrew. "The Eye Turned Inward: Shame and the Self." In *The Many Faces of Shame*. Edited by Donald L. Nathanson. New York: Guilford P, 1987. 271–91.

Nacht, Sacha. "*Le Masochisme*, Introduction." In *Essential Papers on Masochism*. Edited by Margaret Ann Fitzpatrick Hanly. New York: NYUP, 1995. 18–34.

Nathanson, Donald L. "A Timetable for Shame." In *The Many Faces of Shame*. Edited by Donald L. Nathanson. New York: Guilford Press, 1987. 1–63.

Novick, Peter. *The Holocaust in American Life*. New York: Mariner, 2000.

Nygren, Åse. "A World of Story Smoke: A Conversation with Sherman Alexie." *MELUS* 30.4 (Winter, 2005): 149–69.

Ophüls, Marcel. *The Sorrow and the Pity*. Directed by Marcel Ophüls. Cinema 5 Distributing, 1972.

Ozick, Cynthia. "Levitation." In *Levitation: Five Fictions*. New York: E.P. Dutton, 1983.

———. "Toward a New Yiddish: Note." In *Art & Ardor: Essays by Cynthia Ozick*. New York: Knopf, 1985, 152.

———. "Tradition and (or Versus) the Jewish Writer." In *Who We Are: On Being (and Not Being) a Jewish American Writer*. Edited by Derek Rubin. New York: Schocken, 2005. 19–23.

Porter, Laurence M. "Real Dreams, Literary Dreams, and the Fantastic in Literature." In *The Dream and the Text: Essays on Literature and Language*. Edited by Carol Schreier Rupprecht. Albany: SUNY Press, 1993. 32–47.

Provenza, Paul. Director. *The Aristocrats*. DVD. Mighty Cheese Productions, 2005.

Rabinowitz, Paula. "Soft Fictions and Intimate Documents: Can Feminism Be Posthuman?" In *Posthuman Bodies*. Edited by Judith Halberstam and Ira Livingston. Bloomington: Indiana UP, 1995.

Rand, Naomi R. *Silko, Morrison, and Roth: Studies in Survival*. New York: Peter Lang, 1999.

Ravits, Martha A. "The Jewish Mother: Comedy and Controversy in American Popular Culture." *MELUS* 25.1 (2000): 3–31.

Rebhun, Uzi. "Jewish Identity in America: Structural Analyses of Attitudes and Behaviors." *Review of Religious Research* 46.1 (2004): 43–63.

Reich, Annie. "Pathological Forms of Self-Esteem Regulation." In *Essential Papers on Narcissism*. Edited by Andrew P. Morrison, M.D. New York: NYUP, 1986.

Reik, Theodor. *Masochism in Modern Man*. New York: Grove, 1941.

Reuben, Steven Carr. *There's An Easter Egg on Your Seder Plate: Surviving Your Child's Interfaith Marriage*. Westport, CT: Praeger, 2008.

Rody, Caroline. "Jewish Post-Holocaust Fiction and the Magical Realist Turn." In *Moments of Magical Realism in U.S. Ethnic Literatures*. Edited by Lyn Di Iorio Sandín and Richard Perez. New York: Palgrave Macmillan, 2012. 39–63.

Roth, Philip. *The Counterlife*. New York: Penguin, 1986.

———. *Goodbye Columbus*. New York: Vintage, 1987.

———. *Portnoy's Complaint*. New York: Random House, 2002.

Royal, Derek Parker. "Tugging at Jewish Weeds: An Interview with Steve Stern." *MELUS* 32.1 (2007): 139–61.

Sandín, Lyn Di Iorio and Richard Perez, eds. *Moments of Magical Realism in U.S. Ethnic Literatures*. New York: Palgrave Macmillan, 2012.

Sanyal, Debarati. "A Soccer Match in Auschwitz: Passing Culpability in Holocaust Criticism." *Representations* 79 (2002): 1–27.

"Sarah Silverman: Jesus Is Magic (2005)." Rotten Tomatoes. IGN Entertainment. August 30, 2008. http://www.rottentomatoes.com/m/sarah_silverman_jesus_is_magic/.

Schaeffer, Neil. "Lenny Bruce and Extreme Comedy." In *The Art of Laughter*. New York: Columbia UP, 1981.

———. "Reply to George A. Test." *College English* 38.5 (January 1977): 519–21.

Schroeder, Shannin. *Rediscovering Magical Realism in the Americas*. Westport, CT: Praeger, 2004.

Schwartz, Howard. *Gabriel's Palace: Jewish Mystical Tales*. Oxford: Oxford University Press, 1993.

Sellman, Tamara Kaye. "Jewish Magical Realism: Writing to Tell the Tale." *Margin*, April 20, 2006. http://www.angelfire.com/wa2/margin/nonficSellmanJewishMR.html.

Silverman, Kaja. "Masochism and Male Subjectivity." In *Male Subjectivity at the Margins*. New York: Routledge, 1992.

Silverman, Sarah. *Sarah Silverman: Jesus Is Magic*. Directed by Liam Lynch. Roadside Attractions, 2006.

Singer, Isaac Bashevis. *The Collected Stories of Isaac Bashevis Singer*. New York: Farrar, Straus, and Giroux, 1982.

Smirnoff, Victor N. "The Masochistic Contract." In *Essential Papers on Masochism*. Edited by Margaret Ann Fitzpatrick Hanly. New York: NYUP, 1995. 62–73.

Sobchack, Vivian. *Carnal Thoughts: Embodiment and Moving Image Culture*. Berkeley: UCP, 2004.

Sokel, Walter H. "Kafka as a Jew." *New Literary History* 30.4, Case Studies (Autumn 1999): 837–53.

Sollors, Werner. *Beyond Ethnicity: Consent and Descent in American Culture*. Oxford: OUP, 1986.

Stam, Robert. *Literature through Film: Realism, Magic, and the Art of Adaptation*. Malden: Blackwell, 2005.

Stern, Steve. *The Wedding Jester*. Saint Paul, MN: Graywolf, 1999.

Sturken, Marita, and Lisa Cartwright. *Practices of Looking: An Introduction to Visual Culture*. Oxford: OUP, 2001.

Tangney, June Price, and Ronda L. Dearing. *Shame and Guilt*. New York: Guilford Press, 2002.

Telushkin, Joseph. *Jewish Humor: What the Best Jewish Jokes Say about the Jews*. New York: Quill, 1998.

Test, George A. "On 'Lenny Bruce without Tears.'" *College English* 38.5 (1977): 517–19.

Thiem, Jon. "The Textualization of the Reader in Magical Realist Fiction." In *Magical Realism: Theory, History, Community*. Edited by Lois Parkinson Zamora and Wendy B. Faris. Durham, NC: Duke UP, 1995. 235–48.

Tomkins, Silvan. "Shame-Humiliation and Contempt-Disgust." In *Shame and Its Sisters: A Silvan Tomkins Reader*. Edited by Adam Frank, Eve Kosofsky Sedgwick, and Irving E. Alexander. Durham, NC: Duke UP, 1995. 133–78.

Walker, Steven F. "Magical Archetypes: Midlife Miracles in *The Satanic Verses*." In *Magical Realism: Theory, History, Community*. Edited by Lois Parkinson Zamora and Wendy B. Faris. Durham, NC: Duke UP, 1995. 347–70.

Weissman, Gary. *Fantasies of Witnessing: Postwar Efforts to Experience the Holocaust*. Ithaca: Cornell UP, 2004.

Westbrook, Bruce. "There Are No Miracles in Silverman's Stage Show." *The Houston Chronicle*. Chron.com, August 20, 2008.http://www.chron.com/disp/story.mpl/ent/movies/reviews/3503740.html.

Wiesel, Elie. "Trivializing the Holocaust: Semi-Fact and Semi-Fiction." *New York Times*, April 16, 1978: 2, 29.

Wilentz, Gay. *Healing Narratives: Women Writers Curing Cultural Dis-Ease*. New Brunswick: Rutgers UP, 2000.

Wilson, Rawdon. "The Metamorphoses of Fictional Space: Magical Realism." In *Magical Realism: Theory, History, Community*. Edited by Lois Parkinson Zamora and Wendy B. Faris. Durham, NC: Duke UP, 1995. 209–34.

Wirth-Nesher, Hana. *Call It English: The Languages of Jewish American Literature*. Princeton: Princeton UP, 2006.

Zamora, Lois Parkinson, and Wendy B. Faris. "Introduction: Daiquiri Birds and Flaubertian Parrot(ie)s." In *Magical Realism: Theory, History, Community*. Edited by Lois Parkinson Zamora and Wendy B. Faris. Durham: Duke UP, 1995. 1–11.

Index

Aarons, Victoria, 37
Ahmed, Sara, 38, 39, 42
Alexie, Sherman, 127–128
Allen, Woody, 125; *Annie Hall*, 6–7, 13–29, 40; *Hannah and Her Sisters*, 24
American identities, 93; Native American identities, 127–128. *See also* Jewish American identity
American Jewish Identity Politics (Moore), 1–2
American Jews. *See* Jewish Americans
Anderson, Sam, 94
Annie Hall: assimilation in, 26; enigma of difference of Jewish Americans in, 22, 29; Jewish American excess in, 13–14, 15–16, 18–19, 22, 24, 29, 30n7; Jewish American identity in, 18–19, 24–26, 29, 40; Jewish American magical realism in, 6–7, 13, 14, 15, 18–21, 23, 24, 25, 26, 29; Jewish American neurotic in, 14, 29, 30n7, 129; Jewish diaspora and, 16–17; jokes in, 16, 17, 30n16, 30n24; postmodernism in, 6–7, 13–14, 18, 21, 22–23, 26, 27–29; sexual fantasies in, 17–18, 30n26; *The Sorrow and the Pity* in, 15, 21, 24, 27, 28, 49n64
anti-Semitism, 63, 69n53, 82
Antler, Joyce, 34, 89n19, 112n32
The Aristocrats, 98–99
ascent stories, 120
assimilation: in *Annie Hall*, 26; Kafka and, 118–119; in "The Tale of a Kite," 75, 77, 82
Athitakis, Mark, 124
Azlant, Edward, 97

Band, Arnold J., 116
Baumeister, Roy F., 104
Bender, Aimee, 89n2

Benito, Jesús, 125–126
Benn Michaels, Walter, 52, 60
Bial, Henry, 2, 19, 24, 30n7
Biale, David, 29n1, 78, 115
bible, 119–120
Bloom, James D., 76, 80, 100–101
Boskin, Joseph, 103
Brook, Vincent, 115
Brown, Wendy, 62–64
Bruce, Lenny, 97–98, 103, 112n41
Bukiet, Melvin Jules, 8, 10n18, 51, 53–62, 64–67, 67n12–68n13, 121, 128
Butler, Judith, 19

Chalom, Adam, 88
Chanady, Amaryll Beatrice, 95, 110n7
Coen, Joel and Ethan, 125
Cohen, Sacha Baron, 98, 111n23
Coldness and Cruelty (Deleuze), 56
comedy: U.S. culture and, 107. *See also* humor; jokes; magical and comical modes; satire
communications technologies, 102–103, 104, 112n47
corporations, 97, 102
culture. *See* Jewish culture; U.S. culture

Dearing, Ronda L., 35, 36, 39
Delbaere-Garant, Jeanne, 3
Deleuze, Gilles, 56, 59, 60, 61
de Man, Paul, 68n13
Di Iorio Sandín, Lyn, 125, 126–127
Douglas, Susan, 102–103, 104–105, 107
"Dreaming in Polish" (Bender), 89n2
Dundes, Alan, 33–34, 112n32

"Eli, the Fanatic" (Roth), 82
Englander, Nathan: "The Gilgul of Park Avenue," 8, 10n16, 10n18, 71–76, 77–78, 79, 80, 81, 84, 87, 88,

121; Jewish American contemporary communities and, 80

enigma of difference, of Jewish Americans, 77; in *Annie Hall*, 22, 29; of contemporary Jewish Americans, 71, 74, 86; Holocaust, Jewish American identity and, 53, 62, 63, 67; in *Jesus Is Magic*, 93, 95–96, 103, 110; Jewish American culture and, 2, 8; Jewish American identity and, 53, 62, 63, 67, 79, 115; Jewish American literature and, 2, 8, 88; Jewish American magical realism and, 3, 4–5, 9, 88, 115, 122, 123, 127, 129; magical, comical modes and, 71, 80, 83, 88; overview, 2–3; religiosity, ethnicity and, 71, 79, 83, 88; shame and, 7–8, 33, 35. *See also* Jewish American difference

Epstein, Lawrence, 89n19, 112n36

ethnic humor, 107, 112n31. *See also* Jewish humor

ethnic identities: magical realism and dichotomies of, 3–4, 128–129. *See also* Jewish identity

ethnicity: in *Jesus Is Magic*, 100–101, 104, 106–107. *See also* religiosity, ethnicity and

excess: Jewish American excess, 13–14, 15–16, 18–19, 22, 24, 29, 29n4, 30n7; magical realism and, 14–15

Faris, Wendy B., 14–15, 61, 74

Felman, Shoshanah, 55, 66, 68n38

Flight (Alexie), 128

Fortunoff Video Archive for Holocaust Testimonies, 51–52, 68n13

Franco, Dean, 17, 36, 43–44

Freud, Sigmund, 14, 16, 108

Friedlander, Saul, 55

Furman, Andrew, 2, 6, 82–83, 89n3

"The Gilgul of Park Avenue" (Englander): ethnicity and religiosity in, 74, 75–76, 77, 79, 87; *gilgul* and, 121; Jewish American communities and, 74–75, 80, 87, 88; Jewish American difference in, 81; Jewish American identity and, 8, 71,

72, 74, 77–78, 79, 81, 84, 87, 88; Jewish American magical realism in, 8, 10n16, 10n18, 71, 72–76, 77, 84, 88; magical and comical modes in, 71, 74, 75–76, 84, 88; overview, 8, 71–72; religiosity and, 74, 75–76, 77–78, 79, 87

Goldscheider, Calvin, 74–75, 78–79, 85, 88

guilt: Holocaust and, 63; injury, identity and, 64; intermarriage and, 34–35; Jewish American mother stereotype and, 33–34; Jewish Americans and, 33–35; in "Levitation," 7; shame compared to, 7, 33, 35, 36, 38; trauma and, 63

Hartman, Geoffrey H., 52, 68n37

The Haunted Smile: the Story of Jewish Comedians in America (Epstein), 89n19, 112n36

Holocaust: guilt and, 63; "Levitation" and, 44, 46, 49n64; Ozick on, 41, 43; proprietorship of, 64; witnessing and, 43, 45, 48n54, 48n59, 54–55, 68n38. *See also* Jewish American identity, Holocaust and; *The Sorrow and the Pity*

Holocaust testimony: memory and, 7–8, 52, 60; witnessing and, 54–55, 68n38

Holocaust testimony, archiving: Fortunoff Video Archive for Holocaust Testimonies and, 51–52, 68n13; Jewish American identity and, 52; in "The Library of Moloch," 55, 56–60, 61–62, 64, 65, 66–67, 67n12–68n13; masochism and, 53, 55, 56–57, 61, 65, 66

humor: ethnic humor, 107, 112n31; during hard times in Jewish American culture, 17, 30n23–30n24; in *Jesus Is Magic*, 8–9, 108–110; naïve humor, 108; racism and, 108–110; social humor, 103. *See also* comedy; ethnic humor; jokes; magical and comical modes; satire

Hungerford, Amy, 68n37

Hutcheon, Linda, 14

identity: guilt and, 64; injury and, 63–64; marginalized identities and magical realist fiction, 4; social crimes and, 62–63; trauma and, 63. *See also* American identities; ethnic identities

injury: guilt and, 64; identity and, 63–64

Jacobson, Matthew Frye, 36
Jaffe, Daniel M., 119, 121–122
JAP. *See* Jewish American Princess
Jesus Is Magic, 111n12; ascension in, 120; critical reception of, 106, 113n58; enigma of difference of Jewish Americans in, 93, 95–96, 103, 110; ethnicity in, 100–101, 104, 106–107; humor in, 8–9, 108–110; Jewish American identity and, 9, 93, 129; Jewish American magical realism in, 95–96, 101–102, 103, 104, 105, 109, 110; Jewish American mother stereotype in, 101; Jewish American Princess stereotype in, 99–100, 106; Jewish identity in, 100–101; Jewish women stereotypes in, 102; media culture and, 93–94, 99, 101–103, 107–108; narcissistic fantasy in, 93–94, 96–97, 101–105, 110, 129; overview, 8–9, 94–95; pornography in, 102; racism within humor in, 108–110; satire of, 93, 96, 99–100, 101, 103, 106–110, 112n44; September 11th terrorist attack and, 97, 102, 103
"The Jewbird" (Malamud), 123–124
Jewish American communities, 88; as continuously changing, 78–79; Englander and, 80; "The Gilgul of Park Avenue" and, 74–75, 80, 87, 88; religiosity and ethnicity of, 85, 86, 87; Stern and, 80; "The Tale of a Kite" and, 87, 88
Jewish American culture, 1, 2, 115; acculturation and Jewish humor, 13, 29n1; enigma of difference of Jewish Americans and, 2, 8; humor during hard times in, 17, 30n23–30n24

Jewish American difference: in "The Gilgul of Park Avenue," 81; Jewish American identity, Holocaust and, 60; Jewish history and, 36; in "Levitation," 37, 51; shame and, 7, 46; in "The Tale of a Kite," 81–82. *See also* enigma of difference, of Jewish Americans
Jewish American excess, 13, 29n4; in *Annie Hall*, 13–14, 15–16, 18–19, 22, 24, 29, 30n7
Jewish American identity, 101; in *Annie Hall*, 18–19, 24–26, 29, 40; anti-Semitism and, 63, 69n53; as continuously changing, 78–79, 122; defining contemporary, 1–2; enigma of difference of Jewish Americans and, 53, 62, 63, 67, 79, 115; in "The Gilgul of Park Avenue," 8, 71, 72, 74, 77–78, 79, 81, 84, 87, 88; guilt in, 33, 35; interfaith marriage and, 78, 90n32; *Jesus Is Magic* and, 9, 93, 129; Jewish American magical realist films and, 6, 9; Jewish American magical realist short fiction and, 6, 9; Jewish American magical realist works and, 3, 5, 6, 122–123, 129; Jewish diaspora and, 36, 43, 47n20; in "Levitation," 7, 35–36, 38, 41; performance of, 18–19, 24; religiosity and ethnicity in, 71, 73–74, 77–79, 85, 87–88; shame and, 33, 35; social crime and, 63; in "The Tale of a Kite," 8, 71, 74, 76–77, 82–84, 85, 87, 88
Jewish American identity, Holocaust and, 63, 87; archiving Holocaust testimony and, 52; centrality of Holocaust in Jewish identity, 52–53, 62, 67n10; enigma of difference of Jewish Americans and, 53, 62, 63, 67; Jewish American difference and, 60; "The Library of Moloch" and, 8, 51, 53, 62, 64, 67, 67n12, 121; masochism of centralizing, 51; memory, testimony and, 7–8, 52, 60; Native American identities and, 127–128

Jewish American literature, 1, 2, 127; enigma of difference of Jewish Americans and, 2, 8, 88. *See also* Jewish American magical realist literature

Jewish American magical realism: in *Annie Hall,* 6–7, 13, 14, 15, 18–21, 23, 24, 25, 26, 29; enigma of difference of Jewish Americans and, 3, 4–5, 9, 88, 115, 122, 123, 127, 129; in "The Gilgul of Park Avenue," 8, 10n16, 10n18, 71, 72–76, 77, 84, 88; in *Jesus Is Magic,* 95–96, 101–102, 103, 104, 105, 109, 110; Jewish history and, 43; in "Levitation," 7, 10n18, 36, 37, 43, 44, 45–46; in "The Library of Moloch," 10n18, 51, 53, 58, 59, 61, 67, 128; in "The Tale of a Kite," 71, 72, 73–74, 75–77, 83, 84, 86–87, 88, 89n8

Jewish American magical realist filmmakers, 5, 125; enigma of difference of Jewish Americans and, 3. *See also* Allen, Woody; *specific filmmakers*

Jewish American magical realist films, 9; Jewish American identity and, 6, 9. *See also* Jewish American magical realist works; *specific films*

Jewish American magical realist literature, 9; enigma of difference of Jewish Americans and, 88, 122; of Malamud, 123–124; scholarship on, 5, 11n24. *See also* Jewish American magical realist works

Jewish American magical realist short fiction: Jewish American identity and, 6, 9. *See also* Jewish American magical realist literature; *specific works*

Jewish American magical realist works, 115; enigma of difference of Jewish Americans and, 88, 122, 123, 127, 129; Jewish American identity and, 3, 5, 6, 122–123, 129; Jewish mystical literature and, 120–121; scholarship on, 5, 11n24

Jewish American magical realist writers, 5, 124–125; enigma of

difference of Jewish Americans and, 3. *See also specific writers*

Jewish American mother stereotype, 89n19, 112n32; guilt and, 33–34; in *Jesus Is Magic,* 101

Jewish American neurotic, in *Annie Hall,* 14, 29, 30n7, 129

Jewish American Princess (JAP) stereotype, 89n19, 96, 99–100, 106, 112n32

Jewish Americans: guilt and, 33–35, 35; Jewish history and, 36, 47n20; postmodernism and, 115, 122

Jewish American writers, 2, 37. *See also* Jewish American magical realist writers

Jewish culture: Kafka and, 116, 117. *See also* Jewish American culture

Jewish diaspora: *Annie Hall* and, 16–17; Jewish American identity and, 36, 43, 47n20

Jewish history: Jewish American magical realism and, 43; Jewish Americans and, 36, 47n20; Jewish identity and, 43, 87; "Levitation" and, 37–38, 40–41, 42–44, 46; shame in, 42–43, 46–47. *See also* Holocaust

Jewish humor, 76, 107; Jewish American acculturation and, 13, 29n1

Jewish identity: in *Jesus Is Magic,* 100–101; Jewish history and, 43, 87; of Kafka, 116–117, 118. *See also* Jewish American identity

Jewish literature: magical and mystical, 119–121. *See also* Jewish American literature

Jewish magical realism, 115. *See also* Jewish American magical realism

"Jewish Magical Realism: Writing to Tell the Tale" (Sellman), 6, 11n24

"The Jewish Mother: Comedy and Controversy in American Popular Culture" (Ravits), 89n19, 112n32

"Jewish Post-Holocaust Fiction and the Magical Realist Turn" (Rody), 5–6, 11n24

Jewish women stereotypes, 102. *See also* Jewish American mother

stereotype; Jewish American
Princess stereotype
Johnston, Ruth D., 25
jokes: in *Annie Hall*, 16, 17, 30n16,
30n24. *See also* comedy; humor

Kafka, Franz, 9; assimilation and,
118–119; fiction of, 116–117, 118;
Jewish culture and, 116, 117; Jewish
identity of, 116–117, 118; magical
realist fiction of, 4, 11n22, 118–119,
121, 123
Kaufman, Debra Renee, 87

LaCapra, Dominick, 55
Langer, Lawrence L., 60
Laub, Dori, 54–55
Leveen, Lois, 26
Levine, Mordecai H., 34
Levinson, Julian, 124
"Levitation" (Ozick): ascension in, 120;
characterizations in, 37–38, 40,
41–42; guilt in, 7; Holocaust and, 44,
46, 49n64; Jewish American
difference in, 37, 51; Jewish
American identity in, 7, 35–36, 38,
41; Jewish American magical
realism in, 7, 10n18, 36, 37, 43, 44,
45–46; Jewish history in, 37–38,
40–41, 42–44, 46; names in, 40–41;
overview, 37; party in, 37, 38–40, 41,
42, 48n32; self-consciousness in, 37,
39–40; shame in, 7, 35–36, 37, 38, 39,
41, 42, 45–46, 51; witnessing in,
44–45, 45, 46, 49n60
Levitt, Laura, 1, 3, 13
"The Library of Moloch" (Bukiet):
archiving Holocaust testimony in,
55, 56–60, 61–62, 64, 65, 66–67,
67n12–68n13; archiving trauma
testimony in, 51, 54, 64; Jewish
American identity and Holocaust
in, 8, 51, 53, 62, 64, 67, 67n12, 121;
Jewish American magical realism
in, 10n18, 51, 53, 58, 59, 61, 67, 128;
masochism in, 53, 54–55, 56, 58–59,
60–61, 65–66, 67; overview, 8
The Longest Shadow (Hartman), 52,
68n37

Lowe, John, 107
Lynch, Liam, 106

MacKendrick, Karmen, 61
magical and comical discord, between
religiosity and ethnicity: enigma of
difference of Jewish Americans and,
71, 83, 88; in "The Gilgul of Park
Avenue," 74, 75–76; in "The Tale of
a Kite," 74, 75–76, 83
magical and comical modes: enigma of
difference of Jewish Americans and,
71, 80, 83, 88; in "The Gilgul of Park
Avenue," 71, 74, 75–76, 84, 88; in
"The Tale of a Kite," 71, 74, 75–76,
77, 83, 84, 88
magical realism: dichotomies of ethnic
identities and, 3–4, 128–129; excess
and, 14–15; fantasy and science
fiction compared to, 4; overview, 3,
95, 110n7. *See also* Jewish magical
realism
magical realist fiction, 122; of Kafka, 4,
11n22, 118–119, 121, 123;
marginalized identities and, 4;
Native American identities and,
128. *See also* Jewish American
magical realist short fiction
magical realist literature, 3, 5. *See also*
Jewish American magical realist
literature
magical realist works, 80–81; overview,
3, 95, 110n6; as subversive, 74. *See
also* Jewish American magical realist
works
Malamud, Bernard, 123–124
Manzanas, Ana Mª, 125–126
Masoch. *See* Sacher-Masoch, Leopold
von
masochism: archiving Holocaust
testimony and, 53, 55, 56–57, 61, 65,
66; of centralizing Jewish American
identity in Holocaust, 51; language
in tales of, 56; "The Library of
Moloch" and, 53, 54–55, 56, 58–59,
60–61, 65–66, 67; overview, 55–56; in
Sacher-Masoch's *Venus in Furs*, 55,
56, 57, 58, 59, 60–61; trauma
restaging and, 65

McLuhan, Marshall, 112n47
media culture, 93–94, 99, 101–103, 107–108
"The Metamorphosis" (Kafka), 118
Moments of Magical Realism in U.S. Ethnic Literatures (Di Iorio Sandín and Perez), 125, 126–127
Moore, Deborah Dash, 1–2, 52
Morf, Carolyn C., 96, 105
Morgan, Michael L., 52

naïve humor, 108
narcissism: communications technologies and, 102–103, 104; *Jesus Is Magic* and narcissistic fantasy, 93–94, 96–97, 101–105, 110, 129; of Jewish American Princess, 96; media culture and, 103, 108; Reich on, 96, 104, 105
Nathanson, Donald L., 35
Native American identities, 127–128
Novick, Peter, 1, 52, 53

Ozick, Cynthia: on Holocaust, 41, 43; "Levitation," 7, 10n18, 35–36, 37–46, 49n60, 49n64, 51, 120

Perez, Richard, 125, 126–127
Portnoy's Complaint (Roth), 34, 39–40, 89n19, 112n32, 124
postmodernism: in *Annie Hall*, 6–7, 13–14, 18, 21, 22–23, 26, 27–29; Jewish Americans and, 115, 122

Ravits, Martha A., 34, 89n19, 112n32
Rediscovering Magical Realism in the Americas (Schroeder), 5
Reich, Annie, 96, 104, 105
Reik, Theodor, 65
religion: corporate practice and, 97; Silverman on, 97
"Religions Inc.," 97
religiosity: "The Gilgul of Park Avenue" and, 74, 75–76, 77–78, 79, 87; "The Tale of a Kite" and, 74, 75–76, 77, 81–87, 89n4
religiosity, ethnicity and: enigma of difference of Jewish Americans and, 71, 79, 83, 88; in "The Gilgul of Park

Avenue," 74, 75–76, 77, 79, 87; of Jewish American communities, 85, 86, 87; in Jewish American identity, 71, 73–74, 77–79, 85, 87–88; in "The Tale of a Kite," 74, 75–76, 77, 83, 85–87, 89n4. *See also* magical and comical discord, between religiosity and ethnicity
"A Report to an Academy" (Kafka), 118–119
Rhodewalt, Frederick, 96, 105
Rody, Caroline, 5–6, 11n24, 123, 124–125, 127
Roth, Philip, 34, 39, 40, 82, 89n19, 112n32, 124

Sacher-Masoch, Leopold von, 55, 56, 57, 58, 59, 60–61
Sanyal, Debarati, 48n54, 55, 63
satire: of Bruce, 97–98, 103, 112n41; of *Jesus Is Magic*, 93, 96, 99–100, 101, 103, 106–110, 112n44; Schaeffer on, 97, 98, 111n21; of Silverman, 93–94, 97–99, 101, 106, 108, 111n23. *See also* comedy; humor
Schaeffer, Neil, 97, 98, 99, 111n21
Schroeder, Shannin, 5, 18, 74
Schwartz, Howard, 120–121
Sellman, Tamara Kaye, 6, 11n24
September 11th terrorist attack, 97, 102, 103
shame: enigma of difference of Jewish Americans and, 7–8, 33, 35; guilt compared to, 7, 33, 35, 36, 38; Jewish American difference and, 7, 46; Jewish American identity and, 33, 35; Jewish history and, 42–43, 46–47; in "Levitation," 7, 35–36, 37, 38, 39, 41, 42, 45–46, 51
Silverman, Sarah: in *The Aristocrats*, 98–99; Bruce and, 97–98; on corporations, 97, 102; *Jesus Is Magic*, 8–9, 93–94; meta-bigotry of, 94; naïve humor of, 108; narcissistic persona of, 98; overview, 94, 110n2; on religion, 97; satire of, 93–94, 97–99, 101, 106, 108, 111n23
Simal, Begoña, 125–126
Singer, Isaac Bashevis, 40, 123

Smirnoff, Victor N., 55–56
Sobchack, Vivian, 18, 27, 28
social crimes, 62–63
social humor, 103
Sollors, Werner, 93
The Sorrow and the Pity, 15, 21, 24, 27, 28, 49n64
Stam, Robert, 4
Stern, Steve: Jewish American contemporary communities and, 80; on potential of cities, 73; "The Tale of a Kite," 8, 11n29, 71, 72, 73–74, 75–77, 81–87, 88, 89n3–89n4, 89n8, 120
Symbolism: An International Annual of Critical Aesthetics, 11n24

"The Tale of a Kite" (Stern), 11n29, 89n3; ascension in, 120; assimilation in, 75, 77, 82; Jewish American communities and, 87, 88; Jewish American difference in, 81–82; Jewish American identity in, 8, 71, 74, 76–77, 82–84, 85, 87, 88; Jewish American magical realism in, 71, 72, 73–74, 75–77, 83, 84, 86–87, 88, 89n8; magical and comical discord between religiosity and ethnicity in, 74, 75–76, 83; magical and comical modes in, 71, 74, 75–76, 77, 83, 84, 88; overview, 72; potential of cities in, 73; religiosity and, 74, 75–76, 77, 81–87, 89n4; religiosity and ethnicity in, 74, 75–76, 77, 83, 85–87, 89n4
Tangney, June Price, 35, 36, 39
Telushkin, Joseph, 107
Testimony (Laub and Felman), 55, 68n38
trauma: guilt and, 63; identity and, 63; masochism and restaging of, 65

trauma testimony, 60; secondary trauma and, 68n37
trauma testimony, archiving: in "The Library of Moloch," 51, 54, 64; witnessing in, 54–55. *See also* Holocaust testimony, archiving
"The Turn Within: The Irony of Technology in a Globalized World" (Douglas), 102–103, 104, 112n47

Uncertain Mirrors: Magical Realisms in US Ethnic Literatures (Benito, Manzanas, Simal), 125–126
United States (U.S.), ethnic magical realist works of, 3, 4, 5, 10n19, 125–127, 129
U.S. culture: comedy and, 107; media culture, 93–94, 99, 101–103, 107–108. *See also* Jewish culture

Venus in Furs (Sacher-Masoch), 55, 56, 57, 58, 59, 60–61
Vohs, Kathleen D., 104

Weissman, Gary, 52
Wiesel, Elie, 53, 67n10
Wilson, Rawdon, 80
witnessing: archiving trauma testimony and, 54–55; Holocaust and, 43, 45, 48n54, 48n59, 54–55, 68n38; in "Levitation," 44–45, 46, 49n60

You Never Call! You Never Write!: A History of the Jewish Mother (Antler), 34, 89n19, 112n32

Zamora, Lois Parkinson, 14–15, 61, 74
Zelig, 125

About the Author

Aaron Tillman is associate professor of English and Director of the Honors Program at Newbury College in Brookline, MA. His short story collection, *Every Single Bone in My Brain*, was published by Braddock Avenue Books in July, 2017. He earned his M.F.A. in Fiction Writing from Sarah Lawrence College and his Ph.D. in English from the University of Rhode Island where he received an Excellence in Doctoral Research Award and a Distinguished Achievement Award. He has taught seminars on a range of topics, including contemporary American humor, U.S. ethnic magical realism, and Jewish American film.

Lightning Source UK Ltd.
Milton Keynes UK
UKOW04n1606201117
313046UK00001B/9/P